HARDPRESS.NET
HOME OF HARD-TO-FIND BOOKS

The Naval Monument
by Abel Bowen

Address:
HardPress
8345 NW 66TH ST #2561
MIAMI FL 33166-2626
USA
Email: info@hardpress.net

WASHINGTON

INDEPENDENCE

MANLY. TRUXTON. JONES.
PREBLE. BA...LITTLE.
BARRY.

The naval monument

Abel Bowen

J.R.PENNIMAN BOSTON

W.B.Annin Sc

WASHINGTON
INDEPENDENCE
MANLY. TRUXTON. JONES.
PREBLE. BAINBRIDGE. LITTLE.
BARRY.

WE HAVE AND THEY MET THE ENEMY ARE OURS

Inv. et Del. by
J.R. PENNIMAN Boston Mass.

W.B. Annin Sc.

Engd. for the Naval Monument.

James Sampson.

THE

NAVAL MONUMENT,

CONTAINING OFFICIAL AND OTHER ACCOUNTS

OF ALL THE BATTLES FOUGHT BETWEEN

THE NAVIES OF THE

'UNITED STATES AND GREAT BRITAIN,

DURING THE LATE WAR;

AND AN

ACCOUNT OF THE WAR WITH ALGIERS.

WITH

TWENTY-FIVE ENGRAVINGS.

TO WHICH IS ANNEXED

A NAVAL-REGISTER OF THE UNITED STATES,

REVISED AND CORRECTED,

AND BROUGHT DOWN TO THE YEAR 1836.

Bowen, Abel
&c

BOSTON:

PUBLISHED BY GEORGE CLARK.

1838.

DISTRICT OF MASSACHUSETTS, TO WIT : }
DISTRICT CLERK'S OFFICE. }

Be it remembered, that on the 12th day of March, A. D. 1816, and in the 40th year of the independence of the United States of America, ABEL BOWEN, of the said district, has deposited in this Office the title of a book, the right whereof he claims as proprietor, in the words following, *to wit* :

" The Naval Monument, containing Official and other accounts of all the " battles fought between the Navies of the United States and Great Britain, " during the late war ; and an account of the war with Algiers, with " twenty-five Engravings. To which is annexed a Naval Register of the " United States."

In conformity to an act of the Congress of the United States, entitled ᴕ An Act for the encouragement of learning, by securing the copies of Maps, Charts and Books, to the authors and proprietors of such copies during the times therein mentioned ; and also to an act entitled ' An Act supplementary to An Act, entitled an act for the encouragement of learning by securing the copies of Maps, Charts and Books to the authors and proprietors of such copies during the times therein mentioned ; and extending the benefits thereof to the Arts of Designing, Engraving* and Etching Historical and other Prints.' "

JNO. W. DAVIS, Clerk of the District of Massachusetts.

* The Designs and Engravings in this volume were entered as the law directs, Nov. 25, and Dec. 28, 1815, by A. Bowen.

TO

THE OFFICERS

OF

THE UNITED STATES NAVY,

WHO BY THEIR

BRAVERY AND SKILL

HAVE EXALTED THE AMERICAN CHARACTER,

SECURED

THE APPLAUSE OF THEIR COUNTRY,

AND EXCITED THE

ADMIRATION OF THE WORLD:

THIS VOLUME

IS MOST RESPECTFULLY DEDICATED,

BY THEIR

MOST OB'T AND HUMBLE SERV'T.

A. BOWEN.

PREFACE.

THAT a country, but of yesterday among the nations, should already have acquired naval renown, and made the trident tremble in hands that had wielded it for ages, is now not least among the phenomena in the archives of history. Burke was astonished at the growth which, in his time, had happened to this country within the short period of the life of man. 'Whatever England has been growing to by a progressive increase of improvement, brought in by varieties of people, by successions of civilizing conquests and civilizing settlements in a series of seventeen hundred years, you shall see as much added to her by America in course of a single life.' Thus he supposes the genius of Lord Bathurst to have addressed* that nobleman in his youth, foretelling only what, at the moment of uttering this fine imagination, had become fact; and yet to have left his Lordship altogether incredulous and in wonder. But what has not been the progress of this country since Burke's day, and still all within the compass of a single life? America was then under the bonds of colonial subjection. Imagine, at the time he spoke, some sage equally illustrious, had thus addressed the monarch of England. 'Sire, these bonds she shall soon burst. You will struggle to impose others, and to force her sons to your service. They will resist, with a spirit so desperate, and an enterprise so hardy, as shall, 'before you taste of death,' make your ships not safe at home, even within your immediate waters. Your navy, the favorite of your kingdom, that you have been centuries creating, shall strike once and again, in single ships and in squadron, on the ocean and the lakes, in the old world and the new; to a navy, the outcast of its country, and the work of an hour. It will indeed be simply an upstart from its cradle, but you will find it a Hercules there.' Had the sovereign then been thus prophetically 'rapt into times,' but little 'future,' rather than live to behold them, would he not gladly have resigned, at once his crown and life?

* The beginning of this address we supply for the gratification of what we consider laudable, a proper national pride. 'Young man, there is America —which at this day serves for little more than to amuse you with stories of savage men, and uncooth manners ; yet shall before you taste of death, *shew itself equal to the whole of that commerce, which now attracts the envy of the world.'*

Naval history has a charm on the attention of the ardent, from being peculiarly the record of enthusiasm. Every naval man of spirit is an enthusiast. We read of ' the self devoted Decii.' Among naval men self devotion is so common, than an act, evincing this virtue merely, is passed almost without notice. It is looked upon as but duty, and therefore no object for praise. They devote themselves to their country and to their commander, with whom in their minds, indeed, the country is often identified. This spirit pervades not merely officers, but the men. Instances from British history are familiar; and the one from our own, of the sailor who interposed himself between the uplifted scymitar and Decatur, in the first Tripolitan war, and received the blow in its fall, of which he still lingers the living monument, is, we trust, indelibly riveted in the memory of a grateful country, who probably owe to this one act of heroism all the benefit of the subsequent signal services of this gallant captain. Here is disinterestedness that was perfectly pure, unadulterated even by the love of fame. What cared this mariner for fame? His name scarcely is known; and how soon it is every where forgotten, he heeds not. Nay, when all was over, had he not borne upon his body the marks of an act, which subjected him to the teasing of questions as to its cause, home this sailor had probably gone, and, like Samson of old, ' told neither father nor mother of it.' This utter extinction of selfishness, is it not sublime? The fear of death, according to Johnson, ' natural to all,' is, in this class of men, not merely completely overcome. Death is courted by them as glory, or sought from friendship. Is it owing to the progress of Christianity gradually and insensibly improving and elevating the mass of mankind, that the virtues of our ordinary seamen have become thus exalted? What a reform have men's ideas not undergone in the lapse of a few years? Chivalry of character has shifted its element. The world now looks for ' men of honor,' and for ' cavaliers,' not where it looked formerly. To the ocean, which was of late inseparably associated with every thing boisterous and rough; the traversers of which were thought to participate only in the nature of the storms that occasionally desolate its surface; to this ocean are the eyes of mankind now universally directed for all that is valorous and gallant in war, and for much of the virtue, thought peculiar to peace. Tho habiliments of the knight are changed; and the plainness, that most ennobles, has got to be (such are the caprices of fashion) the common, every day dress of the mariner.

The dawn of the American navy was ominous of a glorious day. Not to mention the other exertions at sea in the war of the revolution,* which were all respectable, and, but for an

---

* To show the notice BARNEY then gained, and the favor shown by fair royalty to the American cause, we add as a curiosity, what we do not vouch for as fact. ' A correspondent of the morning Chronicle, who signed ' JEAN

eclipse from greater brightness, would have remained brilliant; the exploits of Paul Jones alone excited an eclat that ensured the whole-extent of success, which has to this day followed. Truxton and the *Constellation* flashed next on the public eye. The scene of naval operations soon shifted to Tripoli. Here Preble was the father of a spirit that now reflects its radiance alike on his memory and country. The warfare was most active. It evinced enterprize the most ardent, and boldness the most daring. In these seas, nearly all the mariners, who have since been eminently distinguished, received their first rudiments of discipline and lessons of danger. The city thrice bombarded; the only frigate the Turks took, and that from her accidentally grounding, fired at the very mouths of their loaded batteries; the infidels chastised into peace; self devotion animating our whole fleet as one band; in the back ground of the picture, Somers, Israel, Wadsworth, kindling their own funeral pyre, and mounting in a blaze to the mansions of light; these were among the objects which then attracted the attention of the world, and forced its admiration.

We have just passed the close of a three years' war. The causes of that war out of the question, the interrogatory is put to the politician, to him who realizes that in the family of nations, no one member has respect from another, but for its power; to him the point is pressed home; is not the *effect* of this war, in the impression produced the world over from the lustre of our arms, cheaply bought by all the blood and the treasure that the conflict hast cost? Is not our flag now looked up to, as an object of triumph, under every heaven? Is not our navy covered with renown?

A good mind is ever grateful for peace. Justice to the merits that have achieved it, is to such a mind among the first of its duties. Has this renown then been justly acquired?

What are the constituents of naval excellence? Bravery, discipline, military and nautical skill. In each of these respects what are the positive merits, and what the comparative, of the American navy.

It is not intended to pursue the answer through details of any great minuteness. It will be rested on the authority principally of this single volume, the references to which will, for the most part, be general.

FRANCIS,' affirms, that the musical bagatelle, called ' *Barney leave the girls alone,*' owes its origin to the kiss publicly bestowed on this American officer by the beautiful Maria Antoinette, and was composed by Count O'L. of the Irish brigade, who was present at court when the royal familiarity took place; and he stated, that the maids of honor were all so eager to follow the gracious examples set by the lovely queen, that Mr Barney became an object of envy and dislike to the entire *beau monde.* The American papers speak favorably of his conduct on the surprise of Washington, and affirm, that of the seamen he commanded, one half were killed and wounded; he was himself badly wounded and taken prisoner.'

Brit. Nav. Chron., 1814.

Bravery may be shown either in enterprize or in actual engagement; as well in the pursuit, as the improvement, of opportunity; in defeat, not less, than in victory.

Bravery of enterprize certainly belongs in common to all of our captains, the oldest at their head, who bearded the lion in his den. They have even been blamed for excess in this particular, and the right of challenge has been absurdly questioned, as if in a strife of mere glory, and to settle the point as to power, it was not highly commendable to seek the opportunity indispensable for the purpose, but which yet happened not to fall in one's way. The challenge given by the *Hornet*, and that taken (for sailing across the harbor, was clearly in substance a challenge) by the luckless *Chesapeake*, under circumstances of obvious disadvantage, before the sailors could have lost the effect of land habits, or have regained their sea legs, are among the countless proofs of an aspiring spirit, steadily intent on one object, namely, never at least to be condemned as failing from not having dared to attempt.

Where is the instance in which Americans have not evinced bravery in battle? The fatal engagement of the *Chesapeake*, even after the boarding, is not, in fairness an exception. Not an officer was now left upon deck. Who are the men, in any navy, that will continue valiant, deprived of the countenance and support of every officer? Of the fights between single vessels, that of the *Wasp* and the *Frolic* is perhaps far the most distinguished for personal intrepidity. But we had battles in squadron. Who ever showed more courage than Perry, passing open boat from ship to ship, within full view and point blank shot of a multiplied foe, each of whose ships was intent on taking his single life, as the object to make victory sure; or than this same commander, breaking the enemy's line, thus doubling his own force, exposing himself of course to shots from each side, to double broadsides at once, and at half pistol shot distance? Who ever evinced greater constancy than Macdonough, awaiting at anchor the approach of an enemy in unknown numbers, by land and water, two states, if not the whole country. in suspense for safety on the issue, or who more glorious collectedness than this same commander in like danger with Paul Jones, his own vessel twice on fire? What perseverance was ever more indefatigable than Chauncey's in pursuit? Unless indeed that of his adversary, in patience.

ADVERTISEMENT.

In making this selection the editor has endeavoured to obtain the most correct and authentic accounts. He cannot however promise himself, that every part of it is perfectly accurate; but he believes that no material error has escaped him. The difficulties of observing exact chronological order in a work like this need not be mentioned, as they will readily occur to the reader. Perhaps some instances of skill and valor have been overlooked, and others given too much at length. The official accounts of the battles represented in the plates are given entire. In many other instances, official letters are curtailed. To have printed them at large would have increased the work beyond the limits prescribed. This is offered as an apology for omitting what otherwise would gladly have been inserted. Many of the periodical publications of the last four years have been examined, but the compiler is particularly, and almost exclusively indebted to the able and indefatigable *Mr Niles*, publisher of the *Baltimore Weekly Register*, a paper in which may be found a full and interesting naval and military history of the late wars against Great Britain and Algiers. The pages of this work might have been enriched with extracts from the *Analetic Magazine* and *Naval Chronicle*; but this is rendered unnecessary by the extensive circulation of that eloquent and excellent work. Whoever wishes to be instructed or delighted on the subject of the American navy, may have his curiosity fully gratified by a perusal of those publications.

The editor cannot but indulge the hope, that he has fulfilled the engagements made in the prospectus, and equalled the expectations of subscribers. Should he meet the approbation of the public, he intends to publish a military history of the war, on a similar plan, entitled the *Military Chronicle.*

Most of the engravings which accompany this volume, are from the designs of Mr Corne. The frontispiece was designed by Mr Penniman. The plate which exhibits the return of the squadron from the Mediterranean, is from a design of Mr Fanning, and was taken from actual survey on board the *Independence.*

For the preface the editor is indebted to the kindness of a literary gentleman, who has furnished to our periodical publications, many interesting articles on the subject of the navy.   A. B.

INDEX TO THE ENGRAVINGS.

Africa   CONSTITUTION   Shannon   Eolus   Guerriere   Belvidera

Constitution's Escape from the British Squadron after a chase of sixty hours.

NAVAL MONUMENT,

The exploits of the American Navy in the late war between the United States and Great Britain, commenced with the escape of the Frigate Constitution from an English squadron.

On July 12th, the Constitution, completely equipped and well manned, left the Chesapeake, bound to New York. On the 16th, saw a frigate and gave chase, with winds too light to reach her. On the 17th discovered the British squadron, consisting of the *Africa* 64, and *Guerriere, Shannon, Belvidera* and *Æolus*, frigates, a brig and a schooner. The *Belvidera* within gun-shot. The 17th was calm and spent in towing, manœuvering and firing. On the morning of the 18th a light breeze sprung up, when the *Constitution* spread all her canvas, and by outsailing the enemy, escaped a conflict, which she could not have maintained with any hope of success, against a force so greatly superior. The chase was continued sixty hours, during which the whole crew remained at their stations.

A gentleman, belonging to an American captured vessel, who was on board the *Shannon*, during the above period, informs us, that all the officers of the British squadron applauded the conduct of Capt. Hull; and though mortified at losing so fine a ship, gave him much credit for his skill and prudence in managing the frigate.

A more particular account is detailed in the following extract from the *Constitution's* log book.

EXTRACTS FROM LOG BOOK.

Friday, July 17, 1812.

Commences with clear weather and fresh breezes from the northward and eastward. At ½ past 1, P. M., sounded in 22 fin's. water. At 2, four sail of vessels in sight. At 3, sounded in 18 ½ fm's. At ½

past 3, tacked to the east. At 4, a ship in sight,
bearing N. E. standing down for us, and three ships
and a brig N. N. W. on the starboard tack. From
4 to 6, light airs from the northward. At 6, the single
ship bearing E. N. E. At ½ past 6, got a light
breeze from the southward and eastward, wore ship and
and stood towards the above sail, keeping her a little
off the larboard bow. At ½ past 7, beat to quarters and cleared ships for action. At 8, light airs ;—
coming up with the ships very slow. At ½ past 10,
made the private signals of the day. At ¼ past 11,
hauled down the signals, not having been answered,
and made sail by the wind, with starboard tacks on
board. From 12 to 4 A. M. light airs from the southward and westward and cloudy. At 4 A. M. the ship
made a signal. At day-light, discovered three sail
astern. At 5, discovered another sail astern, making
two frigates off our lee-quarter, and two frigates and
one ship of the line, one brig, and one schooner, astern.
At ¼ past 5, it being calm and the ship having no
steering way, hoisted out the first cutter and got the
boats ahead to tow ship's head round to the southward,
got a 24 pounder up off the gun-deck for a stern-gun,
and the forecastle gun aft—cut away the taffarel to give
them room, and run two guns out of the cabin windows.
At 6, got the ship's head round to the southward and
set top-gallant studding-sails and stay-sails, one of the
frigates firing at us. At ½ past 6, sounded in 26 fm's.
water. At 7, got a kedge and warped the ship ahead.
At ½ past 7, hoisted the colours and fired one gun
at the ship astern. At 8, calm ;—employed warping
and towing the ship. The other ships having a light
air gaining on us, with their boats ahead, and one of
them using sweeps. At 9, the above ship in close chase
of us, and the nearest frigate gaining on us. At 9
minutes past 9, a light breeze sprung from the southward ; braced up by the wind on the larboard tack,
when the above frigate commenced firing, but her shot
did not reach us ; got the boats along side, run two of
them up. At 10, started 2335 gallons of water and

pumped it out—almost calm—manned the first cutter
to tow ship;—six sail of the enemy's ships off the starboard beam and quarter; perceived that the nearest
frigate had got all the boats from the other ships to tow
her towards us. From 10, A. M. to meridian, employed warping and towing. All sail made by the wind,
one of the ships coming up, apparently having all the
boats from the other ships.

Saturday, July 18

Light airs from the southward and eastward, attended with calms. At ½ after meridian, sent the
first cutter and green cutter ahead to tow ship. At ¼
before 1, P. M. a strange sail discovered two points
abaft off the lee-beam, the four frigates one point off
the starboard-quarter. Line-of-battle ship, brig and
schooner, off the lee-beam. At 7 minutes before 2,
the chasing frigates commenced firing their bow chase
guns, we returned them with our stern chasers. At
½ past 3, still chased by the above ships, one of them
being nearly within gun-shot. At 7, observed the
enemy's ships towing with their boats. Lowered down
the first cutter, green cutter and gig, and sent them
ahead, to tow ship;—light airs, inclinable to calms. At
8, light airs from the southward and eastward. The
first and fifth cutters and gig ahead towing ship. The
enemy's ships in the same position as at 7. From 8
to 9, light airs and cloudy. The enemy's ships still in
chase of us; boats ahead towing ship. At 7 minutes
before 11, a breeze springing up from the southward;
boats came along side, hoisted up the gig and green
cutter, and set the fore-top-mast staysail and main-top-
gallant studding sail. At midnight moderate breezes
and cloudy, the enemy's ships still in chase. At 2,
A. M. discovered one of the ships off the lee-beem. At
½ past 2, took in the studding sails, at daylight four
frigates in sight, three off the lee-quarter and one off
the lee-beam, from two to three miles distant. At 4,
six sail in sight from off the deck, hauled down the fore-
top-mast staysail;—very light breezes. At 20 minutes

past 4, tacked ship to the eastward. At 5, passed about gunshot distance to windward of one of the frigates , hoisted in the first cutter ;—ten sail in sight from the mast-head. At 9, saw a ship to windward, supposed to be an American merchantman, standing towards us. The frigate astern hoisted American colours as a decoy ; we immediately hoisted English colours, got royal studding sails fitted. At 11, A. M. took in sky-sails. At meridian, moderate breezes and pleasant weather, rather leaving the frigates in chase ; the head-most frigate to lee-ward, bearing nearly N. by W. four or five miles distant, the nearest frigate W. N. W. directly in our wake, distant about three and half miles. The line-of-battle ship, N. by W. ½ W. on the larboard tack, hull down. Two frigates off our lee-quarter, N. N. W. ½ W. and N. W. by N. about five miles distant, and a brig bearing about N. by W. Observed, latitude 38° 47′ N. which, with the soundings got at ½ past 10, A. M. and allowing for the distance since run, gives our long. about 73° 53′ W. from which we date our departure.

July 19.

Fresh breezes from the southward and pleasant. At 1 P. M. hauled down the royal staysails and set the middle staysail. At 2, got shifting backstays on the top-gallant mast, and set them well up, took in the gaft–topsail and mizen-top-gallant staysail. At ½ past 2, set the mizen-top-gallant and main royal staysails and main skysail. At 4, a moderate breeze from the S. S. W. and cloudy ; four sail of the enemy still in chase, the nearest about six miles off, bearing N. N. W. and one off the weather quarter, W. by N. ½ N. At ½ past 7, the leewardmost ship N. N. W. ½ W. and the weathermost ship, N. W. by ¾ W.—the other two more astern, and hull down. At ½ past 9, the wind hauled round to the southward and westward. At ½ 10 P. M. the wind backed round again. At 11, could just discover the weather-bow ship to have got in our wake. At midnight, moderate breezes and pleasant. From midnight to 4 A. M. moderate breezes. At 1-2 past 4, hauled up to S. E. by S. four sail in sight astern, all of them hull down. At 1-2 past 6, more moderate ;—employed wetting the sails aloft. At 8, four ships still in sight chasing us. At 1-2 8 A. M. all the ships in chase stood to the northward and eastward.

CAPT. HULL'S OFFICIAL LETTER.

Constitution at sea, off Nantucket,
SIR,   *July* 20, 1812.

The Constitution is on her way to Boston for your orders, having been chased by a British squadron off New-York, and very near being taken. The chase continued three days and nights, by a line-of-battle ship, four frigates, a brig and a schooner.

I shall call off Boston and write from there, and continue crusing in the bay until I hear from you.

Respectfully,

Hon. PAUL HAMILTON,   ISAAC HULL.
Sec'y of Navy.

On Sunday, the 26th of July, the Constitution arrived in Boston harbour. On Tuesday the 28th, Capt. Hull came up to town. On his landing and reaching State Street, he was received by his fellow citizens with repeated huzzas.

[The following card was inserted, at the request of Capt HULL, in the Exchange Coffee-House Books.]

" Capt. HULL, finding his friends in Boston are *correctly* informed of his situation when chased by the British squadron off New-York, and that they are good enough to give him more credit by escaping them than he ought to claim, takes this opportunity of requesting them to make a transfer of a great part of their good wishes to Lt. MORRIS, and the other brave officers, and the crew under his command, for their very great exertions and prompt attention to orders while the enemy were in chase. Capt. HULL has great pleasure in saying, that notwithstanding the length of the chase, and the officers and crew being deprived of sleep, and allowed but little refreshment during the time, not a murmur was heard to escape them.

Interesting particulars.

Capt. HULL, in the management of his ship, during her chase by the squadron under Com. BROKE, displayed the most skilful and accomplished seamanship.

At a time when the wind was very light, the sails of the *Shannon* were all furled, and the boats of the squadron were all put to tow her directly to windward toward the *Constitution;* at the same time Capt. HULL was kedging his ship forward faster than the enemy was able to advance by towing; he had gained a considerable distance, before the enemy, who were constantly observing him with their glasses, perceived the manner in which he was leaving. They then kedged in their turn, but not with the same rapidity, owing probably in some measure to the precaution observed by Capt. HULL, when his boats came home, instead of making them fast to the ship, of hoisting them up at the davids. This manœuvre of *kedging* a ship at sea, in 25 or 30 fm's. water, was an ingenious and novel experiment; it was first suggested, it is understood, by *Lieut.* [now Com.] *C. Morris.*

When the squall struck the *Constitution,* by which she ultimately escaped, *Capt. H.* availed himself of another stratagem to gain time. He was to windward —the squall was powerful, and pressed her huge side low in the water; he immediately let every thing go by the run, apparently in the utmost confusion, as if unable to show a yard of canvass—his sails were hauled up by the brails and clewlines; the enemy, perceiving this, hastened to get every thing snug, before the gust should reach them:—but, no sooner had they got their sails furled, than Capt. HULL had his courses and topsails set, and the *Constitution* darted forward with great rapidity. So coolly however did he pro-

THE CONSTITUTION BEARING DOWN FOR THE GUERRIERE.

ceed, that he would not suffer one of his boats to be cut adrift, but, though pressed by a pursuing enemy, attended personally to hoisting in his launch and other boats, while the ship was going nine or ten knots through the water. This is a fact which will appear astonishing to a sailor; and he seemed to be the only person in the ship who conceived it feasible :—the British squadron cut adrift all their boats, and, after they abandoned the chase, spent two or three whole days in cruising to pick them up.

CAPTURE OF THE NAUTILUS.

Soon after the escape of the Constitution, the U. S. brig Nautilus, 12 guns, Lt. Crane, was captured by the above British squadron. The following letter is honorary to Lt. Crane:

The Sec. of the navy to Lt. Crane, late of the Nautilus.
SIR, *Navy department,* 7 *Oct.* 1812.
The following is the opinion of the court of inquiry, convened agreeably to your request, for the loss of the U. S. brig *Nautilus.*

The court were unanimously and decidedly of opinion, that in the capture of the late U. S. brig *Nautilus,* Lieut. Crane, her late commander, and his officers, are entirely free from the least blame, or censure, and do consider Lt. Crane did every thing to prevent said capture, that a skilful and experienced officer could possibly do.

This opinion of the court, Sir, only confirms the impression confidently entertained with respect to your conduct on the occasion, to which it refers.

I have the honour to be respectfully,
Sir, your ob't serv't,
WILLIAM M. CRANE, Esq. PAUL HAMILTON.
of the navy, Boston.

CONSTITUTION AND GUERRIERE.

U. S. Frigate Constitution, off Boston Light,
SIR, *August* 30, 1812.
I have the honor to inform you that on the 19th
2

inst. at 1 P. M. being in lat. 41° 42′ and long. 55° 48′, with the *Constitution* under my command, a sail was discovered from the mast head bearing E. by S. or E. S. E. but at such a distance we could not tell what she was. All sail was instantly made in chase, and soon found we came up with her. At 3 P. M. could plainly see that she was a ship on the starboard tack under easy sail, close on a wind; at ¼ past 3 P. M. made her out to be a frigate; continued the chase until we were within about three miles, when I ordered the light sails to be taken in, the courses hauled up, and the ship cleared for action. At this time the chase had backed his maintop-sail, waiting for us to come down. As soon as the *Constitution* was ready for action, I bore down with intention to bring him to close action immediately; but on our coming within gun-shot she gave us a broadside and filed away, and wore, giving us a broadside on the other tack, but without effect; her shot falling short. She continued wearing and manœuvering for about three quarters of an hour, to get a raking position, but finding she could not, she bore up, and run under her top-sails and gib, with the wind on her quarter. I immediately made sail to bring the ship up with her, and five minutes before 6 P. M. being along side within half pistol-shot, we commenced a heavy fire from all our guns, double shotted with round and grape, and so well directed were they, and so warmly kept up, that in 15 minutes his mizen mast went by the board, and his main yard in the slings and the hull, rigging, and sails very much torn to pieces. The fire was kept up with equal warmth for 15 minutes longer, when his mainmast and foremast went, taking with them every spar, excepting the bowsprit. On seeing this we ceased firing, so that in thirty minutes after, we got fairly along side the enemy; she surrendered, and had not a spar standing, and her hull below and above water so shattered, that a few more broadsides must have carried her down.

After informing you, that so fine a ship as the *Guerriere*, commanded by an able and experienced officer, had been totally dismasted, and otherwise cut to pieces so as to make her not worth towing into port, in the short space of thirty minutes, you can have no doubt of the gallantry and good conduct of the officers and ship's company I have the honor to command; it only remains therefore for me to assure you, that they all fought with great bravery; and it gives me great pleasure to say, that from the smallest boy in the ship to the oldest seaman, not a look of fear was seen. They all went into action, giving three cheers, and requested to be laid close along side the enemy.

Enclosed I have the honor to send you a list of killed and wounded on board the *Constitution*, and a report of the damages she has sustained; also a list of killed and wounded on board the enemy, with his quarter bill, &c.

I have the honor to be, with very great respect,

Sir, your ob't servt,

Hon. PAUL HAMILTON, &c.   ISAAC HULL.

Return of killed and wounded on board the U. S. Frigate Constitution, Isaac Hull Esq. Captain, in the action with H. M. ship Guerriere, Jas. R. Dacres, Esq. Captain, on the 20th day of Aug. 1812.

KILLED—Wm. S. Bush,* 1st Lt. marines; Jacob Sago, seaman; Robert Brice, do; John Brown, do; James Read, do.; Caleb Smith, do.; James Ashford, do.

WOUNDED—Chas. Morris, 1st Lt. dangerously; John C. Alwyn, master, slightly; Richard Dunn, seaman, dangerously; Geo. Reynolds, ord. seaman, dangerously; Daniel Lewis, do. dangerously; Owen Taylor, do. dangerously; Francis Mullen, marine, slightly.

Recapitulation.

KILLED—One Lt. of marines and six seamen.—Total killed 7.

---

* Lieut. William S. Bush, was a native of Wilmington (Delaware.) His father, Capt. John Bush was a meritorious officer in the revolutionary war, and he was the nephew of the brave Major Lewis Bush, who fell supporting the cause of his country at the battle of Brandywine.

Wounded—Two officers, four seamen and one marine. Total wounded 7.

Total killed and wounded, 14.

ISAAC HULL, *Capt.*

U. S. *Frigate Constitution,* T. J. CHEW, *Purser.* *Aug.* 21, 1812.

List of killed and wounded on board the Guerriere.

Killed—H. Ready, 2d Lt. and fourteen petty officers, seamen and marines.

Wounded—James R. Dacres, Capt. ; Bart. Kent, Lt. ; Robert Scott, master ; Samuel Grant, master's mate ; James Enslie, midshipman, and fifty seven petty officers, seamen and marines.

Missing—Lt. James Pullman, Mr. Gaston, and twenty two seamen and marines.

The following particulars of the action, are communicated by an officer of the *Constitution,* and may be considered as essentially correct.

Lat. 41° 42′ N. lon. 55° 33′ W. Thursday, Aug. 20, fresh breeze from N. W. and cloudy ; at 2 P. M. discovered a vessel to the southward, made all sail in in chase ; at 3, perceived the chase to be a ship on the starboard tack, close hauled to the wind ; hauled S. S. W. ; at ½ past 3 made out the chase to be a frigate ; at 4, coming up with the chase very fast ; at ¼ before 5, the chase laid her main-top-sail to the mast ; took in our top-gallant-sails, stay-sails and flying-gib ; took a second reef in the top-sails, hauled the courses up, sent the royal yards down, and got all clear for action ; beat to quarters, on which the crew gave three cheers ; at 5 the chase hoisted three English ensigns, at 5 minutes past 5 the enemy commenced firing ; at 20 minutes past 5, set our colours, one at each masthead, and one at the mizen-peak, and began firing on the enemy, and continued to fire occasionally, he wearing very often, and we manœuvering to close with him, and avoid being raked ; at 6 set the main-top-gallant sail, the enemy having bore up ; at 5 minutes past six,

THE CONSTITUTION IN CLOSE ACTION WITH THE GUERRIERE.

brought the enemy to close action, standing before the wind; at 15 minutes past 6, the enemy's mizen-mast fell over on the starboard side; at 20 minutes past 6, finding we were drawing ahead of the enemy, luffed short round his bows, to rake him; at 25 minutes past 6, the enemy fell on board of us, his bow-sprit foul of our mizen rigging. We prepared to board, but immediately after, his fore and main mast went by the board, and it was deemed unnecessary. Our cabin had taken fire from his guns; but soon extinguished, without material injury; at 30 minutes past 6, shot ahead of the enemy, when the firing ceased on both sides; he making the signal of submission by firing a gun to leeward; set fore-sail and main-sail, and hauled to the eastward to repair damages; all our braces and much of our standing and running rigging and some of our spars being shot away. At 7 wore ship, and stood under the lee of the prize—sent our boat on board, which returned at 8, with Capt. DACRES, late of his Majesty's ship *Guerriere*, mounting 49 carriage guns, and manned with 302 men; got our boats out and kept them employed in removing the prisoners and baggage from the prize to our own ship. Sent a surgeon's mate to assist in attending the wounded; wearing ship occasionally to keep in the best position to receive the boats. At 20 minutes before 2 A. M. discovered a sail off the larboard beam, standing to the south; saw all clear for another action: at 3 the sail stood off again; at day light was hailed by the Lieut. on board the prize, who informed he had four feet of water in the hold, and that she was in a sinking condition; all hands employed in removing the prisoners, and repairing our own damage through the remainder of the day. Friday the 21st, commenced with light breezes from the northward, and pleasant; our boats and crew still employed as before. At 3 P. M. made the signal of recal for our boats, having received all the prisoners. They immediately left her on fire, and ¼ past 3 she blew up. Our loss in the action was 7 killed and 7 wounded; among the former, Lieut. BUSH, of marines, and among the latter, Lieut. MORRIS, severely ; and Mr. AYLWIN, the master slightly.   On the part of the enemy, 15 men killed, and 64 wounded.   Among the former, Lieut. READY, 2d of the ship ; among the latter, Capt. DACRES, Lieut. KENT, 1st, Mr. SCOTT, master, and master's mate.

During her short cruise, the *Constitution*, beside the above gallant achievement, has destroyed two English brigs ; one with lumber, the other in ballast, and. recaptured the *Adeline* of Bath, from London, with dry goods, which had been taken by the British sloop *Avenger*, Capt. Johnston, of 16 guns ;—and which Capt. Hull manned and ordered for America.

When the *Guerriere* first came in sight of the *Constitution*, she stood toward her as if with an intention of bringing her to immediate action, and the latter put herself under easy sail for her reception : but after approaching sufficiently near, to observe her with accuracy, she bore up, stood broad off from the wind, and seemed inclined to take French leave ; Capt. Hull was compelled to crowd a press of sail upon his ship in order to overtake his antagonist, who when he got within gun-shot, commenced a cannonade ; not a gun was returned from the Constitution, whose men were cooly turned up to reef topsails, send down top-gallant yards and swing the lower yards with chains ; this business being effected with deliberation and precision under a galling fire from the enemy, and without herself returning a single shot, the *Constitution* was ranged along side of the enemy, and her fire opened with such terrible effect, that in 25 minutes the *Guerriere* was demolished !

When the *Guerriere's* mizen mast was shot away, Capt. H. in the enthusiasms of the moment, swung his hat round his head, and in true sailor's phraze, exclaimed, "*Huzza ! my boys ! we have made a brig of her !*"

It is well known that when Lieut. Bush of the marines received his mortal wound, the *Guerriere's* bowsprit was engaged in the mizen rigging of the *Constitution*, and he was on the quarter for the purpose of boarding. Lieut. Morris was in the same situation, and received a musked ball through his body. Capt. Hull was about joining them for the same purpose, and when stepping upon the armchest, he was drawn back by a sailor, who begged *he would not get up there unless he took off those* SWABS, pointing to his epaulets. At that moment the two ships were so near together, that one of our sailors, having discharged his boarding pistol, and missed his object, threw the pistol itself, and struck him in the breast.

The flag being shot away from the *Constitution's* main-top-gallant mast head, John Hogan, a young sailor, ascended amid a shower of bullets and lashed it to the mast. This brave fellow enjoys a pension for his intrepidity.

Lieutenant, (now COM.) MORRIS, has since been promoted to the command of the frigate *Adams*, of 32 guns. He has ever been distinguished in the navy for his unremitted application in the acquirement of nautical information ; for activity, intelligence, and zeal in the faithful discharge of his duty. His gallant conduct, while under Commodore Preble, in the Tripolitan war, gained him the confidence of his commander, the admiration of his companions in arms, and the applause of his countrymen. He was the first man who gained the deck of the frigate Philadelphia, on that ever memorable night, when under the batteries of the enemy, she was wrapt in flames by the Spartan band, under Lieut. Decatur ; for which brilliant exploit the President most justly gave the latter a Captain's commission. When the *Constitution* made her escape from the British squadron off the Capes of the Chesapeake—to Lieut. Morris did the magnanimous Hull give much of the credit acquired in that masterly retreat. Those who personally know the sterling worth and intrinsic merit of Capt. Morris, cannot but rejoice that his manly virtues and naval talents have now a more ample field of exertion in his country's cause.

Capt. Hull, in a letter to the secretary of the navy, passed a handsome eulogium of Capt Morris, in the following passage: "I cannot but make you acquainted with the very great assistance I received from that valuable officer, Lieut. Morris, in bringing the ship into action, and in working her whilst along side the enemy ; and I am extremely sorry to state, that he is badly wounded, being shot through the body. We have yet hopes of his recovery, when, I am sure, he will receive the gratitude of his country for this and the many gallant acts he has done in the service."

WASP AND FROLIC.

OFFICIAL LETTER OF CAPT. JONES.

Copy of a letter from Capt. Jones, late of the United States' sloop of war, the Wasp, to the Secretary of the Navy.

SIR,   *N. York, 24 Nov.* 1812.

I HERE avail myself of the first opportunity of informing you of the occurrences of our cruise, which terminated in the capture of the *Wasp* on the 18th of October, by the *Poictiers* of seventy four guns, while a wreck, from damages received in an engagement with the British sloop of war *Frolic*, of twenty two guns, sixteen of them 32lb. carronades, and four twelve pounders on the main deck, and two twelve pounders, carronades, on the top-gallant forecastle, making her superior in force to us by four twelve pounders. The *Frolic* had struck to us, and was taken possession of about two hours before our surrendering to the *Poictiers*.

We had left the Delaware on the 13th. The 15th had a heavy gale, in which we lost our jib-boom and two men. Half past eleven, on the night of the 17th, in latitude 37° north, and longitude 65° west, we saw several sail, two of them appearing very large; we stood from them some time, then shortened sail, and steered the remainder of the night the course we had

THE WASP BOARDING THE FROLIC.

perceived them on.   At day-light on Sunday the 18th, we saw them ahead ; gave chase, and soon discovered them to be a convoy of six sail under the protection of a sloop of war : four of them large ships, mounting from sixteen to eighteen guns.   At 32 minutes past eleven A. M. we engaged the sloop of war, having first received her fire, at the distance of fifty or sixty yards, which space we gradually lessened until we laid her on board, after a well supported fire of 43 minutes ; and although so near while loading the last broadside that our rammers were shoved against the sides of the enemy, our men exhibited the same alacrity which they had done during the whole of the action.   They immediately surrendered upon our gaining their forecastle, so that no loss was sustained on either side after boarding.

Our main-top mast was shot away between 4 and 5 minutes from the commencement of the firing, and falling together with the main topsail yard across the larboard fore and fore topsail braces, rendered our head yards unmanageable the remainder of the action.   At eight minutes the gaft and mizen top-gallant mast came down, and at 20 minutes from the beginning of the action, every brace and most of the rigging was shot away. A few minutes after separating from the *Frolic*, both her masts fell upon deck ; the mainmast going close by the deck and the foremast twelve or fifteen feet above it.

The courage and exertions of the officers and crew fully answered my expectations and wishes.   Lieut. Biddle's active conduct contributed much to our success, by the exact attention paid to every department during the engagement, and the animating example he afforded the crew by his intrepidity.   Lieuts. Rodgers, Booth, and Mr. Rapp, shewed, by the encessant fire from their division, that they were not to be surpassed in resolution or skill.   Mr. Knight, and every other officer, acted with a courage and promptitude highly honorable, and I trust have given assurance that they may be relied on whenever their services may be required.

3

I could not ascertain the exact loss of the enemy, as many of the dead lay buried under the masts and spars that had fallen upon deck, which two hours' exertion had not sufficiently removed.   Mr. Biddle, who had charge of the *Frolic,* states, that from what he saw, and from information from the officers, the number of killed must have been about 30, and that of the wounded about 40 or 50.   Of the killed is her first Lieut. and sailing master ; of the wounded, Capt. Whinyates, and the second Lieutenant.

We had 6 killed and 5 wounded, as per list : the wounded are recovering.   Lieut. Claxton, who was confined by sickness, left his bed a little previous to the engagement ; and though too indisposed to be at his division, remained upon deck, and showed by his composed manner of noting its incidents, that we had lost by his illness the services of a brave officer.

I am respectfully yours,

Hon. PAUL HAMILTON,   JACOB JONES.*
  Sec'y of Navy.

It is on the navy of the United States that our national pride, and our hopes of glory repose.   We have never been able to look without the highest satisfaction on that fearless profession, the nursery of generous courage, and of high-minded patriotism——to whose followers every form of danger is alike familiar and without terror.

> Nor toil, nor hazard, nor distressd, appear
> To sink the *seamen* with unmanly fear ;
> Who from the face of danger strive to turn,
> Indignant from the social hour they spurn ;
> No future ills, unknown, their souls ap'pal,
> *They know no danger, or they scorn it all.*

But we have no language to convey our admiration of the young and gallent spirits, who in the first essays of their strength, have triumphed over the veteran science, and the disciplined valor, of the habitual conquerors of the ocean.   They have retrieved all our

* Capt. Jones is a native of Kent county, state of Delaware.

disasters ; they have shed new lustre on our arms, and sustained, even in the midst of mortifying reverses, the loftiest tone of national enthusiasm. Their only anxiety has been to find the enemies of their country ; and, wherever they have met them, their valor has rendered victory certain, whilst their skill has made it easy.

Devoted, as is this monument, to all that can add honor or distinction to the national character, it has no fairer pages than those which record instances of bravery like the following, the account of which we have rendered scrupulously minute and authentic.

The United States' sloop of war the *Wasp*, commanded by Capt. Jacob Jones, was crusing in long. 65° W. and lat. 37° N. the track of vessels passing from Bermuda to Halifax, when, on Saturday, the 17th of October, about 11 o'clock, in a clear moon-light evening, she found herself near five strange sail, steering eastward. As some of them seemed to be ships of war, it was thought better to get farther from them. The Wasp therefore haled her wind, and having reached a few miles to windward, so as to escape or fight as the occasion might require, followed the strange sail through the night. At daybreak, on Sunday morning, Capt. Jones found that they were six large merchant ships, under convoy of a sloop of war which proved to be the *Frolic*, Capt. Whinyates, from Honduras to England, with a convoy, strongly armed and manned, having all forty or fifty men ; and two of them mounting sixteen guns each. He determined, however, to attack them, and as there was a heavy swell of the sea, and the weather boisterous, got down his top-gallant yards, close reefed the topsails, and prepared for action. About eleven o'clock the Frolic showed Spanish colors; and the Wasp immediately displayed the American ensign and pendant. At thirty-two minutes past eleven, the Wasp came down to windward, on her larboard side, within about sixty yards, and hailed. The enemy hauled down the Spanish colors, hoisted the British ensign, and opened a fire of cannon and musketry. This the Wasp instantly returned ; and, coming nearer to the enemy, the action became close, and without intermission. In four or five minutes the main topmast of the Wasp was shot away, and, falling down with the main topsail yard across the larboard, fore and fore topsail braces, rendered her head yards unmanageable during the rest of the action. In two or three minutes more her gaft and mizen top-gallant sail were shot away. Still she continued a close and constant fire. The sea was so rough that the muzzles of the Wasp's guns were frequently in the water. The Americans, therefore, fired as the ship's side was going down, so that their shot went either on the enemy's deck or below it, while the English fired as the vessel rose, and thus her balls chiefly touched the rigging, or were thrown away. The Wasp now shot ahead of the Frolic, raked her, and then resumed her position on her larboard bow. Her fire was now obviously attended with such success, and that of the Frolic so slackened, that Capt. Jones did not wish to board her, lest the roughness of the sea might endanger both vessels; but, in the course of a few minutes more, every brace of the Wasp was shot away, and her rigging so much torn to piece, that he was afraid that his masts, being unsupported, would go by the board, and the Frolic be able to escape. He thought, therefore, the best chance of securing her was to board, and decide the contest at once. With this view, he wore ship, and, running down upon the enemy, the vessels struck each other, the Wasp's side rubbing along the Frolic's bow, so that her jib-boom came in between the main and mizen rigging of the Wasp, directly over the heads of Capt. Jones and the first Lieutenant, Mr. Biddle, who were at that moment standing together near the capstan. The Frolic lay so fair for raking, that they decided not to board until they had given a closing broadside. Whilst they were loading for this, so near were the two vessels, that the rammers of the Wasp were pushed against the Frolic's sides, and two of her guns went through the bow ports of the Frolic, and swept the whole length of her deck.

At this moment, *Jack Lang*,* a seaman of the Wasp, a gallant fellow, who had been once impressed by a British man of war, jumped on his gun with his cutlass, and was springing on board the Frolic: Capt. Jones, wishing to fire again before boarding called him down; but his impetuosity could not be restrained, and he was already on the bowsprit of the Frolic, when, seeing the ardour and enthusiasm of the Wasp's crew, Lieut. Biddle mounted on the hammoc cloth to board. At this signal the crew followed; but Lieut. Biddle's feet got entangled in the rigging of the enemy's bowsprit, and midshipman Baker, in his ardor to get on board, laying hold of his coat, he fell back on the Wasp's deck. He sprang up, and as the next swell of the sea brought the Frolic nearer, he got on her bowsprit, where Lang and another seaman were already. He passed them on the forecastle, and was surprised at seeing not a single man alive on the Frolic's deck, except the seaman at the wheel and three officers. The deck was slippery with blood, and strewed with the bodies of the dead. As he went forward, the Captain of the Frolic, with two other officers, who were standing on the quarter deck, threw down their swords, and made an inclination of their bodies, denoting that they had surrendered. At this moment the colors were still flying, as, probably, none of the seamen of the Frolic would dare to go into the rigging for fear of the musketry of the Wasp. Lieut. Biddle, therefore, jumped into the rigging himself, and hauled down the British ensign, and possession was taken of the Frolic in 43 minutes after the first fire. She was in a shocking condition; the birth deck, particularly, was crowded with dead, and wounded, and dying; there being but a small proportion of the Frolic's crew who had escaped. Capt. Jones instantly sent on board his surgeon's mate, and all the blankets of the Frolic were brought from the slop room for the comfort of the wounded. To increase

---

*John Lang was a native of New Brunswick, in New Jersey. We mention with great pleasure, the name of this brave American seaman, as a proof that conspicuous valor is confined to no rank in the naval service.

this confusion, both the Frolic's masts soon fell, covering the dead and every thing on deck, and she lay a complete wreck.

It now appears that the Frolic mounted sixteen 32lb. carronades, four 12 pounders on the main deck, and two 12lb. carronades. She was, therefore, superior to the Wasp, by exactly four twelve pounders. The number of men on board, as stated by the officers of the Frolic, was one hundred and ten—the number of seamen on board the Wasp, was one hundred and two ; but it could not be ascertained, whether in this one hundred and ten, were included marines and officers ; for the Wasp had, besides her one hundred and two men, officers and marines, making the whole crew about one hundred and thirty five.—What however, is . decisive, as to their comparative force is, that the officers of the Frolic acknowledged that they had as many men as they knew what to do with, and, in fact, the Wasp could have spared fifteen men. There was, therefore, on the most favorable view, at least an equality of men, and an inequality of four guns. The disparity of loss was much greater. The exact number of killed and wounded on board the Frolic could not be precisely determined ; but from the observations of our officers, and the declarations of those of the Frolic, the number could not be less than about thirty killed, including two officers ; and of the wounded, between forty and fifty ; the Captain and second Lieut. being of the number. The Wasp had five men killed, and five slightly wounded.

All hands were now employed in clearing the deck, burying the dead, and taking care of the wounded, when Captain Jones sent orders to Lieut. Biddle to proceed to Charlestown, or any southern port of the United States ; and, as there was a suspicious sail to the windward, the Wasp would continue her cruise. The ships then parted. The suspicious sail was now coming down very fast. At first it was supposed that she was one of the convoy, who had all fled during the engagement, and who now came for the purpose of attacking the prize. The guns of the Frolic were, therefore, loaded, and the ship cleared for action ; but the enemy, as she advanced, proved to be a seventy-four, the *Poictiers*, Capt. Beresford. She fired a shot over the Frolic ; passed her ; overtook the Wasp, the disabled state of whose rigging prevented her from escaping; and then returned to the Frolic, who could of course, make no resistance. The Wasp and Frolic were carried into Bermuda. It is not the least praise due to Capt. Jones, that his account of this gallant action, is perfectly modest and unostentatious. On his own share in the capture, it is unnecessary to add any thing. "The courage and exertion of the officers and crew," he observes, "fully answered my expectations and wishes. Lieut. Biddle's active conduct contributed much to our success, by the exact attention paid to every department, during the engagement, and the animating example he afforded the crew by his intrepidity Lieut. Rodgers and Booth, and Mr. Rapp, showed by the incessant fire from their divisions, that they were not to be surpassed in resolution or skill. Mr. Knight and every other officer, acted with a courage and promtitude highly honorable. Lieut. Claxton, who was confined by sickness, left his bed a little previous to the engagement ; and, though too weak to be at his division, remained upon deck, and showed, by his composed manner of noting its incidents, that we had lost, by his illness, the services of a brave officer."

UNITED STATES AND MACEDONIAN.

Message of the President of the United States, communicating to congress the official letters of Captains Decatur and Jones.

To the Senate and House of Representatives of the United States.

I TRANSMIT to Congress a copy of a letter to the Secretary of the navy, from Capt. Decatur, of the frigate *United States*, reporting his combat and capture of the British frigate *Macedonian*.

Too much praise cannot be bestowed on that officer and his companions on board, for the consummate skill and conspicuous valour by which this trophy has been added to the naval arms of the United States.

I transmit also a letter * from Capt Jones, who commanded the sloop of war *Wasp*, reporting his capture of the British sloop of war, the *Frolic*, after a close action, in which other brilliant titles will be seen to the public admiration and praise.

A nation feeling what it owes to itself, and its citizens, could never abandon to arbitrary violence on the ocean, a class of men, which gives such examples of capacity and courage, in defending their rights on that element ; examples, which ought to impress on the enemy, however brave and powerful, a preference of justice and peace to hostility against a country whose prosperous career may be accelerated, but cannot be prevented by the assaults made on it.

JAMES MADISON.

Washington, Dec. 11, 1812.

COM. DECATUR'S OFFICIAL LETTER TO THE SECRETARY OF THE NAVY.

U. S. ship, United States, at sea.

SIR,   Oct. 30, 1812.
I have the honor to inform you, that on the 25th inst. being in latitude 29° N. longitude 29° 30′ W. we fell in with, and after an action of an hour and a half, captured his Britannic Majesty's ship *Macedonian*, commanded by captain John Carden, and mounting 49 carriage guns, (the odd gun shifting.) She is a frigate of the largest class two years old, four months out of dock, and reputed one of the best sailers in the British service. The enemy, being to windward, had the advantage of engaging us at his own distance,

---

* Which see ante. p. 14.

THE UNITED STATES AND MACEDONIAN.

which was so great, that for the first half hour, we did not use our caronades, and at no moment was he within the complete effect of our musketry and grape; to this circumstance, and a heavy swell, which was on at the time, I ascribe the unusual length of the action.

The enthusiasm of every officer, seaman and marine on board this ship, on discovering the enemy—their steady conduct in battle, and precision of their fire, could not be surpassed. Where all met my fullest expectations, it would be unjust in me to discriminate. Permit me, however, to recommend to your particular notice, my first Lieut. William H. Allen. He has served with me upwards of five years, and to his unremitted exertions in disciplining the crew, is to be imputed the obvious superiority of our gunnery exhibited in the result of this contest.

Subjoined is a list of the killed and wounded on both sides. Our loss compared with that of the enemy, will appear small. Amongst our wounded you will observe the name of Lieut. Funk, who died a few hours after the action; he was an officer of great gallantry and promise, and the service has sustained a severe loss in his death.

The *Macedonian* lost her mizen mast, fore and main topmasts and main yard, and was much cut up in her hull.—The damage sustained by this ship was not such as to render her return into port necessary; and had I not deemed it important that we should see our prize in, should have continued our cruise.

With the highest consideration and respect, I am, sir, your obedient humble servant,

Hon. PAUL HAMILTON.   STEPHEN DECATUR.

List of killed and wounded on board the United States.

KILLED—One seaman and five marines.

WOUNDED—John Musser Funk, Philadelphia, Lieut. and six others.

On board the *Macedonian*, there were thirty-six killed, and sixty-eight wounded: among the former were

4

the boats·vain, one master's mate and the school-master; of the latter, were the first and third Lieuts. one master's mate and two midshipmen.

At a meeting of the young men of Lancaster, *Pa.* the following resolution, honorary to Lieut. Funk, was passed:

Whereas, with the deepest regret we have been apprised of the untimely death of our friend and fellow citizen, Lt. John Musser Funk, who fell gloriously fighting in the cause of his country, in the engagement between the frigate *United States* and the *Macedonian*, which ended in the brilliant victory of the *United States* over the British frigate.

Resolved, That as a testimony of our grief at the loss of the companion of our youth, our respect for his virtues, and the high estimation in which we hold his memory, we will wear crape on the left arm for the space of thirty days.

John Archibald died of his wounds soon after. He left three children to the mercy of the world and a worthless mother, who had abandoned them. When his father went on board the frigate to claim the wages and property of his son, an inquiry into the circumstances of the family took place, and a plan was agreed upon by the seamen for the relief of the orphans, and two dollars apiece was immediately subscribed, amounting to about eight hundred, for the maintenance and education of the bereaved infants to be placed in the hands of suitable trustees.

Address of Thanks.

The father of the deceased John Archibald, who fell in the gallant action on board the *United States*, under the command of the heroic Com. Stephen Decatur, avails himself of thus publicly returning his most sincere thanks to the commander for his humanity and benevolence to him, and also to his gallant officers and seamen, many of whom, are personally acquainted with the deceased's father, for having contributed largely and honourably towards the support of the said de-

ceased's three orphan children; which clearly demon-
strate that the American seamen are possessed both of
courage and humanity.

Capt. Carden spoke in the highest terms of approbation of the conduct of Com. Decatur and his officers.
All the private property of the officers and men on
board the *Macedonian* was given up. That claimed
by Capt. Carden, (including a band of musick and
several casks of wine) valued at about 800 dollars, the
Comodore—whose soul is as liberal as brave—paid him
for. Generosity could not have been more properly
applied. Capt. Carden has been distinguished for his
civilities to such Americans as he met at sea before the
war.

The frigate *United States* is 176 feet deck, and 42
feet beam—her gun deck is 6 feet 6 inches high—she
has 15 port holes on a side—and carries 24 pounders
on her main deck.

The *Macedonian*, is 166 feet deck—42 feet 8 inches beam—her gun deck is 6 feet 10 inches high—she
has 15 port holes on a side—and carries 18 pounders
on her main deck. The *Macedonian* is said to be the
best model for a frigate, and was accounted the most
completely fitted vessel in the service.

An officer of the *United States* frigate, speaking of
Decatur's victory, says,

" I am well aware it will be said, the *Macedonian*
is a little ship, with five guns less than the *United
States*, and a hundred men less, and carries lighter
metal &c. Well, all this is true—she is inferior in all
these, but she is just such a ship as the English have
achieved all their single ship victories in ; it was in
such a ship that Sir ROBERT BARLOW took the *Afri-
caine*, that Sir MICHAEL SEYMOUR took the *Brune*,
and afterwards the *Niemen*, that Capt. MILNE took
the *Vengeance*, Capt. COOKE the *La forte*, Capt. LA-
VIE, the *Guerriere*, Capt. ROWLEY, the *Venus*, and
God knows how many others :—She is in tonnage,
men and guns, such a ship as the English prefer to all
others, and have, till the *Guerriere's* loss, always

thought a match for any single decked ship afloat. You will observe the ship was just out of dock, her masts were better than the *Guerriere's.* She had taken no prizes ; her complement was full. She was not built of fir, thirty years ago, as was said of that ship, but of the best English oak, two years since.

CONSTITUTION AND JAVA.

House of Representatives of the United States,
Monday, February 22, 1813.

To the Senate and House of Representatives.

I LAY before congress a letter with accompanying documents from Capt. Bainbridge, now commanding the United States frigate " the *Constitution,*" reporting his capture and destructon of the British frigate "*Java.*" The circumstances and the issue of this combat afford another example of the professional skill and heroic spirit which prevail in our naval service. The signal display of both by Capt. Bainbridge, his officers and crew command the highest praise. This being the second instance in which the condition of the captured ship, by rendering it *impossible* to get her into port, has barred a contemplated reward for successful valor, I recommend to the consideration of congress equity and propriety of a general provision, allowing in such cases, both past and future, a fair proportion of the value which would accrue to the captors on the safe arrival and sale of the prize.

JAMES MADISON.

U. S. frigate Constitution, St. Salvador,

SIR,   *January 3, 1813.*

I HAVE the honor to inform you that on the 29th ult. at 2 P. M., in south lat. 13° 6', and west long. 38°, about 10 leagues distant from the coast of Brazil, I fell in with and captured his B. M. frigate *Java*, of 49 guns and upwards of 400 men, commanded by Capt. Lambert, a very distinguished officer. The action lasted 1

THE JAVA SURRENDERING TO THE CONSTITUTION.

hour 55 minutes, in which time the enemy was completely dismasted, not having a spar of any kind standing. The loss on board the *Constitution*, was 9 killed and 25 wounded, as per enclosed list. The enemy had 60 killed and 101 wounded, certainly, (among the latter Capt. Lambert, mortally) but by the enclosed letter, written on board this ship, by one of the officers of the *Java*, and accidentally found, it is evident that the enemy's wounded must have been much greater than as above stated, and who must have died of their wounds previously to their being removed. The letter states 60 killed and 170 wounded.

For further details of the action, I beg leave to refer you to the enclosed extracts from my Journal. The *Java* had, in addition to her own crew, upwards of one hundred supernumerary officers and seamen to join the British ships of war in the East Indies : also Lieut. General Hislop, appointed to the command of Bombay : Maj. Walker and Capt. Wood of his staff, and Capt. Marshall, master and commander in the British navy, going to the East Indies to take command of a sloop of war there.

Should I attempt to do justice by representation to the brave and good conduct of all my officers and crew during the action, I should fail in the attempt ; therefore suffice it to say, that the whole of their conduct was such as to merit my highest encomiums. I beg leave to recommend the officers particularly to the notice of the government, as also the unfortunate seamen who were wounded, and the families of those brave men who fell in the action.

The great distance from our own coast and the perfect wreck we made the enemy's frigate, forbade every idea of attempting to take her to the United States ; I had therefore no alternative but burning her, which I did on the 31st ult, after receiving all the prisoners and their baggage, which was very hard work, only having one boat left out of eight, and not one left on board the *Java*.

On blowing up the frigate *Java*, I proceeded to

this place, where I have landed all the prisoners on their parole to return to England, and there remain until regularly exchanged, and not to serve in their professional capacities in any place, or in any manner whatsoever against the United States of America, until their exchange shall be affected.

I have the honor to be, &c.
(Signed)   W. BAINBRIDGE.
To the Secretary of the Navy.
List of killed and wounded on board the Constitution.

KILLED—Jonas Ongrain, seamen ; Joseph Adams, do.; Patrick Conner, do.; Barney Hart, do. ; John Cheever, do.; Mark Snow, do.; John D. Allen, do.; Wm. Cooper, do.; Thomas Hanson, private marine.

WOUNDED—Wm. Bainbridge, commander, severely ; John C. Aylwin, lieut. do.; Chas. F. Waldo, masters's mate, do.; and twenty one others.
(Signed)   AMOS R. EVANS, *Surgeon,*
R. C. LUDLOW, *Purser,*
W. BAINBRIDGE.

John Cheever was mortally wounded in the late action with the *Java.* Whilst lying on the deck, apparently dying, the word was passed the enemy had struck. He raised himself up with one hand, gave three cheers, fell back, and expired ! Heroic specimen of the genuine patriotism of American tars ! He had a brother, Joseph P. Cheever, killed in the same action. They have left an aged and helpless mother at Marblehead, who depended entirely on the fruits of their industry for a subsistence.

At a public dinner, at the Exchange Coffee house, in Boston, given in honor of Capt. Bainbridge, March 2, 1813, the Hon. Christopher Gore, president of the day, announced in an affecting and eloquent address, that the money arising from the subscription, which was usually appropriated to decorations, had been on this occasion, reserved for the benefit of the widow Cheever, who had lost in the battle with the *Java,* her only two sons, her stay and support ; and he offered this to the Commodore as an apology for an omission of dec-, orations of the hall, as had been usual, and doubted not it would be acceptable. The Commodore expressed his grateful sense of the compliment implied in the apology ; and all present felt that the compliment was justly due.

Lieut. Aylwin died, at sea, Jan. 28, 1813, on board the U. S. frigate *Constitution*, of wounds received in the action with the *Java*. He entered the service about the time war was declared, as a sailing master, and was promoted to a lieutenant for his gallant conduct in the action with the *Guerriere*. He was an officer of great merit, much esteemed by all who had the pleasure of his acquaintance. In him his country has suffered great loss. He had seen much of the world, and improved his opportunities of observation ; possessed a strong mind, and a benevolent disposition.

In the action with the *Guerriere*, he stood on an elevated situation by the side of his comrades, Morris and Bush, at the time the two vessels came in contact, and was wounded in the left shoulder by a musket ball. In the late action he commanded the forecastle division ; and his deliberate bravery and marked coolness throughout the contest, gained him the admiration of his commander, and all who had an opportunity of witnessing it. When boarders were called to repel boarders, he mounted the quarter deck hammock-cloths ; and, in the act of firing his pistol at the enemy, he received a ball through the same shoulder. Notwithstanding the serious nature of his wound, he continued at his post until the enemy struck. A few days after the action, although labouring under considerable debility, and the most excruciating pain, he left his bed, and repaired to quarters, when an engagement was expected with a ship, which afterwards proved to be the *Hornet*. He bore his pain with great and unusual fortitude, and expired without a groan.

The following is a list of his Britannic Majesty's military and naval officers and crew, paroled at St. Salvador (Brazil) by Com. William Bainbridge, 3d Jan. 1813.

1 Lieutenant general, 1 major, 1 captain, military officers ; 1 post captain, 1 master and commandant, 5 lieutenants, 3 lieutenants of marines, 1 surgeon, 2 assisting surgeons, 1 purser, 15 midshipmen, 1 gunner, 1 boatswain, 1 master, 1 carpenter, 2 captain's clerks, 38 ; and 323 petty officers, seamen, marines and boys, exclusive of 9 Portuguese seamen liberated and given up to the governor of St. Salvador, and 3 passengers, private characters, whom the Commodore did not consider prisoners of war, and permitted them to land without any restraint.

EXTRACT FROM COM. BAINBRIDGE'S JOURNAL.

"Tuesday December 29, 1812—At 9 A. M.discovered two strange sails on the weather bow.   At 10 discovered the strange sails to be ships : one of them stood in for the land, and the other stood off shore, in a direction towards us.   At 45 minutes past 10 A. M. we tacked ship to the northward and westward, and stood for the sail standing towards us ; at 11 A. M. tacked to the southward and eastward, hauled up the mainsail and took in the royals.   At 30 minutes past 11, made the private signal for the day, which was not answered, and then set the mainsail and royals to draw the strange sail off from the neutral coast, and separate her from the sail in company.

"Wednesday, 30 Dec. (*nautical time*) lat. 13° 6' S. lon. 31° W. ten leagues from the coast of Brazil, commenced with clear weather and moderate breezes from E. N. E. hoisted our ensign and pendant.   At 15 minutes past meridian, the ship hoisted her colours, an English ensign, having a signal flying at main.

" At 26 minutes past 1 P. M. being sufficiently from land, and finding the ship to be an English frigate, took in the main sail and royals, tacked ship, and stood for the enemy.   At 50 minutes past 1 P. M. the enemy bore down with an intention of raking us which we avoided by wearing.   At 2 P. M. the enemy being within half a mile of us, and to windward, and having hauled down his colours, except the union jack at the

mizen mast head, induced me to give orders to the officer of the third division to fire a gun ahead of the enemy, to make him show his colours, which being done,
brought on a fire from us of the whole broadside, on
which the enemy hoisted his colors, and immediately
returned our fire. A general action, with round and
grape, then commenced ; the enemy keeping at a much
greater distance than I wished : but could not bring
him to a closer action, without exposing ourselves to
several rakes. Considerable manœuvres were made
by both vessels to rake and avoid being raked. The
following minutes were taken during the action :

"At 10 minutes past 2 P. M. commenced the action
within good grape and canister distance, the enemy to
windward, (but much farther than I wished.) At 30
minutes past 2, our wheel was shot entirely away.
At 40 minutes past 2, determined to close with the enemy, notwithstanding his raking. Set the fore and
mainsail, and luffed up close to him. At 50 minutes
past 2, the enemy's jib-boom got foul of our mizen
rigging. At 3, the head of the enemy's bowsprit and
jib-boom shot away by us. At 5 minutes past 3, shot
away the enemy's foremast by the board. At 15 minutes past 3, shot away his main topmast just above the
cap. At 40 minutes past 3, shot away the gaft and
spanker boom. At 55 minutes past 3, shot away his
mizen mast nearly by the board. At 5 minutes past 4,
having silenced the fire of the enemy completely, and
his colours in the main rigging being down, we supposed he had struck ; we then hauled down courses
and shot ahead to repair our rigging, which was extremely cut ; leaving the enemy a complete wreck; soon
after discovered that the enemy's flag was still flying.
Hove to, to repair some of our damage. At 20 minutes past 4, the enemy's mainmast went nearly by the
board. At 50 minutes past four, wore ship and stood
for the enemy. At 25 minutes past 5, got very close
to the enemy in a very effectual raking position, ath-
wart his bows, and was at the very instant of raking
him when he most prudently struck his flag—for had

5

he suffered the broadside to have raked him, his **additional** loss must have been extremely great, as he laid an unmanageable wreck upon the water."

The following correspondence exhibits the character of Capt. Bainbridge in a light so honorable, and so well calculated to exalt the national character, that we are happy in the opportunity of giving it publicity.

GENERAL HISLOP TO COM. BAINBRIDGE.

Dear Sir,   *St. Salvador, January 3, 1813.*

I am justly penetrated with the fullest sense of your very handsome and kind treatment, ever since the fate of war placed me in your power, and I beg once more to renew to you my sincere acknowledgments for the same.

Your acquiescence with my request in granting me my parole, with the officers of my staff, added to the obligations I had previously experienced, claims from me this additional tribute of my thanks. May I now finally flatter myself, that in the further extension of your generous and humane feelings, in the alleviations of the misfortunes of war, that you will have the goodness to fulfil the only wish and request I am now most anxious to see completed, by enlarging on their parole (on the same conditions you have acceded to with respect to myself) all the officers of the *Java* still on board your ship, a favour I shall never cease duly to appreciate by your acquiescence thereto.

I have the honour to subscribe myself, dear sir,
your most obliged and very humble servant,
          (*Signed*)   T. HISLOP.
Com. Bainbridge.

ANSWER OF COM. BAINBRIDGE.

United States frigate Constitution.

Dear Sir,   *St. Salvador, Jan. 3, 1813.*

I have received your letter of this date conveying, sentiments of your feelings for my treatment towards you since the fate of war placed you in my power. The kind expressions which you have been pleased to use, are justly appreciated by me, and far overbalance those common civilities shewn by me, and which are always due to prisoners. I regret that the lumbered state of my ship prevented me from making you as comfortable on board, as I sincerely wished to have done. I have complied with your last request, respecting paroling all the officers of the *Java.* In doing so, your desire, in addition to my disposition to ameliorate as much as possible the situation of those officers, considerably influenced me.

Permit me to tender you (notwithstanding our respective countries are at war) assurances of sincere esteem and high respect, and to assure you that I shall feel at all times highly gratified in hearing of or from you.

With fervent wishes for the recovery of the gallant Capt. Lambert, I have the honor to subscribe myself, very respectfully, &c.

(Signed)   W. BAINBRIDGE.

Lieut. Gen. Hislop, of the British army.

GENERAL HISLOP TO COM. BAINBRIDGE.

DEAR SIR,   *St. Salvador, Jan. 4. 1813.*

Allow me once more to express my sincerest acknowledgments for this last instance of your kind attention to my wishes, by having complied with my request in behalf of the officers of the *Java.* Lieut. Chads delivered to me your very polite and obliging letter, and be assured that I shall feel no less gratification at all times to hear of and from you, than that which you are so good as to express you will derive in receiving information respecting myself.

May I request now that you will be so good as to cause to be looked for a small chest, containing articles of plate, more valuable to me on account of having been presented to me by the colony of Demarara, where I commanded for several years.

I have the honor to be &c.

(Signed)   T. HISLOP.

COM. BAINBRIDGE.

Lieut. Chads presents his compliments to Com. Bainbridge, and is extremely sorry to inform him, Capt. Lambert died a short time since.
St. Salvador, Monday 11 *o'clock.*

COM. BAINBRIDGE TO LIEUT. CHADS

January 4, 1813.

Com. Bainbridge has learnt with real sorrow the death of Capt. Lambert. Though a political enemy, he could not but greatly respect him for the brave defence he made with his ship : and Com. Bainbridge takes this occasion to observe, in justice to Lieut. Chads, who fought the *Java* after Capt. Lambert was wounded, that he did every thing for the defence of that ship, which a brave and skilful officer could do, and that further resistance would have been a wanton effusion of human blood.

Size of the Java.

The *Java* is rated in Steel's list a 38 gun frigate. Her real force was 28 eighteen pounders on the main deck—14 thirty-two pounders, on the quarter deck—4 thirty-two pounders, and 2 large twelve pounders on the forecastle—and one shifting gun, a twénty-four pounder.

The British rate their ship from the number of guns on a particular deck ; and a frigate carrying 28 eighteen pounders on her main deck, is regularly called by them a 38, which rate has frequently fifty-two mounted.

There are on board the *Constitution* some of the *Java's* shot, from which it has been ascertained, that there is scarcely three pounds difference between her eighteens and the American twenty-fours, so called ; and that the thirty-two pound shot of the *Java* is heavier than the thirty-two pound shot of the *Constitution.*

The officers of the *Java,* while on board the *Constitution,* mentioned, that this frigate was formerly the French ship *La Renome,* taken off Madagascar, May 20, 1811, in company with *La Neriede,,* after a

THE HORNET BLOCKADING THE BONNE CITOYENNE.

severe action, by the *Phœbe*, *Astrea* and *Galatea*. At the time of capture, *La Renome* mounted 44 guns —The British added five guns.

HORNET AND BONNE CITOYENNE.

Capt. LAWRENCE, while off the harbour of St. Salvador, in the Hornet, sent a challenge to Capt. Greene, of the *Bonne Citoyenne*, to try the superiority of their vessels in action ; which was conveyed through the American Consul, as follows :

"When I last saw you, I stated to you my wish to meet the *Bonne Citoyenne*, and authorized you to make my wish known to Capt. Greene. I now request you to state to him, that I will meet him whenever he may be pleased to come out, and pledge my honor that neither the *Constitution*, nor any other American vessel shall interfere.

Com. Bainbridge, of the *Constitution* frigate, confirms to me (says the consul) the request of Capt. Lawrence, in these words :—" If Capt. Greene wishes to try equal force, *I pledge my honor* to give him an opportunity, by being out of the way or not interfering."

The following letter from Mr. Frederick Landeman, the English Consul to the American Consul, conveys Capt. Greene's reply to the challenge.

SIR, "*Fort de St. Pedro, Dec.* 29, 1812.

I transmitted your letter to me, of yesterday, to Capt. P. B. Greene, to whom the substance is directed ; and, having received his reply, I herewith insert it verbatim.

"I hasten to acknowledge the favour of your communication, made to me this morning from Mr. Hill, consul to the United States of America, on the subject of a challenge, stated to have been offered through Mr. Hill, by Capt Lawrence, of the United States sloop of war the *Hornet*, to myself, as commander of his Britannic Majesty's ship the *Bonne Citoyenne,* anchored in this port, pledging his honor, as well as that of Com. Bainbridge, that no advantage shall be taken by the *Constitution* or any other American vessel whatever on the occasion. I am convinced, sir, if such rencontre were to take place, the result could not be long dubious, and would terminate favourably to the ship which I have the honor to command ; but I am equally convinced that Com. Bainbridge could not swerve so much from the duty he owes to his country, as to become an inactive spectator, and see a ship, belonging to the very squadron under his orders, fall into the hands of an enemy ; this reason operates powerfully on my mind for not exposing the *Bonne Citoyenne* to a risk, upon terms so manifestly disadvantageous as those proposed by Com. Bainbridge ; indeed, nothing could give me greater satisfaction than complying with the wishes of Capt. Lawrence; and I erneastly hope that chance will afford him an opportunity of meeting the *Bonne Citoyenne* under different circumstances, to enable him to distinguish himself in the manner he is now so desirous of doing. I further assure you, that my ship will, at all times, be prepared, wherever she may be, to repel any attacks made against her, and I shall also act offensively, wherever I judge it proper to do so.

I am, sir, with great regard, &c."

HORNET AND PEACOCK.

CAPT. LAWRENCE'S LETTER TO THE SEC'Y OF THE NAVY.

SIR,
U. S. ship Hornet, Holmes' Hole,
March 19, 1813.

I HAVE the honor to inform you of the arrival at this port of the United States ship *Hornet,* under my command, from a cruise of 145 days ; and to state to you, that after Com. Bainbridge left the coast of Brazils, (Jan. 6) I continued off the harbour of St. Salvador, blockading the *Bonne Citoyenne,* until the 24th, when the *Montague* 74 hove in sight, and chased me into the harbour ; but night coming on, I wore and stood out to the southward. Knowing that she had left Rio Janeiro for the express purpose of relieving the *Bonne Citoyenne* and the packet, [which I had also blockaded for 14 days, and obliged her mail to go to Rio, in a Portuguese smack] I judged it most prudent to shift my cruising ground, and hauled by the wind to the eastward, with the view of cruising off Pernambuco, and on the 4th of February captured the English brig *Resolution*, of 10 guns, from Rio Janeiro, bound to Morahnam, with coffee, jerked beef, flour, fustic, and butter, and about 23,000 dollars in specie. As she sailed dull and I could not spare hands to man her, I took out the money and set her on fire. I ran down the coast of Morahnam, and cruised there a short time : from thence ran off Surinam. After cruising off that coast from the 15th to the 22d of Feb. without meeting a vessel, I stood for Demerara, with an intention, should I be fortunate on that station, to run through the West Indies, on my way to the United States. But, on the 24th in the morning, I discovered a brig to the leeward, to which I gave chase ; ran into quarter less four, and not having a pilot, was obliged to haul off, the fort at the entrance of Demerara river at this time bearing S. W. distant about two and a half leagues. Previous to giving up the chase, I discover-ed a vessel at anchor without the bar, with English colours flying, apparently a brig of war, In beating round Corobano Bank, in order to get at her, at half past 3 P. M, discovered another sail on our weather quarter, edging down for us. At 20 minutes past 4, she hoisted English colours, at which time we discovered her to be a large man-of-war brig—beat to quarters, cleared ship for action, and kept close by the wind, in order, if possible, to get the weather gage. At 10 minutes past 5, finding I could weather the enemy, I hoisted American colours and tacked. At 25 minutes past 5, in passing each other, exchanged broadsides within half pistol shot. Observing the enemy in the act of

ed. Our loss was trifling in comparison. John Place, killed ; Samuel Coulson, and John Delyrumple severely wounded ; George Coffin and Lewis Todd severely burnt by the explosion of a cartridge. Todd survived only a few days. Our rigging and sails are much cut. One shot through the foremast ; and the bowsprit slightly injured. Our hull received little or no damage. At the time I brought the *Peacock* to action, the *L'Espiegle* (the brig mentioned as being at anchor) mounting sixteen 32 pound carronades and two long nines, lay about six miles in shore of me, and could plainly see the whole of the action. Apprehensive that she would beat out to the assistance of her consort, such exertions were made by my officers and crew repairing damages, &c. that by nine o'clock my boats were stowed away, new set of sails bent, and the ship completely ready for action. At 2 A. M. got under way and stood by the wind to the northward and westward, under easy sail.

On mustering next morning, found we had two hundred and seventy seven souls on board, including the crew of the American brig *Hunter*, of Portland, taken a few days since by the *Peacock*. As we had been on two thirds allowance of provisions, for some time, and had but 3,400 gallons of water on board, I reduced the allowance to three pints a man, and determined to make the best of my way to the United States.

The *Peacock* was deservedly styled one of the finest vessels of her class in the British navy. I should judge her to be about the tonnage of the *Hornet.* Her beam was greater by five inches ; but her extreme length not so great by four feet. She mounted sixteen 24 pound carronades, two long nines, one 12 pound carronade on her top-gallant forecastle, as a shifting gun, and one 4 or 6 pounder, and two swivels mounted aft. I find, by her quarter bill, that her crew consisted of 134 men, 4 of whom were absent in a prize.

The cool and determined conduct of my officers and crew during the action, and their almost unexam-

6

pled exertions afterwards, entitle them to my warmest acknowledgments, and I beg leave most earnestly to recommend them to the notice of government.

By the indisposition of Lieut. Stewart, I was deprived of the services of an excellent officer. Had he been able to stand the deck, I am sure his exertions would not have been surpassed by any one on board. I should be doing injustice to the merits of Lieut. Shubrick, and acting Lieuts. Conner and Newton, were I not to recommend them particularly to your notice. Lieut. Shubrick was in the actions of the *Guerriere* and *Java*. Capt. Hull and Com. Bainbridge can bear testimony of his coolness and good conduct on both occasions. I have the honor to be, sir, your obedient servant,

Hon. WM. JONES,   JAMES LAWRENCE.
Secretary of the Navy.

P. S. At the commencement of the action, my sailing-master and seven men were absent in a prize ; and Lieut. Stewart and six men were on the sick list.

As there is every prospect of the wind being to the eastward in the morning, I shall make the best of my way to New-York.

Liberality of American tars.

It is a fact worthy of note, and in the highest degree honorable to our brave tars, that, the day preceeding the destruction of his Britannic Majesty's brig *Peacock* the crew of the *Hornet* made a subscription, and supplied the prisoners, who had lost almost every thing, with two shirts, a blue jacket and trowsers, each.

Tribute of gratitude.

SIR,   *New-York, March 27, 1813.*

We, the surviving officers of his Britannic Majesty's brig *Peacock*, beg leave to return you our grateful acknowledgments for the kind attention and hospitality we experienced during the time we remained on board the United States sloop *Hornet*. So much was done to alleviate the distressing and uncomfortable situation, in which we were placed when received on board the sloop you command, that we cannot better express our feelings, than by saying, "we ceased to consider ourselves prisoners," and every thing that friendship could dictate, was adopted by you, and the officers of the *Hornet*, to remedy the inconveniences we should otherwise have experienced from the unavoidable loss of the whole of our property and clothes by the sudden sinking of the *Peacock*.

Permit us then, sir, impressed, as we are, with a grateful sense of your kindness, for ourselves and the other officers and ship's company, to return you, and the officers of the *Hornet*, our sincere thanks, which we shall feel obliged, if you will communicate to them in our name, and believe us to remain with a high sense of the kind offices you have rendered us, your humble servants,

F. A. WRIGHT, 1st Lieutenant,
C. LAMUERT, 2d Lieutenant.
EDWARD LOTT, Master.
I. WHITAKER, Surgeon.
F. D. UNWIN, Purser.

JAMES LAWRENCE, *Esq.*
Commander U. S. Sloop Hornet.

The demolition of the *Peacock* by the *Hornet* appears to have been a master-piece of American gunnery. When the *Leopard*, a 50 gun ship, attacked the *Chesapeake* of 36 guns, she poured her broadsides for nearly 20 minutes, without cessation, and close aboard, into an unresisting, cluttered and inferiour ship. Yet only three were killed, and a proportionate number wounded. The *Wasp*, in 43 minutes cut down the *Frolic* from 119 men to 20, capable of doing duty ; and the *Hornet*, in only 15 minutes, killed 9, wounded 35, and totally shivered her superior antagonist to atoms !

CHESAPEAKE AND SHANNON.

*The following account of the capture of the Chesa-
peake, appeared in a Boston newspaper on Friday, 4th June, 1813.*

ON Tuesday forenoon, 1st of June, the British
frigate *Shannon*, Capt. Broke, appeared off our harbour, and displayed her colours.

The United States frigate *Chesapeake*, Capt. Lawrence, was then at anchor, just below fort Independence. As soon as the enemy was seen, she fired a
gun, and hoisted her colors. Preparations were immediately made for sailing, and when the officers had
assembled on board, and the tide served, she got under way. The *Shannon* proceeded down the bay, the
Chesapeake following under a press of sail.

Spectators were collected on every place in Boston,
which commanded a view of the sea, but the frigates
proceeded to the eastward till lost sight of from the
town, and our citizens on shore were thereby spared
the distress of witnessing the result, a pain which those
had to encounter, who were spectators of the conflict
in boats and vessels ; and from whom the particulars
of the battle, as far as at present known here, are obtained.

The *Chesapeake* had a colour at each mast head.
That on the fore royal mast was white, and appeared
to have some inscription on it. She was put under
her topsails on approaching the enemy, fired a gun,
and 10 or 12 minutes before 6 the cannonade became
general and severe, and the *Shannon* experienced some
injury in her spars and rigging, while the *Chesapeake*
suffered no visible damage ; and appeared to have the
advantage of her antagonist. About 6, the *Chesapeake*,
which was to windward, ran on board the enemy, and
the contest continued yard-arm to yard-arm. In about
5 minutes there was a great explosion on board the
Chesapcake, but whether caused by accident, or any
new combustible used by the enemy, is uncertain. Soon
after the smoke thus caused had dispersed, the ships

THE CHESAPEAKE & SHANNON.

separated, and the English colour (a blue flag) was seen over the American ensign inverted ; and both vessels then stood to the eastward, undoubtedly for Halifax. From the manner in which the action was fought, neither of the frigates were essentially injured in their masts or rigging.

We know not that any written challenge was received by Capt. Lawrence, but one intended for him reached Salem just after he sailed from Boston. If one was delivered on board the *Chesapeake*, duplicates were written.

The *Chesapeake* was rated 39 guns, but we understand mounted 49, the *Shannon* was rated 38, but, it is said, mounted 52—and was superiour in weight of metal. The number of men probably about equal. The *Chesapeake* had been refitted for a cruise and was nearly ready for sea.

Capt. Lawrence took the command of the Chesapeake a few days since. Some changes had also occurred in the other officers, and the 1st lieutenant was sick on shore.* For the same officers to be long associated, we should conceive an advantage. Many of the sailors were fresh recruits, and little or no opportunity had been afforded to discipline them, as the business of equipping the vessel for sea was not completed. The enemy, on the contrary, there is reason to believe, was prepared. All her officers and men had been for several months in the same relative situations—the complement in each respect was full—and the seamen had had every chance of being thoroughly exercised. From these circumstances Capt. Lawrence might, without impropriety, have delayed the interview, but he yielded to the impulse of his intrepid

* Lieut. Octavius Augustus Page died at Boston, of the lung fever, on Friday the 4th of June, three days after the battle, aged 28. He was a son of the late Governor Page of Virginia, one of the oldest Lieutenants in the navy of the United States, and the 1st of the *Chesapeake*. This gentleman is deeply lamented as a brave and skilful officer. Capt. Lawrence deplored the necessity of proceeding to sea without him, and Lieut. Page, during his illness, seemed to forget his own sufferings in regret of his inability to rejoin his ship, and in anxiety for the fate of his gallant companions in arms.

spirit as soon as he saw the foe, and whatever specu-
lations there may be as to what would have been the
mode of battle deserving preference (speaking after the
event,) no one doubts the bravery of the commander,
officers and crew, and that he did what he considered
best.

OFFICIAL ACCOUNT

From Lieut. Budd to the Secretary of the navy dated
   SIR,   *Halifax, June* 15, 1813.

The unfortunate death of Capt. James Lawrence,
and Lieut. Augustus C. Ludlow, has rendered it my
duty to inform you of the capture of the late United
States frigate *Chesapeake.*

On Tuesday June 1st, at 8 A. M. we unmoored ship,
and at meridian got under way from President's roads,
with a light wind from the southward and westward,
and proceeded on a cruise. A ship was then in sight
in the offing, which had the appearance of a ship of
war, and which, from information received from pilot
boats and craft, we believed to be the British frigate
Shannon. We made sail in chase and cleared ship
for action. At ½ past 4 P. M. she hove to, with her
head to the southward and eastward. At 5 P. M. took
in the royals and top-gallant sails, and at ½ past 5 hauled the courses up. About 15 minutes before 6 P. M.
the action commenced within pistol shot. The first
broadside did great execution on both sides, damaged
our rigging, killed among others Mr. White, the sailing master, and wounded Capt. Lawrence. In about
12 minutes after the commencement of the action, we
fell on board of the enemy, and immediately after,
one of our arm chests on the quarter deck was blown
up by a hand grenade, thrown from the enemy's ship.
In a few minutes one of the Captain's Aids came on
the gun deck to inform me that the boarders were called. I immediately called the boarders away, and proceeded to the spar deck, where I found that the enemy
had succeeded in boarding us, and had gained possession of our quarter deck. I immediately gave orders

to haul on board the foretack, for the purpose of shooting the ship clear of the other, and then made an attempt to regain the quarter deck, but was wounded and thrown down on the gun deck. I again made an effort to collect the boarders, but in the mean time the enemy had gained complete possession of the ship. On my being carried down to the cockpit, I there found Capt. Lawrence and Lieut. Ludlow both mortally wounded; the former had been carried below previously to the ship's being boarded; the latter was wounded in attempting to repel the boarders. Among those who fell early in the action was Mr. Edward J. Ballard, the 4th lieutenant, and Lieut. James Broom of marines.

I herein enclose to you a return of the killed and wounded by which you will perceive that every officer, upon whom the charge of the ship would devolve, was either killed or wounded previously to her capture. The enemy report the loss of Mr. Watt, their 1st lieutenant; the purser; the captain's clerk, and 23 seamen killed; and Capt. Broke, a midshipman, and 56 seamen wounded.

The *Shannon* had, in addition to her full complement, an officer and 16 men belonging to the *Belle Poule*, and a part of the crew belonging to the *Tenedoes.*

I have the honour to be, with very great respect, &c.

Hon. WM. JONES, GEORGE BUDD.

Sec'y of Navy.

KILLED—Edw. J. Ballard, acting lieutenant; James Broom, 1st lieutenant of marines; Wm. A. White, sailing master; Pollard Hopewell, midshipman; John Evans do.; Courtland Livingston, do.; Daniel Burnham, quarter master; James Woodbury do.; Michael Kelly, quarter gunner; John Carter, boatswain's mate,—also, twenty-six seamen, and eleven marines.

WOUNDED—James Lawrence, Esq. captain (since deceased:) Aug. C. Ludlow, lieutenant, (since deceased;) Geo. Budd, lieutenant, Wm. Cox, acting do.; Samuel Livermore, acting chaplain; Francis Nichols,

Walter abbot, Wm. A. Weaver, Edmund M. Russell, Wm. Barry, midshipmen. Peter Adams, boatswain, (since dead;) Jefferson Griffith, quarter master; James A. Lewis, quarter master; Forbes Dela, quarter gunner, (since dead;) Samuel Hutson, sail maker's mate; Thomas Finnagan, gunner's yeoman; Thomas Smith 2d, quarter gunner; John Veazy, do.; John Giles, do.; Thomas Rouse, do.; and Thomas Jackson 2d, quarter master, and fifty seven seamen,—eight of whom afterwards died of their wounds.

Marines—Twenty marines were also wounded and one died of his wounds.

Killed 47; wounded 99; wounded, since dead, 14. The British return states the loss of the *Shannon* to be 27 killed and 58 wounded.

FUNERAL OF CAPTAIN LAWRENCE.

The following orders were issued the day previous to the funeral :—

GARRISON ORDERS.

Halifax 7th June, 1815.

A funeral party will be furnished to-morrow, by the 64th regiment, consisting the 300 rank and file, with a proper proportion of officers, and to be supplied with three rounds of blank cartridges each man; to inter the remains of Capt. Lawrence, late of the American frigate *Chesapeake*, from the King's Wharf, at ¼ past 1 oclock, P. M.

The band of that corps will attend, and the party will be commanded by Lieut. Col. Sir J .Wardlow.

The officers of the garrison will be pleased to attend the commandant there, at ¼ before 2, to march in procession, wearing a piece of black crape round their left arm.

    (*Signed*)   F. T. THOMAS,
                                  Major of Brigade.

NAVY ORDER.

The body of the commander of the late United

States frigate *Chesapeake*, will be interred to-morrow at 2 o'clock. The captains and commanders, with a portion of lieutenants and midshipmen, agreeably to the following order of procession, will attend the funeral, and will assemble precisely at 1 o'clock along side of the *Chesapeake*, for that purpose.

THOMAS M. CAPEL,
Capt. and senior officer at Halifax.

ORDER OF PROCESSION FROM THE SHIP.

Pall bearers		Pall bearers
Abreast of the corpse.		Abreast of the corpse
Capt. BAKER,		Capt. HEAD,
	THE BODY.	
PEARSE,		PERCHEL,
COLLIER,		BLYTE.

Boats two and two, with midshipmen and lieutenants, commanders or lieutenants commanding vessels.

Commanders.
Post captains.

ORDER OF PROCESSION ON SHORE.

Funeral firing party.

Pall bearers { THE BODY } Pall bearers.

Officers of Privateers.
American naval officers.
English naval officers.
Midshipmen.
Lieutenants.
Officers of garrison according to rank.
Post captains.
Staff officers.
General and Senior officers.

7

The respect due to a brave enemy was yesterday shewn to the remains of Capt. Lawrence.—The corpse was landed from the *Chesapeake*, under a discharge of minute guns, and at 2 o'clock reached the King's wharf—the American ensign was spread as a pall over the coffin, on which was placed the sword of the deceased—six captains of the navy officiated as pall-bearers—six companies of the 64th regiment, commanded by Sir John Wardlow, preceded the corpse—the officers of the Chesapeake followed it as mourners—the officers of the navy generally attended—Sir Thomas Saumarez, the staff, and officers of the garrison—and the procession was closed by a number of respectable inhabitants.—The funeral service was performed by the Rev. Rector of St. Paul's and three vollies discharged by the troops over the grave.

EXTRACT OF A LETTER.

June 19, 1813.

"I suppose the newspapers and letters sent from Halifax, by such of the officers, whose wounds would permit them to write, will give you all the particulars of the loss of our frigate *Chesapeake*, which had arrived there. She came in eight or nine miles ahead of the *Shannon*, and appeared to out-sail her fast. When she saluted one of the forts six miles from the town, and shewed the English over the American colours, the Halifax people thought it was the *President*, a prize, and there was a general shout. But I undeceived all whom I could speak to, as I knew the ship; and when they found it to be the *Chesapeake*, and that her captain was dead, not a huzza was heard, except I believe on board a brig. I was near *La Hogue*, a 74, and am certain her crew did not cheer. Capt. Lawrence was highly respected for his humanity to the crew of the *Peacock*; and marks of real grief were seen in the countenances of all the inhabitants I had a chance to see. I can say truly, that all appeared to lament his death; and I heard several say, they considered the blood which had been shed on the *Chesa-*

peake's deck as dear as that of their own countrymen. They also speak against the war as cruel and unnatural ; and hope the States will not compel them to continue it. I saw three mahogany coffins carried on board the *Chesapeake* the day of the funeral. In one of them Capt. Lawrence was placed, and the coffins put into a twelve-oared barge, which rowed minute strokes, followed by a procession of boats. The corpse was received at the king's wharf, by a regiment of troops, and a full band of music. Six of the oldest navy captains carried the pall, which was one of the colours of the *Chesapeake* ; which they said was considered a particular mark of respect by naval men, as it was a token that he had defended his colours bravely, and that at his tomb they should not be separated from him. The procession was very long, and every thing was conducted in the most solemn and respectful manner and the wounded officers of both nations, who followed in the procession, made the scene very affecting. I never attended a funeral in my life when my feelings were so much struck. There was not the least mark of exultation that I saw, even among the commonest people.

The *Shannon* received five or six shots in her hull, near wind and water, but they were stopped and leaded. She was lying in the harbor, and they were overhauling and shifting her rigging. They expected to get her to sea shortly.

Capt. Broke and Capt. Lawrence were both delirious from their wounds ; and the ships were both brought in by very young officers. Capt. Broke we consider as very dangerously wounded, having his head cut from the top to near his mouth by the ear. When Capt. Lawrence could speak, he would say, 'Don't give up the ship.' He was first wounded in the leg, which bled much, and weakened him ; but he would not be carried below ; when he received a grape shot in the lower part of his belly, of which he died. Capt. Broke was stated to have received his wound in stooping down, trying to save the life of one of the

Chesapeake's crew, which one of his own men was mangling and whose head he cut off.''

Shortly after the fate of the *Chesapeake* and her brave defenders was known in the United States, B. W. Crowninshield Esq. of Salem, solicited the American government for permission to sail with a flag of truce to Halifax, for the purpose of obtaining the entombed bodies of Capt. Lawrence and Lieut. Ludlow: the permission being granted, Mr. Crowninshield sailed in a vessel, manned by himself and ten other masters of vessels, and on application to the British admiral, commanding on that station, obtained the object of his request. On their arrival at Salem the funeral obsequies of the brave deceased were again celebrated in the most solemn and impressive manner.

Business was suspended, and the whole town was crowded either to perform or to witness the funeral honors to the fallen heroes. About noon the bodies were removed from the cartel *Henry*, accompanied by eight boats, manned by sailors in uniform, rowing minute-strokes; the cartel brig and the U. S. brig of war *Rattlesnake*, Capt. Creighton, firing minute guns during their passage. The bodies were landed, and the coffins placed on hearses, which were lent by the Board of Health of Boston; the U. S. flag covering the hearses. At one o'clock the procession, consisting of the officers of the U. S. navy and army, the clergy of all denominations, the different corporate bodies, the several marine societies, together with citizens and strangers from Boston and the vicinity, moved under the escort of the elegant company of light infantry, commanded by Capt. J. C. King. Minute guns were fired during the whole procession by the Salem artillery, under Capt. Peabody, which was stationed on Washington-Square. The movement was deeply impressive. The sides of the streets were crowded, and the windows were filled with spectators, and many were on the tops of houses. The tolling of the deep toned bells—the solemn melody of the music—the slow and melancholy-inspiring pace of the procession—the appearance of the sable coffins with their accompaniments—and the awe-striking report of the minute guns, rendered the whole a scene of solemn woe. Two hours elapsed while the procession was moving to the church ; and the multitude was so great, that a small part only could be accomodated to hear the Eulogy by the Hon. Judge Story. After the orator had concluded, the bodies were entombed with the customary military and masonic ceremonies. The church was shrouded in the sable habiliments of woe, and the sacred services of religion, and the musick, were appropriate.

During the day, our own, as well as the neutral merchant vessels in the harbour wore their colours at half mast.

In the procession were several officers of high military rank—Maj. Gen. H. Dearborn, Brig. Gen. T. H. Cushing, &c.

We have understood that the remains are to be reembarked in the cartel *Henry*, and carried to New-York, and there to be at the disposal of their respective relatives.

A great number of the citizens of Boston attended the funeral rites in Salem. Minute guns were fired at 1 o'clock, and the flags were displayed half-mast from the frigate *Constitution*, the vessels in the harbour, the forts, gun-houses, and public buildings. A company of artillery left town for Salem on Sunday evening, to assist in the funeral honors.

Their remains were soon after conveyed to New-York, where a procession was formed, which, with the spectators, it is supposed, amounted to fifty thousand. The burial service was once more performed, and the dead committed to the tomb.

LOSS OF LAWRENCE AND THE CHESAPEAKE.
"Pro Patria"

Of the sea-fight in the time of the Commonwealth, it is said, by a British historian, "that Blake, who was victor, gained not more honor than Tromp, who was vanquished." The remark is alike true of the recent engagement. The perseverance of Broke was equalled by the promptness of Lawrence. This vessel was met the instant it was ascertained there was no other to meet. His very first movement was announced to the foe, who, in plain sight, was challenging battle and crushing defiance. His going into action was to be full as gallant as his reception. But he met his fate in the first ball. "Give not up the ship," he said, and fell, no officer unwounded near, to bear him up in his fall. He cared only for victory and his country ; never for life.

No restlessness for battle betrayed him into action. He had fought and conquered ; had realized the glory of victory, and helped to establish the honor of his country. Not to go out would be an acknowledgement of victory. The result of a meeting could be no more. True, she had a crew picked from the squadron. But were not American seaman equal to any ? Her captain and men well known to each other. Can mine want confidence in me ? Has she not been long upon the cruise, and preparing for the purpose ? What then ? Are we not always ready ? And what if she be the better sailer ? The challenger will not dare to retreat ; and I shall willingly spare him the trouble of pursuit.

The die was cast ; and let those event-enlightened reasoners who have now the presumtion to think it was then cast in rashness, ask themselves the question, what they would not have said, and what others would not have said had the *Chesapeake* to this hour remained in port, supinely at anchor, beholding the British flag, day by day, cross and recross the harbour, waving, triumphantly, from a frigate not so decidedly her superior, as to be deemed generally much more than a match. As for Lawrence, if he had had " forty thousand lives,"he would have thought the loss of all was gain to the surviving such a sight.

If not rash in going out, still less can this imputation be cast upon his commencing the battle. He was not only so cautious as not to waste a single ball at a fruitless distance ; but so gloriously collected as to hold himself in reserve, and receive his enemy's successive fires, until within musket shot he was able to pour in his whole broadside at once. To what then was owing the sudden termination of this deadly conflict ? Not indeed to an explosion that swept the deck of its officers. Mistaking only the cause, never was conjecture more fatally right as to the affect. The captain, every lieutenant without exception, officers of marines, many of the midshipman, the sailing master, the boatswain, were all, early in the action, levelled with the deck ; and at the precise point of time, when it was most of all important that the *Chesapeake* should gain a particular position, at the instant of boarding, the loss of an assential part of her rigging threw her into the wind, and gave to the enemy the decisive advantage. The desperation not over, Broke now led his boarders ; an effort, Lawrence doubtless had equalled, but for his previous disability ; and had probably made his adversary bitterly repent his daring temerity. Nothing is farther than blame from any single officer on board. Ludlow, the 1st lieutenant, received three balls in the fight, and has since carried them to the grave. Every man did his duty. The enemy have gained a battle, in which it may be said, without disparagement to their prowess, that certainly their valour and their skill could not have been greater than was their good fortune. We grudge them not the only laurel they have won. Under these circumstances, were it not deeply drenched in the blood of her sons, our country could say to the enemy, "take it, and welcome."

Most probably the annals of the world may in vain be challenged to furnished another instance of so short an engagement, and on each side such tremendous execution.

Capt. Lawrence, at the time of his death, had been nearly sixteen years in the service, with only one furlough, and that of six weeks. In September, 1798, he entered as midshipman; and in two years was promoted to an acting lieutenant in the *Adams*, Capt. Robinson, in which capacity he continued, till the reduction of the navy; an event which alone prevented his appointment being confirmed. He, however, was not to remain midshipman long. In the war with Tripoli he was promoted to a lieutenancy, and was originally the 1st officer of the *Enterprize*, but afterwards removed to the *John Adams*. He signalized himself in this memorable warfare by volunteering as first lieutenant, with about seventy men and Decatur in the ketch *Intrepid* of 4 guns, to destroy the *Philadelphia*, of 44, in the harbour of Tripoli, and at the very mouth of the Bashaw's cannon. He returned to this country with Preble; and to Tripoli as commander of gun boat No. 6. Nearly five years in all he served against the Turks; and was afterwards constantly engaged; in the *Constitution* as first lieutenant—and in the *Vixen, Wasp, Argus* and *Hornet*, as commander. His first cruise the present war was under Com. Rodgers; and we all remember what interest his countrymen took in that remonstrance, temperate, yet firm, which he made so immediately after his return, against the unprecedented promotion of the gallant Morris, and in which he contrived, with delicacy and spirit, at once to save the feelings of a brother, and to vindicate his own. Under the countenance of Rodgers and of Bainbridge he urged his appeal, but left it to its fate, and sailed with the latter upon that brilliant cruise which eventuated so gloriously to his country, his commander and himself. Of the right and fitness of challenging in a public war and at sea, we have, no doubt. This whole business of naval warfare, incalculable as it is in its importance to a commercial nation, is yet a strife only for glory. It is not to enrich or augment one fleet at the expense of another; to support a country by spoils, or extend empire by the conquest of ships. It is a contest for superiority, a mere struggle for distinction; and the opportunity, which cannot otherwise be met, may very fairly be sought. But let those refined minds, those nicely scrupulous souls, who quarrel upon principle with the right of challenge, consider how Lawrence was circumstanced ; and either withhold their censure, in this instance at least, from his challenge to the *Bonne Citoyenne*, or avow, at once, their utter unwillingness to pardon any thing to "poor human nature." He had left a country, which he had certainly reason to distrust as regardless of his claims, and when he was as yet uncertain what was their fate. Unless those claims were answered, he was publickly pledged to go into retirement on his return, to the minds of some men perhaps with doubtful dignity, to the forfeiture of his only object in life, and to the rendering utterly useless all his habits of living. To this, however, he was equal. But "a wounded spirit who can bear ?" The *Bonne Citoyenne* however did not come out ; and as far as may be infered from the fate of the *Peacock*, a vessel equal in force to the *Bonne Citoyenne*, there was no rashness in giving this challenge, since, had she come out, her fate, in all human probability had been the same. But she saved her money and lost her credit. The challenge declined was pronounced by high authority "a victory gained." But the character of James Lawrence not to be left to any constructive victory, however fair the construction. On his way home he fell in with the *Peacock*, which in less than 15* minutes he compelled to make signs of distress as her signal for surrender ; and, to his eternal honor be it recorded, lost more men in saving, than in conquering the enemy. One man only was killed in the battle. Three of his "brave fellows" went down in attempting to save the vanquished from the sinking vessel.

---

* It is said that Capt. L. stated in conversion, on his last visit to this town, that the interval between firing his first shot and the *Peacock's* hoisting her flag, union down, was only 11 minutes by the watch ; but as his clerk had got it down 15, he thought that time short enough, and would not correct it. This certainly justified the statement in the Halifax papers, " that a vessel, moored for the purpose of experiment, could not have been sunk sooner."

It is with delight the most exquisite ; with pleasure the most elevated ; that we dwell upon incidents like these, which have invariable characterized all our naval achievements. Truly our ocean heroes are humanely glorious. Such has been their humanity, it is difficult to say, whether the enemy have more of dread of their valour as warriours, or of admiration at their magnanimity as victors.

This engagement with the *Peacock* has been pronounced by Lieut. Ludlow, whom we name with pride, and certainly not without sympathy, not to have been surpassed " for brilliancy of design and boldness of execution," by any of all the bold and brilliant events, that at sea have distinguished this war.

Capt. Lawrence was as amiable in his private, as he was admirable in his professional life.* The domestic were in the same circle with the ocean virtues, each heightening the charm of the others. As a husband, such was the ardour of his affection, that there is a sacredness in the griefs of the chief mourner of his country upon which we dare not suffer even our sympathies abruptly to intrude. As a Christian, his proof of faith in our Father in Heaven was love to every brother upon earth. Reduced foreigners in our own metropolis realized the munificence of his private charity. As a companion, he looked on you only to smile, and with that blandness which is characteristic of child-like simplicity. If in him the gentleman forgot not the sailor, the sailor certainly ever remembered the gentleman. As a citizen, believing order to be " heaven's first law," and content with filling up completely his own department, he left to civilians the civil. To political opinions he had however a right, which he exercised without disguise. But satisfied that it must forever be patriotism to fight for one's country, he desired no better naval creed than Blake's

---

* With a heart of a most magnanimous texture, the lamented Lawrence took under his particular care a youth, whose father being killed in the *Peacock*, was left an orphan, bereaved of parents, and had it not been for our hero, would have been left in his tender years exposed to the shocks of a boisterous world.

under Cromwell. *"It is still our duty to fight for our country, into what hands soever the government may fall."*

The funeral solemnities of Capt. Lawrence took place abroad.

' By strangers honor'd and by strangers mourn'd !'

His enemies were his mourners; or rather the enemies of his country; for personal enemies Lawrence had none. The tears of Britons evinced how much rather they would have shewn homage to his person, than respectful attention to his remains. That flag, from which he had parted but with life, was restored to him in death.

"His signal once, but now his shroud !" *

The publication of the subsequent is due to the memory of the heroes, who on that disastrous day, so gallantly sacrificed their lives for their country.

The members of the court were Com. Bainbridge, and Captains Hull and Smith, names indentified with chivalry, and dear to Americans; and their report contains the only authentic account of the engagement with the *Shannon*.

Capt. Lawrence's sailing orders were peremptory; and when the enemy hove in sight, the *Chesapeake's* crew were mutinous, on account of the non-payment prize-money. The commander could not have disobeyed his orders with impunity; and mutiny was to be overawed by energy. He passed the day in preparation for action, and in the encouragement of his men; and before night-fall, the whole ship was animated with his heroic soul.

The unexampled destruction of the *Guerriere* was

* We would have every opportunity improved of being just to an enemy. As Capt. Broke had not his senses till after his arrival at Halifax; and as his 1st lieutenant was killed in the action, the command of two frigates devolving upon a 2d lieutenant at a time when the precise extent of the injury to either could not be ascertained, and when each was a sort of human slaughter house; his paramount, if not his only duty was to make the best of his way to Halifax, especially as Capt. Lawrence was so badly wounded, that his end might have been accelerated by any attempt at removing him out of the vessel. The utmost then in their power to do in this case, has been done, and done well.

accomplished in less than 18 minutes, and the vanquished ship had 63 killed and wounded. One third more metal is thrown by the *Constitution's* than the *Chesapeake's* broadside; and the *Shannon* was so cut in her hull, by eight minutes' broadsiding, that it was with difficulty she could be kept afloat during the night; and she numbered 88 killed and wounded. It has been truly remarked, "that the world never witnessed so destructive a fire from so limited a broadside in so short a space." Lawrence fell! and the remainder of the fight, if fight it may be called, was as disgraceful as the first eight minutes were brilliant. The moment after Capt. Lawrence was carried below, Capt. Broke boarded our quarter deck at the head of 20 men. Nothing but desperation could have prompted or justified the measure. Lieut. Budd, the senior officer, had now gained the spar deck, where there were, with those who had come up, from 60 to 75 well men. No attempt was made to bring more men from the gun-deck, and none on the spar deck to rally the men and charge the boarders. This melancholy pause continued, as Mr. Budd has testified, 3 minutes. In the mean time, Capt. Broke, without making any attack, had collected near 100 men, and proceeded to the attack on the starboad side of the ship. Mr. Budd now perceived a British uniform, and concluded that the men on the quarter deck were the enemy, at whose approach our men fled to the forecastle, precipitated themselves through the fore hatchway to the gun-deck, and from thence to the birth-deck, without an effort to prevent them. A few only of the enemy were killed or wounded by involuntary and accidental blows, and the fire from the tops; and he continued his unresisted havoc, till not a man was left on either deck. Although Lawrence was prostrate, his soul was in arms. From the cockpit he issued his memorable orders—"keep the guns going"—"fight her till she strikes or sinks"—and when he knew that the enemy had carried the spar deck, he sent the emphatic message to the gun deck, "don't give up the ship."

When he was apprised of the issue, he only remarked, "then the officers of the deck hav'nt toed the mark— the *Shannon* was whip'd when I left."

The officer-like conduct of this gallant martyr, on this day, has been impeached by some of the survivors of that dreadful conflict. The inevitable disadvantages under which he fought a superior ship, perfectly prepared; the chivalry with which he courted the contest; and the brilliancy of it before he fell, should alone rescue his memory from censure. Cruel sacrilege to profane the sanctuary of the tomb to shield living defection from merited disgrace! Every witness upon the court-martial, under a close cross-examination, not only repelled the foul slander, but decidedly established his high character as a commander.

In a very unreserved conversation, Com. Decatur, with whom Capt. Lawrence had served much, was asked, "whether his intrinsic merit as an officer, justified the enthusiastic veneration in which the nation held his memory?" After a short pause he answered, "yes, sir, it did; and the fellow died as well as he lived; but it is a part of a soldier's life to die well. He had no talk; but he inspired all about him with ardour: he always saw the best thing to be done; he knew the best way to execute it; and had no more dodge in him than the mainmast," *Laudatum est, a laudato viro.* This vindication is due to the ashes of the inured patriot.

When the ill starred fortunes of this ship are recalled to memory; when we recollect that her deck was the death scene of our favourte hero, with victory almost in his grasp, we involuntary adopt the language of Milton's monody upon his shipwrecked friend,—

" It was that fatal and perfidious bark ;
" Built in the eclipse ; and rigged with curses dark ;
" That sunk so low that sacred head of thine ; "

REPORT.

The court are unanimously of opinion, that the *Chesapeake* was gallantly carried into action by her late brave commander ; and no doubt rests with the court from comparison of the injury respectively sustained by the frigates, that the fire of the *Chesapeake* was much superior to that of the *Shannon*. The *Shannon* being much cut in her spars and rigging, and receiving many shot in and below the water line was reduced almost to a sinking condition, after only a few minutes cannonading from the *Chesapeake ;* while the *Chesapeake* was comparatively uninjured. And the court have no doubt, if the *Chesapeake* had not accidentally fallen on board the *Shannon*, and the *Shannon's* anchor got foul in the after quarter port of the *Chesapeake*, the *Shannon* must have very soon surrendered or sunk.

It appears to the court, that as the ships were getting foul, Capt Lawrence ordered the boarders to be called ; but the bugle man, Wm. Brown, stationed to call the boarders by sounding a bugle, had deserted his quarters, and when discovered and ordered to call, was unable, from fright, to sound his horn ; that midshipmen went below immediately to pass the word for the boarders ; but not being called in the way they had been usually exercised, few came upon the upper deck; confusion prevailed ; a greater part of the men deserted their quarters, and ran below. It appears also to the court, that when the *Shannon* got foul of the *Chesapeake*, Capt. Lawrence, his 1st lieutenant, the sailing master, and lieutenant of marines were all killed or mortally wounded, and thereby the upper deck of the *Chesapeake* was left without any commanding officer, and with only one or two young midshipmen. It also appears to the court, that previously to the ships getting foul, many of the *Chesapeake's* spar deck division had been killed and wounded, and the number stationed on that deck thereby considerably reduced; that these being left without a commissioned officer, or even a warrant officer, except one or two inexperienced, midshipmen, and not being supported by the boarders from the gun deck, almost universally deserted their quarters. And the enemy, availing himself of this defenceless state of the *Chesapeake's* upper deck, boarded and obtained possession of the ship with very little opposition.

From this view of the engagement and careful examination of the evidence, the court are unanimously of opinion, that the capture of the late United States frigate *Chesapeake*, was occasioned by the following causes ; the almost unexampled early fall of Capt. Lawrence, and all the principal officers ; the bugleman's desertion of his quarters, and inability to sound his horn ; for the court are of opinion if the horn had been sounded when first ordered, the men being then at their quarters, the boarders would have promptly repaired to the spar deck, probably have prevented the enemy from boarding—certainly have repelled them, and might have returned the boarding with success ; and the failure of the boarders on both decks to rally on the spar deck, after the enemy had boarded, which might have been done successfully, it is believed from the cautious manner in which the enemy came on board.

The court cannot, however, perceive in this almost unexampled concurrence of disastrous circumstances that the national flag has suffered any dishonour from the capture of the United States frigate *Chesapeake*, by the superior force of the British frigate *Shannon*, of 52 carriage guns, and 396 men. Nor do this court apprehend that the result of this engagement will in the least discourage our brave seamen from meeting the enemy hereafter on equal terms.

The court being also charged to inquire into the conduct of the officers and men during and after the engagement, and thereupon having strictly examined and maturely considered the evidence as recorded, do find the following causes of complaint :

First. Against Lieut. Cox ; that being stationed in command of the second division on the main deck, he left his division during the action, while his men were at their quarters, and went upon the upper deck ; that when there and the enemy boarding, or on the point of boarding, he left the deck to assist Capt. Lawrence below, went down with him from the spar deck to the birth deck; did not return to his division, but went forward on the gun deck; that while here and the men retreating below, he commanded them to go to their duty without enforcing his commands. But as a court of inquiry allows an accused person no opportunity of vindicating his conduct, the members of this court trust that their opinion on the conduct of Lieut. Cox, may not be deemed conclusive against him, without trial by court martial.

Second. Against Midshipman Forrest; that he left his quarters during the action, and did not return to them, and now assigns no reason for his conduct satisfactory to this court.

Third. Against Midshipman Freshman; that he behaved in an unofficer-like manner at Halifax, assuming a false name at the office of commissary of prisoners, when obtaining his parole, and was paroled by the name of William Brown.

Fourth. Against the crew generally; that they deserted their quarters, and ran below after the ships were foul, and the enemy boarded. But it appearing that they behaved well at their quarters before, and fired on the enemy with great rapidity and precision, the court ascribe their misconduct to the confusion naturally incident to the early loss of their officers, and the omission of the call of boarders in the accustomed manner.

Yet this court is very far from exculpating those who are thus criminal. It is unable to designate by name all the individuals who thus abandoned their duty, because most of the officers had recently joined the ship, some only a few days preceding the engagement, and of course could not distinguish the men. The court, therefore, respectfully submit to higher authority, the expediency of withholding the wages of the crew. The persons whom the court are able to designate by name, as deserters from their stations, are William Brown, bugleman, Joseph Russel, captain of second gun, Peter Frost and John Joyce, seamen.

The court further find, that the following persons entered the British service at Halifax, viz. Henry Ensign, Peter John, Andrew Simpson, Peter Langrun, Magness Sparring, Joseph Galla, Martin Anderson, Francis Paris, John White, boy, Thomas Arthur, Charles Reynolds, John Pierce jun. Andrew Denham, Thomas Jones, Charles Goodman, Joseph Antonio, Christopher Stevens, Charles Bowden, Chas. Westbury, Joseph Smith, George Williams, and George Cordell.

The court further find and report, that William Wainwright, William Worthington, and James Parker, the last of whom was born in Salem, Massachusets, were claimed by the enemy as British subjects, and sent on board of the enemy's ships of war.

This court respectfully beg leave to superadd, that unbiassed by any illiberal feelings towards the enemy, they feel it their duty to state, that the conduct of the enemy after, boarding and carrying the *Chesapeake*, was a most unwarrantable abuse of power after success.

The court is aware that in carrying a ship by boarding the full extent of the command of an officer cannot be readily exercised ; and that improper violence may unavoidably ensue. When this happens in the moment of contention, a magnanimous conquered foe will not complain. But the fact has been clearly established before this court, that the enemy met with little opposition on the upper deck, and none on the gun-deck. Yet after they had carried the ship, they fired from the gun-deck down the hatchway upon the birth-deck, and killed and wounded several of the *Chesapeake's* crew, who had retreated there, were unarmed and incapable of making any opposition ; that some balls were fired even into the cockpit : and what excites the utmost abhorrence, this outrage was committed in the presence of a British officer standing at the hatchway.

W. BAINBRIDGE, *President.*

9

The following is a copy of the letter, denominated a chal-
lenge, sent from the commander of the British frigate
Shannon to the commander of the American fri-
gate Chesapeake. Capt. Lawrence sailed before this
letter reached Boston.

LETTER FROM CAPT. BROKE TO CAPT. LAWRENCE.

His Britanic Majesty's ship Shannon,
Sir,   *Off Boston, June,* 1813.

As the *Chesapeake* appears now ready for sea, I request you will do me the favor to meet the *Shannon*
with her, ship to ship, to try the fortune of our respective flags. To an officer of your character, it requires some apology for proceeding to further particulars. Be assured, sir, that it is not from any doubt
I can entertain of your wishing to close with my proposals, but merely to provide an answer to any
objection which might be made, and very reasonable,
upon the chance of our receiving unfair support.

After the diligent attention which we had paid to
Com. Rodgers; the pains I took to detach all force but
the *Shannon* and *Tenedos* to such a distance that they
could not possibly join in any action fought in sight of
the Capes ; and the various verbal messages which
had been sent into Boston to that effect ; we were
much disappointed to find the commodore had eluded
us by sailing on the first chance, after the prevailing
easterly winds had obliged us to keep an offing from
the coast. He perhaps wished for some stronger assurance of a fair meeting. I am therefore induced to
address you more particularly, and to assure you, that
what I write I pledge my honor to perform to the utmost of my power. The *Shannon* mounts twenty-
four guns upon her broadside, and one light boat gun;
eighteen pounders on her main deck, and thirty-two
pound carronades on her quarter deck and forecastle ;
and is manned with a complement of three hundred
men and boys (a large proportion of the latter,) besides thirty seamen, boys and passengers, who were

taken out of re-captured vessels lately. I am thus minute, because a report has prevailed in some of the Boston papers that we had one hundred and fifty men additional, lent us from *La Hogue*, which really was never the case. *La Hogue* is now gone to Halifax for provisions, and I will send all other ships beyond the power of interfering with us, and will meet you wherever it is most agreeable to you: From six to ten leagues east of Cape Cod Light House, from eight to ten leagues east of Cape Ann Light on Cashe's Ledge in lat. 43 ° N. at any bearing and distance you please to fix off the south breakers of Nantucket, or the shoals off St. George's Bank.

If you will favor me with any plan of signals or telegraph, I will warn you (if sailing under this promise) should any of my friends be too nigh or any where in sight, until I can detach them out of the way, or I would sail with you under a flag of truce to any place you think safest from our cruisers, hauling it down when fair to begin hostilities.

You must, sir, be aware that my proposals are highly advantageous to you, as you cannot proceed to sea singly in the *Chesapeake* without imminent risk of being crushed by the superior force of the numerous British squadrons which are now abroad, where all your efforts, in case of rencontre, would however gallant, be perfectly hopeless. I entreat you, sir, not to imagine that I am urged by mere personal vanity to the wish of meeting the *Chesapeake;* or that I depend only upon your personal ambition for your acceding to this invitation : we have both higher and nobler motives. You will feel it as a compliment if I say, that the result of our meeting may be the most grateful service I can render to my country ; and I doubt not that you, equally confident of success, will feel convinced, that it is only by repeated triumphs in even combats that your little navy can now hope to console your country for the loss of that trade it can no longer protect. Favor me with a speedy reply.

We are short of provisions and water, and cannot stay long here.

> I have the honor to be, sir,
> your obedient humble servant.
> (*Signed*)   P. B. V. BROKE,
> *Capt. of H. B. M. ship Shannon.*

N. B.   For the general service of watching your coast, it is requisite for me to keep another ship in company, to support me with her guns and boats when employed near the land, particularly to aid each other if either ship in chase should get on shore.

You must be aware that I cannot, consistently with my duty, wave so great an advantage for this general service by detaching my consort, without any assurance on your part, of meeting me directly; and that you will neither seek or admit aid from any other of your armed vessels, if I detach mine expressly for the sake of meeting you.——Should any special order restrain you from thus answering a formal challenge, you may yet oblige me by keeping my proposal a secret, and appointing any place you like to meet us (within 300 miles of Boston) in any given number of days after you sail; as, unless you agree to an interview, I may be busied on other service, and perhaps be at a distance from Boston when you go to sea. Choose your terms—but let us meet.

To the Commander of the United
States frigate Chesapeake.

ENDORSEMENT ON THE ENVELOP.

We have thirteen American prisoners on board, which I will give you for as many British sailors, if you will send them out, otherwise being privateersmen, they must be detained.

ARGUS AND PELICAN.

Extract of a letter from James Inderwick, surgeon of the late United States brig Argus, to the Secretary of the Navy.

Boston, September 5, 1814.

Having been appointed by Com. Decatur, as acting surgeon on board the late United States brig *Argus,* a short time previous to her departure from New-York, and having served in that capacity until the unfortunate termination of her cruise ; I was, with her surviving officers, detained as a prisoner of war, on parole, in England. I have now, Sir, however, the honor of reporting to you my arrival on the the 3d inst. at this port, in the cartel ship *Saratoga*, having at length obtained my release and passport as a noncombatant. As Lieut. Watson, our surviving commanding officer, has been unable, under parole restrictions, to transmit any official documents, relative to the action and capture of the *Argus,* I have the honor to enclose, for your information, a report of the casualties attending that event. I regret that I have not yet been able to furnish the wounded with *regular certificates ;* it was impossible without personal communication with them to obtain the information necessary to the filling up the blanks, with the precision, enforced by the orders of your honorable department.

The list of killed and wounded, as given by Dr. Inderwick, is omitted, as a more complete account is given by Lieut. Watson, in his official letter.

Letter from Lieut Watson, 1st of the late United States brig Argus, to the Secretary of the Navy.

Sir, *Norfolk, March 2, 1815.*

Cirumstances during my residence in England having heretofore prevented my attention to the painful duty which devolved on me by the death of my gallant commander, Capt. Wm. H. Allen, of the late U. S. brig *Argus,* I have now the honor to state for your information, that having landed the Minister Plenipotentiary (Mr. Crawford) and suite at L'Orient, we proceeded on the cruise which had been directed by the department, and after capturing twenty vessels (a list of the names and other particulars of which I have the honor to enclose,) being in lat. 52° 15' N. long. 5° 50' W. on the 14th Aug. 1813, we discovered at 4 o'clock A. M. a large brig of war standing down under a press of sail upon our weather quarter, the wind being at south, and the *Argus* close hauled on the starboard tack : we immediately prepared to receive her ; and at 30 minutes after 4, being unable to get the weather gage, we shortened sail, and gave her an opportunity of closing. At 6, the brig having displayed English colours, we hoisted our flag ; wore round, and gave her the larboard broadside (being at this time within grape distance) which was returned, and the action commenced within the range of musketry. At 4 minutes after 6, Capt. Allen was wounded, and the enemy shot away our main braces, main spring-stay, gaff, and trysail-mast. At 8 minutes after 6, Capt Allen, being much exhausted by the loss of blood, was taken below. At 12 minutes after 6, lost our spritsail-yard and the principle part of the standing rigging on the larboard side of the foremast. At this time I received a wound on the head from a grape shot, which for a time rendered me incapable of attending to duty, and was carried below ; I had, however, the satisfaction of recollecting on my recovery, that nothing which the most gallant exertions could effect, would be left undone by Lieut. W. H. Allen, jun. who succeeded to the command of the deck.

Lieut. Allen reports, at 14 minutes after 6, the enemy being in our weather quarter, edged off, for the purpose of getting under our stern, but the *Argus* luffed close to, with the main topsail aback, and giving him a raking broadside, frustrated his attempt. At 18 minutes after 6, the enemy shot away our preventer, main-braces and main-topsail-tye ; and the *Argus* having lost the use of her after sails, fell on before the wind, when the enemy succeeded in passing our stern, and ranged on the starboard side. At 25 minutes after 6, the wheel ropes and running rigging of every discription being shot away, the *Argus* became unmanageable ; and the enemy, not having sustained any apparent damage, had it completely in his power to choose a position, and continued to play upon our starboard quarter, occasionally shifting his situation, until 30 minutes after 6, when I returned to the deck, the enemy being under our stern, within pistol shot, where she continued to rake us until 38 minutes after 6, when we prepared to board, but, in consequence of our shattered condition, were unable to effect it ; the enemy then passed our broadside, and took a position on our starboard bow. From this time until 47 minutes after 6, we were exposed to a cross or raking fire, without being able to oppose but little more than musketry to the broadside of the enemy, our guns being much disabled and seldom brought to bear.

The *Argus* having now suffered much, in hull and rigging, as also in killed and wounded, among the former of whom (exclusive of our gallant captain) we have to lament the loss of two meritorious young officers in Midshipmen Delphy and Edwards ; and being exposed to a galling fire, which from the enemy's ability to manage his vessel, we could not avoid, I deemed it necessary to surrender, and was taken possession of by his Britannic majesty's sloop the *Pelican*, of twenty-one carriage guns, viz. sixteen 32 pound carronades, four long 6's, and one 12 pound carronade. I hope this measure will meet your approbation, and that the result of this action, when the superior size and metal of our opponent, and the fatigue which the crew, &c, of the *Argus* underwent from a very rapid succession of captures, is considered, will not be thought unworthy of the flag under which we serve.

I have the honor to inclose a list of killed and wounded, and feel great satisfaction in reporting the general good conduct of the meritorious officers engaged on this occasion, and particularly the zeal and activity displayed by Lieut. Allen, who you will observe for a time commanded on deck.

I have the honour to be, Sir, with great respect,
your obedient servant,

Hon. B. CROWNINSHIELD,   W. H. WATSON,
Sec'y of the navy.   Late of the U. S. brig Argus.

KILLED. Richard Delphy, Wm. W. Edwards, midshipman; Joshua Jones, Wm. Finley, Wm. Knowlton, George Gardner, seamen.

DIED OF THEIR WOUNDS. William H. Allen, captain; James White, carpenter; Joseph Jordan, boatswain's mate; Francis Eggert, and Charles Backster, seamen.

WOUNDED. William H. Watson, 1st lieutenant; Colin M'Leod, boatswain; John Sniffer, carpenter's mate; John Young, quarter master; and eight seamen.

During a few weeks preceding the loss of the *Argus*, she had captured 23 British vessels, of various sizes, some of great value.

The tonage of the *Argus** is given as follows;

Length of keel for tonnage 80 feet,
Breadth of beam   do.   28 do.   } 298 68-95 tons
Depth of hold   do.   12 ft. 8 in. }

A London paper has the following: the *Pelican* brig of 18 guns, which so nobly captured the *Argus* sloop or war, was commanded by Capt. Searle, when she beat the French frigate *Medea*, of 44 guns, into Guadaloupe, after an action of two hours in the year 1799.

FUNERAL OF CAPT. ALLEN.

At Plymouth Eng. on the 21st of August, was interred with military honors, William Henry Allen, Esq. late commander of the United States sloop of war *Argus*, who lost his left leg in an action with his Majesty' sloop of war *Pelican*, J. F. Maples Esq.

---

* Built in Boston, by Mr. Edmund Hart.

captain, in St. George's Channel on the 14th; of which wound he died in the Mill-prison Hospital, on the 18th following.

The procession left Mill-prison at 12 o'clock: the coffin was covered with a velvet pall, on which was spread the American ensign, under which the action was fought, and upon which the hat and sword of the deceased were laid. On the coffin being removed to the hearse, the guard saluted; and when deposited in the hearse the procession moved forward, the band playing the "Dead March in Saul." On arrival, near the church, the guard clubbed arms, single files inward, through which the procession passed to the church, into which the corpse was carried and placed in the centre aisle, while the funeral services were read by the Rev. Vicar; after which it was removed and interred in the south yard (passing through the guard in the same order from as to the church,) on the right of Mr. Delphy, midshipman of the *Argus*, who lost both legs in the same action, and was buried the preceeding evening.

ORDER OF PROCESSION.

Guard of Honor.
Lieut. Col. of Royal Marines,
with two companies of that corps.
The Captains, Subalterns, and field Adjutants, (Officers with hat bands and scarfs.)
Royal Marine Band.
Vicar and Curate of St. Andrew's.
Clerk of ditto.
THE HEARSE
With the corpse of the diseased Captain,
attended by eight seamen, late of the *Argus*, with crape round their arms, tied with white crape ribbons;
Also, eight British Captains of the Royal Navy, as Pall bearers,
With hat bands and scarfs.
Captain Allen,s servants in mourning.
10

The Officers, late of the *Argus*, in uniform, with crape
sashes, and hat bands, two and two.
John Hawker Esq. late American Vice-Consul,
and his Clerks.
Captain Pellowe, Commissioner for Prisoners of war.
Dr. McGrath, Chief Medical Officer at Mill-prison
Depot.
Captains of the Royal Navy in port, two and two.
Marine and Army Officers, two and two.
Servants of the American Officers, two and two.
Followed by a very numerous and respectable retinue
of Inhabitants.

EXTRACT FROM THE BRITISH NAVAL CHRONICLE.

"As several misstatements have appeared in the
public prints relative to the death of the late Capt. Allen, we subjoin the following particulars, communicated to us by a friend, which may be depended on :
Capt. Allen's left thigh was amputated by his own
surgeon, in a very proper manner, about three quarters of an hour after the close of the action.——On the
morning after the arrival of the *Argus*, ('Tuesday,)
the chief medical officer from Mill-prison attended
him, and soon discovered, that dangerous symptoms,
which had escaped the observation of his surgeon,
who thought favourably of his situation, were insidious-
ly approaching, and accordingly communicated his apprehensions, and recommended such remedies as were
deemed advisable.   In the evening he was again visited, when the prognostic given in the morning was
found too visibly verified.   On the following day his
symptoms were much aggravated, and his immediate
removal to Mill-prison Hospital was strongly recommended, in order to obtain the most prompt remedies,
and where he might have all the care and attention his
situation demanded.   He arrived about noon ; but in
spite of every effort, gradually sunk, until he breathed
his last, about 11 o'clock that night, during which period he was never left by his physician.   We understand he was not conscious of the danger of his situa-

tion, but conversed familiarly with those present with him until about three quarters of an hour before he died. His death was conceived to be chiefly occasioned by the great loss of blood which he sustained previous to amputation, by his persisting in remaining on deck after he was wounded. Throughout the whole, he bore his sufferings with that manly, determined fortitude and composure, which might be expected of a brave and gallant officer, and never once complained of pain ; but his mind constantly dwelt on the loss of his ship, which he regretted in the most feeling and manly manner. In person he was about six feet high, a model of symmetry and manly comeliness, and in his manner and conversation a highly finished and accomplished gentleman.

William Henry Allen* was an officer, no less distinguished by his bravery, than the uniform courtesy and amenity of his manners. In ordinary life we discovered nothing of those high qualities, for which, in the hour of danger, he was found to be so preeminent. He relaxed into all the mildness of the polished and amiable gentleman, stated his opinions with modesty, and carefully abstained from irritating or insulting language. His conversation, although peculiarly unostentatious, was luminous and instructive, and combined the elegance of a scholar with the sound practical sense of a man of intercourse with the world. He studied naval tactics as a science, and laboured to adorn and decorate the stern and masculine character of the sailor, with the milder graces and softer embellishments. In this he succeeded completely, and was capable of turning to the view the stern and intrepid side of his character, or the milder and more amiable, as occasion required. In his friendships he was ardent and constant. All these advantages were rendered still more conspicuous by a noble masculine deportment, and the fine forms which he inherited from nature A stranger in his company, and perfectly ignorant of his character, would find his heart drawn powerfully to-

*Lieut. Allen was a native of Rhode Island.

wards him, by the predominant and pervading sympathy, which such endearing qualities excite.　He would be disposed to converse more with him, and to cultivate his friendship.　Every hour he would feel this attachment growing stronger, as the varied excellences of his character were disclosed in succession.　Such was William Henry Allen.　He had adorned his name by his bravery, which was so conspicuous in the affair of the *Macedonian.*　This enlarged his ideas and made him pant for fame, that last infirmity of noble minds.　He has fallen, indeed, but for all the purposes of life he had lived long enough.　He had enjoyed the confidence of his county, and died in the performance of his duty.　This humble wreath is not less a tribute to individual friendship, than to justice.

The following is from an Irish news-paper.

It would be injustice not to notice the excellent conduct of Capt. Allen, of the *Argus.*　He allowed the passengers and crews of the *Betsey* and *Mariner* to remove every article of their private property, and in order that they might have liberty to do so, he would not suffer one of his officers or crew to be present below, whilst they were employed in packing up their effects.　Capt. Gilbert, of the *Mariner*, had left some articles of cabin furniture behind, which Capt. Allen sent after him in his boat.　A great coat, belonging to an officer of one of the captured ships, was missing, and it was found in the possession of one of the crew of the *Argus.*　Capt. Allen immediately ordered the man to be tied up, and he actually received a severe flogging.　Considerable sums in specie were saved by the passengers, as Capt. Allen would not allow his men to touch a single article.

COURT OF INQUIRY.

The following decision and opinion of the court of inquiry, convened at Baltimore, in April last, to investigate the causes of the loss of the *Argus*, have been received and approved by the secretary of the navy.

THE ENTERPRIZE AND BOXER.

The court, in pursuance of the authority by which they were convened, having carefully examined into the causes of the loss by capture of the U. S. sloop of war *Argus*, under the command of the late W. H. Allen, master commandant in the navy of the United States, and also into the conduct of the officers and crew of the said sloop of war, before and after her surrender to the enemy's ship *Pelican*, and having maturely deliberated upon all the testimony, they find the following facts :

1. It is proved, that in the number of her crew, and in the number and calibre of her guns, the *Pelican* was decidedly superiour to the *Argus*.

2. They find that the crew of the *Argus* was very much exhausted by the continued and extraordinary fatigue and exposure to which they had been subjected for several weeks, and particularly for twenty four hours immediately preceding the action.

3. They find that every officer and man of the *Argus*, (with the exception of one man, Jacob Allister, and one boy, Hendrick) made use of every practicable exertion to capture the British sloop of war *Pelican*.

They are therefore of opinion, that every officer and man, with the exception before mentioned, displayed throughout the engagement, a zeal, activity, and spirit in defence of the vessel and flag committed to their protection, which entitles them to the undiminished confidence and respect of their government and fellow citizens, and do therefore honorably acquit them.

ENTERPRIZE AND BOXER.

LETTER FROM COM. BAINBRIDGE TO THE SECRETARY OF THE NAVY.

Boston September 7, 1813.

THE enclosed letters will give you the information of a brilliant victory, gained by the United States brig *Enterprize,* over his Britannic Majesty's brig *Boxer*, of considerable superiority of force.   Nothing that I can say would add to the lustre of the gallant action, which so decidedly speaks for itself. But I cannot restrain my deep regret for the loss of so valuable an officer as the brave Lieut. Burrows.

I have the honor to be, with great respect,
your obedient servant,
Hon. WILLIAM JONES,   W. BAINBRIDGE.
Sec'y of the navy.

LETTER FROM CAPT. HULL TO THE SEC'Y OF THE NAVY.
Sir,   *Portland, September* 7, 1813

I had the honor last evening to forward you, by express, through the hands of Com. Bainbridge, a letter, received from Samuel Storer Esq. navy agent at this place, detailing an account of the capture of the British brig *Boxer*, by the United States brig *Enterprize*.

I now have to inform you, that I left Portsmouth this morning, and have this moment arrived, and, as the mail is closing, I have only time to enclose you the report of Lt. M'Call, of the *Enterprize*, and to assure you that a statement of the situation of the two vessels, as to the damage they have received, &c, shall be forwarded as soon as surveys can be made   The *Boxer* has received much damage in her hull, masts, and sails; indeed it was with difficulty she could be kept afloat to get her in.   The *Enterprize* is only injured in her masts and sails.

I have the honor to be, &c.
Hon. WILLIAM JONES,   ISAAC HULL.
Secr'y of the navy.

OFFICIAL ACCOUNT.

United States brig Enterprize,
SIR,   *Portland, Sept.* 7, 1813.

In consequence of the unfortunate death of Lieut. William Burrows, late commander of this vessel, it devolves, on me to acquaint you with the result of my cruise.   After sailing from Portsmouth, on the first inst. we steered to the eastward; and on the morning of the 3d, off Wood Island, discovered a schooner, which we chased into this harbour where we anchored. On the morning of the 4th weighed anchor, and swept out, and continued our course to the eastward. Having received information of several privateers being off Manhagan, we stood for that place ; and on the following morning, in the bay near Penguin Point, discovered a brig, getting under way, which appeared to be a vessel of war, and to which we immediately gave chase. She fired several guns, and stood for us, having four ensigns hoisted. After reconnoitring and discovering her force, and the nation to which she belonged, we hauled upon a wind, to stand out of the bay, and at 3 o'clock shortened sail, tacked to run down, with an intention to bring her to close action. At 20 minutes after 3 P. M. when within half pistol shot, the firing commenced from both, and after being warmly kept up, and with some manœuvering, the enemy hailed, and said they had surrendered, about 4 P. M. *their colours being nailed to the masts, could not be hauled down.* She proved to be his B. M. brig *Boxer*, of 14 guns, Samuel Blythe, Esq. commander, who fell in the early part of the engagement, having received a cannon shot through the body. And I am sorry to add, that Lieut. Burrows, who had gallantly led us into action, fell also about the same time by a musket ball, which terminated his existance in 8 hours.

The *Enterprize* suffered much in spars and rigging, and the *Boxer* in spars, rigging, and hull, having many shots between wind and water.

It would be doing injustice to the merit of Mr. Tillinghast, 2d lieutenant, were I not to mention the able assistance I received from him during the remainder of the engagement by his strict attention to his own division and other departments, and of the officers and crew generally, I am happy to add, their cool and determined conduct have my warmest approbation and applause.

As no muster roll, that can be fully relied on, has come into my possession, I cannot exactly state the number killed and wounded on board the *Boxer*, but from· information received from the officers of that vessel, it appears there were between 20 and 35 killed, and 14 wounded.   Enclosed is a list of the killed and wounded on board the *Enterprize*.

I have the honor to be, &c.

EDWARD R. M'CALL, Senior officer.

· Isaac Hull, Esq. *Commanding*
naval officer on the eastern station.

List of killed and wounded on board the United States brig Enterprize, in the engagement with the British brig Boxer, the 5th of September 1813.

Killed, Nathaniel Garren, seaman.

Wounded, William Burrows Esq., commander, (since dead ;) Kervin Waters, midshipman, mortally ; Elisha Blossom, carpenter's mate, (since dead,) David Norton, quartermaster : Russel Coats, do. ; Thomas Owings, do. ; Benjamin Cammon, boatswain's mate ; four seamen and one marine.

Killed, 1.   Wounded, 13.   Since dead of wounds, 3.

EDWARD R. M'CALL, Senior officer.

LETTER FROM ISAAC HULL ESQ. TO THE SECRETARY OF THE NAVY.

U. S. Navy Yard, Portsmouth,

Sir,   *September,* 14, 1813.

I have the honor to forward you by mail the flags of the late British brig *Boxer*, which were nailed to her mast heads at the time she engaged, and was captured by the U. S. brig *Enterprize.* Great as the pleasure is that I derive from performing this part of my duty, I need not tell you how different my feelings would have been, could the gallant Burrows have had this honor.   He went into action most gallantly, and the difference of injury done the two vessels proves how nobly he fought.

I have the honor to be &c.

ISAAC HULL.

EXTRACT OF A LETTER FROM COM. HULL TO COM. BAINBRIDGE.

September, 10, 1813.

"I yesterday visited the two brigs, and was astonished to see the difference of injury sustained in the action.

The *Enterprize* has but one 18 pound shot in her hull, and one in her mainmast, and one in her foremast ; her sails are much cut with grape shot, and there are a great number of grape lodged in her sides, but no injury done by them.——The *Boxer* has eighteen or twenty 18 pound shot in her hull, most of them at the water's edge, several stands of 18 pound grape stick in her side, and such a quantity of small grape, that I did not undertake to count them. Her masts, sails, and spars are literally cut to pieces, several of her guns dismounted, and unfit for service ; her topgallant forecastle nearly taken off by the shot, her boats cut to pieces, and her quarters injured in proportion. To give you an idea of the quantity of shot about her, I inform you, that I counted in her mainmast alone three 18 pound shot holes, 18 large grape shot holes, 16 musket ball holes, and a large number of smaller shot holes, without counting above the cat harpins.

We find it impossible to get at the number killed ; no papers are found, by which we can ascertain it. I however counted upwards of 90 hammocks, which were in her netting with beds in them, besides several beds without hammocks ; and she has excellent accommodations for all her officers below in state rooms ; so that I have no doubt, that she had 100 men on board. We know that she has several of the *Rattler's* men on board, and a quantity of wads was taken out of the *Rattler*, loaded with four large grape shot, with a small hole in the centre, to put in a cartridge, that the inside of the wad may take fire when it leaves the gun : in short, she is in every respect completely fitted, and her accomodations exceed any thing I have seen in a vessel of her class."

11

Remarks. There have been various opinions respecting the relative force of the vessels ; and some ungenerous attempts have been made to diminish the splendor of the victory. The foregoing extracts settle the question of force and skill. It appears, that in number of men the enemy were equal ; in number of guns it is well known the enemy were superior ; and the vast difference of execution confirms (if confirmation were wanted) the fact of the high degree of the superiority of our seamen in the art of gunnery.

In addition to the particulars officially given we have the following from other sources. The *Enterprize* rates as 12 guns, but carries 16, viz. 14 eighteen pound carronades and 2 long 9s ; her officers and crew consisted of 102 persons, and her burthen is about 265 tons. The *Boxer* rates as a 14 gun brig, but carries 18, viz. sixteen 18 pound carronades, and 2 long 9s ; her force, at the time of the action, was 104 men, and her burthen is about 300 tons. The first is an old, light built vessel, the latter is new and very strong.

For several days before the *Boxer* sailed from St. John's, great exertions were made by the government, officers, as well as the magistrates of the place, to man and equip her in a perfect manner to fight the *Enterprize* . Capt. Blythe sailed with the most confident belief of speedily returning to port, crowned with the same laurels, that decked the brow of Broke.

Soon after the arrival of the *Enterprize*, and her prize at portland, the bodies of the two commanding officers, Lieut. Burrows and Capt. Blythe, were brought on shore in tenoared barges, rowed at minute strokes, by masters of ships, accompanied by most of the barges and boats in the harbour, while minute guns were fired from the two vessels. A grand procession was then formed, which moved through the principle streets, to the Rev. Mr. Paysons meeting house, where the rites of sepulture were performed, with appropriate music, and from thence to the place of interment.

The order of procession was as follows :

Military escort,

Composed of a rifle company and two companies of infantry.

Selectmen of Portland.

Town Treasurer and Sheriff of the county.

Town Clerk and other municipal officers.

The Reverend Clergy.

MR. LE SASSIER, MR. SHIELDS,

MR. O'NEAL, BODY OF BURROWS. MR. TURNER,

MR. TILLINGHAST, MR. M'CALL.

Chief mourners

Dr. Washington, Capt. Hull.

Officers of the brig *Enterprize*.

Crew of the brig *Enterprize*.

———

LEMUEL WEEKS, Jun. WILLIAM MERRILL,

SETH BARNES, BODY OF BLYTHE. JAMES COMBS,

JOSHUA KNIGHTS, JOHN ALDEN.

Officers of the brig *Boxer*, as mourners,
and Officers on Parole.

Crew of the brig *Boxer*.

Officers of the United States Navy.

Ship masters and Mates.

Marshall of Maine.

Navy Agent, and

The late Consul General to the Barbary powers.

Collector of the Port, and Surveyor.

Superintendant General of Military Supplies.

Officers of the Army of the United States.

Military Officers of the State, in uniform.

Judges, and other Civil Officers of the United States.

Members of Congress.

Judiciary of the Commonwealth.

Members of the State Legislature.

Civil Officers of the State.

Portland Marine Society.

Presidents, Directors and Officers of the Banks, and Insurance offices.

Citizens in general.

The funeral was attended with all the honors that the civil and military authorities of the place, and the great body of the people could bestow. The whole scene was strikingly impressive. The bells were tolled, and two companies of artillery fired minute guns, which were repeated from forts Preble and Scammel.

Lieut. Burrows was a young man of uncommon worth. He was the son of Col. Burrows, of South Carolina, formerly of the marine corps. He lived with honor, and died with glory. By his early death * his country has lost an able commander, and his two surviving sisters a brother, whose excellencies they will never cease to remember. He was intelligent, intrepid, generous and humane. He was ambitious to add lustre to the American navy, and eagerly rushed into a combat, which issued in a signal victory over a superior force. He received a mortal wound at the commencement of the action, but refused to be carried below until the sword of his enemy was presented to him. He siezed it with both hands, and exclaimed, " *I am satisfied, I die contented,*" and soon expired. Of Lieut, M'Call † the public will judge by the termination of the fight, and his modest account of it.

Capt. Blakely, late of the *Enterprize*, to whom certainly some part of the credit is due for the complete discipline of the men, had a short time before left that vessel, to superintend the building and fitting out of a new sloop of war, which he was to command.

Capt. Blythe, killed on board the *Boxer*, had distinguished himself at the conquest of Cayenne, and received of the Prince Regent of England a handsome present in money, to purchase a sword or some other memorial. His opponent, the invincible Burrows, had little or no experience in the business of a battle, and Lieut. M'Call, on whom the command of the *Enterprize* devolved, had never seen a fight.

*He had just entered his twenty eighth year.
†Lieut. M'Call was a native of South Carolina.

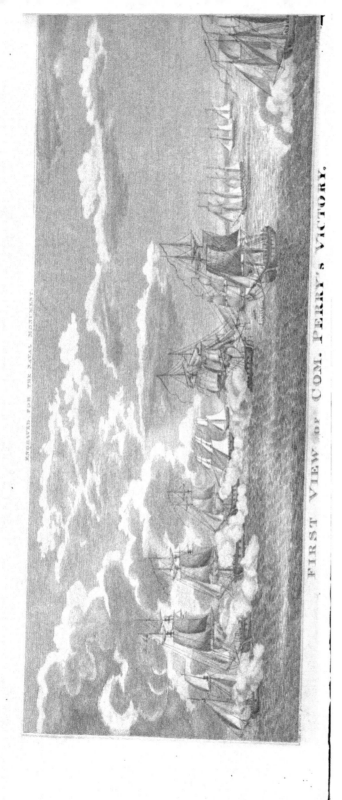

ENGRAVED FOR THE NAVAL MONUMENT.

FIRST VIEW OF COM. PERRY'S VICTORY.

BATTLE OF LAKE ERIE.

COPY OF A LETTER FROM COM. PERRY TO THE SECRETARY
OF THE NAVY.

U. S. Brig Niagara, off the Western Sister,
SIR,   *Lake Erie, Sept.* 10, 1813.

It has pleased the Almighty to give to the arms of the United States a signal victory over their enemies on this lake. The British squadron, consisting of 2 ships, 2 brigs, 1 schooner, and one sloop, have this moment surrendered to the force under my command, after a sharp conflict.

I have the honor to be, Sir, very respectfully,
your obedient servant,

Hon, WILLIAM JONES   O. H. PERRY.*
   Sec'y of the navy.

LETTERS FROM COM. PERRY TO MAJ. GEN. HARRISON.

U. S. Brig Niagara, off the Western Sister,
DEAR GENERAL,   *Lake Erie, Sept.* 10, 1813.

We have met the enemy ; and they are ours ! 2 ships, 2 brigs, 1 schooner, and 1 sloop.

Yours with great respect and esteem,
GEN. HARRISON.   O. H. PERRY.

DEAR SIR,   *September* 11. 1813

We have a great number of prisoners, which I wish to land : will you be so good as to order a guard to receive them ; and inform me of the place ? Considerable numbers have been killed and wounded on both sides. From the best information, we have more prisoners than we have men on board our vessels. In great haste,

yours very truly,
GEN. HARRISON.   O. H. PERRY.

---

*Com. Perry is a native of Newport R. I. and son of Com. Christopher R. Perry, who formely commanded the frigate *General Green.*

COPY OF A LETTER FROM COM. PERRY TO THE SECRETARY
OF THE NAVY.

U. S. Schooner Ariel, Put-in-Bay,

SIR,   *September* 13, 1813.

In my last I informed you that we had captured the
enemy's fleet on this lake. I have now the honor to
give you the most important particulars of the action.
On the morning of the 10th instant, at sunrise they
were discovered from Put-in-Bay, where I lay at anchor with the squadron under my command. We got
under way, the wind light at S. W. and stood for
them. At 10 A. M. the wind hauled to S. E. and
brought us to windward : formed the line and bore up.
At 15 minutes before 12, the enemy commenced firing ; at 5 minutes before 12, the action commenced on
our part. Finding their fire very destructive, owing
to their long guns, and its being mostly directed at
the *Lawrence*, I made sail and directed the other vessels to follow for the purpose of closing with the enemy. Every brace and bow-line being shot away, she
became unmanageable, notwithstanding the great exertions of the sailing master. In this situation she
sustained the action upwards of 2 hours within cannister distance, until every gun was rendered useless, and
the greater part of her crew either killed or wounded.
Finding she could no longer annoy the enemy, I left
her in charge of Lieut. Yarnall, who I was convinced,
from the bravery already displayed by him, would do
what would comport with the honor of the flag. At
half past two, the wind springing up, Capt. Elliott was
enabled to bring his vessel, the *Niagara*, gallantly into close action : I immediately went on board of her,
when he anticipated my wish by volunteering to bring
the schooners which had been kept astern by the lightness of the wind, into close action. It was with un-
speakable pain, that I saw, soon after I got on board
the *Niagara*, the flag of the *Lawrence* come down,
although I was perfectly sensible that she had been
defended to the last, and that to have continued to

make a show of resistance would have been a wanton sacrifice of the remains of her brave crew. But the enemy was not able to take possession of her, and circumstances soon permitted her flag again to be hoisted. At 45 minutes past 2, the signal was made for "close action." The *Niagara* being very little injured, I determined to pass through the enemy's line, bore up and passed ahead of their two ships and a brig, giving a raking fire to them from the starboard guns, and to a large schooner and sloop from the larboard side at half pistol shot distance. The smaller vessels at this time having got within grape and cannister distance, under the direction of Capt. Elliot, and keeping up a well directed fire, the two ships, a brig and a schooner surrendered, a schooner and sloop making a vain attempt to escape.

Those officers and men who were immediately under my observation evinced the greatest gallantry, and I have no doubt that all others conducted themselves as became American officers and seamen. Lieut. Yarnall, first of the *Lawrence*, although several times wounded, refused to quit the deck. Midshipman Forrest (doing duty as lieutenant) and sailing-Master Tailor, were of great assistance to me. I have great pain in stating to you the death of Lt. Brooks of the marines, and Midshipman Laub, both of the *Lawrence*, and Midshipman John Clarke of the *Scorpion:* they were valuable and promising officers. Mr. Hambleton, purser, who volunteered his services on deck, was severely wounded late in the action. Midshipmen Claxon and Swartwout of the *Lawrence*, were severely wounded. On board of the Niagara, Lieutenants Smith and Edwards, and Midshipman Webster (doing duty as a sailing master,) behaved in a very handsome manner. Capt. Breevoort of the army, who acted as a volunteer in the capacity of a marine officer, on board that vessel, is an excellent and brave officer, and with his musketry did great execution. Lieut. Turner, commanding the *Caledonia*, brought that vessel into action in the most able manner, and is an officer that in all situations may be relied on.

The *Ariel*, Lieut. Packet, and *Scorpion*, Sailing-Master Champlin, were enabled to get early into action, and were of great service. Capt. Elliott speaks in the highest terms of Mr. Magrath, purser, who had been despatched in a boat on service previous to my getting on board the *Niagara* ; and, being a seaman, since the action has rendered essential service in taking charge of one of the prizes. Of Capt. Elliott, already so well known to the government, it would be almost superfluous to speak. In this action he evinced his characteristic bravery and judgment, and, since the close of the action, has given me the most able and essential assistance.

I have the honor to enclose you a return of the killed and wounded, together with a statement of the relative force of the squadrons. The captain and 1st lieutenant of the *Queen Charlotte* and the 1st lieutenant of the *Detroit* were killed : Capt. Barclay, senior officer, and the commander of the *Lady Prevost*, severely wounded : the commander of the *Hunter* and *Chippeway* slightly wounded. Their loss in killed and wounded I have not yet been able to ascertain ; it must however have been very great.

Very respectfully, I have the honor to be,
Sir, your obedient servant,
Hon. WILLIAM JONES,   O. H. PERRY.
Sec'y of the navy.

EXTRACT OF A LETTER FROM COM. PERRY.

U. S. Schooner Ariel, Put-in-Bay,
SIR,   *September* 13, 1813.

I have caused the prisoners taken on the 10th inst. to be landed at Sandusky, and have requested Gen. Harrison to have them marched to Chilicothe, and there wait until your pleasure shall be known respecting them.

The *Lawrence* has been entirely cut up : it is absolutely necessary she should go into a safe harbor. I have therefore directed Lieut. Yarnall to proceed to

SECOND VIEW OF COM. PERRY's VICTORY.

Erie in her, with the wounded of the fleet, and dismantle and get her over the bar as soon as possible.

The two ships in a heavy sea this day at anchor lost their masts, being much injured in the action. I shall haul them into the inner bay at this place, and moor them for the present. The *Detroit* is a remarkably fine ship, sails well, and is very strongly built. The *Queen Charlotte* is a much superior vessel to what has been represented. The *Lady Prevost* is a large, fine schooner.

I also beg your instructions respecting the wounded. I am satisfied, Sir, that whatever steps I might take, governed by humanity, would meet your approbation. Under this impression, I have taken upon myself to promise Capt. Barclay, who is very dangerously wounded, that he shall be landed as near Lake Ontario as possible, and I had no doubt you would allow me to parole him. He is under the impression that nothing but leaving this part of the country will save his life.

There is also a number of Canadians among the prisoners, many of whom have families.

I have the honor to be, Sir,
very respectfully, your obed't serv't,
Hon WILLIAM JONES,   O. H. PERRY.
Sec'y of the navy.

STATEMENT OF THE FORCE OF THE BRITISH SQUADRON.

Ship Detroit,* - - 19 guns—1 on pivot, and 2 howitzers.
Queen Charlotte, 17 do.   1   do.
Sch. Lady Prevost, 13 do,   1   do.
Brig Hunter,   -   10 do.
Sl'p Little Belt,   3 do.
Sch. Chippeway,   1 do. and 2 swivels—Total, 63 guns.

STATEMENT OF THE FORCE OF THE U. S. SQUADRON.

Brig Lawrence, - 20 guns.
    Niagara - - 20 do.
    Caledonia, - 3 do.

* The Detroit is a new ship, very strongly built, and mounts long 24s, 18s and 12s.

12

Sch. Ariel,	- -	4 guns. (one burst early in the action.)
Scorpion	-	2 do.
Somers	-	2 do. and 2 swivels.
Sl'p Trippe,		1 do.
Sch. Tigress,		1 do.
Porcupine,		1 do.—Total, 54 guns.

The exact number of the enemy's force has not been ascertained, but I have good reason to believe that it exceeded ours by nearly one hundred men.

List of killed and wounded on board the United States squadron, under command of O. H. Perry Esq. in the action of 10th September, 1813.

On board the Lawrence. KILLED—John Brooks, lieutenant of marines ; * Henry Laub, midshipman ; Christian Mayhew, quarter master ; eleven seamen, and one sail maker, one carpenter, one private, and three marines.

WOUNDED—John J. Yarnall, 1st lieutenant, slightly ; Dulaney Forrest, 2d do. do. ; William N. Taylor, sailing master, do. ; Samuel Hambleton, purser, severely ; Thomas Claxton, Augustus Swartwout, midshipmen, severely ; Jonas Stone, carpenter slightly ; William C. Keen, master at arms, do ; Francis Mason, John Newen, quarter masters, severely ; Joseph Lewis, Ezekiel Fowler, quarter masters, slightly ; John E. Brown, quarter gunner, severely ; William Johnson, boatswain's mate, do ; James Helan, do. slightly ; George Cornell, carpenter's mate, do. and forty five seamen and marines.

[On the morning of the action, the sick list of the *Lawrence* contained 31 unfit for duty.]

On board the Niagara. KILLED—Peter Morel, seamen, Isaac Hardy, ord. seamen.—2

WOUNDED.—John J. Edwards, lieutenant ; John C. Cummings, midshipman ; and twenty one seamen and marines.

---

* A son of the late Gov. Brooks of Medford, Mass. He was an accomplished gentleman and brave officer.

[On the morning of the action, the sick list of the *Niagara* contained 28 unfit for duty.]

On board the Caledonia. WOUNDED — James Artus, Isaac Perkins, James Phillips, slightly—3.

On board the Somers. WOUNDED—Charles Ordeen, Godfrey Bowman—2.

On board the Ariel. KILLED—John White, boatswain's mate—1.

WOUNDED—William Sloss, ord. seaman, slightly; Robert Wilson, seaman, do; John Lucas, landsman, do.—3.

On board the Trippe. WOUNDED—Isaac Green, soldier, 26th regiment, badly; John Failes, do. 17th, slightly—2.

On board the Porcupine. None killed or wounded.

On board the Scorpion. KILLED—John Clark, midshipman; John Sylhamamer, landsman—2.

On board the Tigress. None killed or wounded.

[Two days previous to the action, 57 men unfit for service in the small vessels.]

RECAPITULATION.

	Killed.	Wounded.	Total.
Lawrence,	22	61	83
Niagara,	2	25	27
Caledonia,	0	3	3
Somers,	0	2	2
Ariel,	1	3	4
Trippe,	0	2	2
Scorpion,	2	0	2
	27	96	123

S. HAMBLETON, *Purser.*
O. H. PERRY, *Captain.*
and senior officer.

Of the 96 wounded in the battle of Lake Erie, only four died: most of the wounded were fit for duty in a short time.

Just before the battle, Com. Perry hoisted the union jack, having for a motto the dying words of Lawrence, "dont give up the ship." It was received with repeated huzzas by the officers and crews.

The victory of Com. Perry was the result of skill, courage, and enterprise, against superior force. Both the quality and amount of the force he had to contend with ought to have given a triumph to the other side ; and at the time of the surrender, the odds were increased against him, since his own ship after having suffered more than perhaps a vessel of the same size and force ever did before, had been compelled to strike. The immediate termination of the battle appears to have been decided by the bold Nelsonian measure, of breaking through the British line and coming to close action.

EXTRACT OF A LETTER FROM A NAVAL OFFICER AT ERIE.

October 7, 1813.

"Had I been able, I should before now have sent you some particulars of the action of the memorable 10th of September. As we have not many letter writers in our squadron, the public will have to put up with the Commodore's 'round, unvarnished tale ;' which however is very well told. All the fault I find with it is, that he himself is too much in the back ground.

"In no action fought this war has the conduct of the commanding officer been so conspicious or so evidently decisive of the fate of the battle, as in this. When he discovered that nothing further could be done in the *Lawrence*, he wisely removed to the *Niagara*, and by one of the boldest and most judicious manœuvres ever practised, decided the contest at once. Had the *Niagara* shared the fate of the *Lawrence*, it was his intention to have removed to the next best vessel, and so on as long as one of his squadron continued to float. The enemy saw him put off, and acknowledge that they fired a broadside at him. With his usual gallantry he went off standing up in the stern of the boat ; but the crew insisted on his sitting down. The enemy speak with admiration of the manner in which the *Lawrence* bore down upon them. She continued her course so long and so obstinately, that they thought we were going to board them. They had a great advantage in having long guns. Many of our men were killed on the birth deck and in the steerage, after they were taken below to be dressed—Midshipman Laub was of this number. One shot went through the light room, and knocked the snuff of the candle into the magazine—The gunner happened to see it immediately, and extinguished it with his hand : 2 shot passed through the magazine ; 2 through the cabin ; 3 or 4 came into the ward room—but I believe only one went quite through, and that passed a few inches over the surgeon's head as he sat in the cockpit. Our short guns lodged their shot in the bulwarks of the *Detroit ;* where a number of them now remain. Her bulwarks however were vastly superior to ours, being of oak and very thick. Many of their grape shot came through ours. They acknowledge that they threw combustible matter on board of us, which set our sails and rigging on fire in several places. I am clearly of opinion, that they were better manned than we were. They had a much greater number—they had veteran troops—their men were all well. We had as motley a crew as ever went into action ; and our vessels looked like hospital ships.

"During the whole of the action the most complete order prevailed on board the *Lawrence.* There was no noise, no bustle, no confusion. As fast as the men were wounded they were taken below and replaced by others. The dead remained where they fell until the action was over. Capt. Perry exhibited that cool, collected, dignified bravery, which those acquainted with him would have expected. His countenance all the time was just as composed as if he had been engaged in ordinary duty. As soon as the action was over he gave all his attention to the securing of the prisoners and to the wounded on both sides. Capt. Barclay declared to one of our officers, several days after the action, that Capt. Perry had done himself immortal honor by his humanity and attention to the wounded prisoners. The action was fought on Friday—we got into harbor next day. On Sunday all the officers on both sides, who fell, were buried on South Bass Island, at Put-in-Bay, with the honors of war.

"I am sorry to inform you that Midshipman Claxton died of his wounds this morning.

"There were two Indian chiefs on board the *Detroit*. The 2d lieutenant informed me, that as soon as the action became general they ran below."

The suite of Com. Perry, on his arrival at Newport, R. I. consisted of his brother, and the four sailors that rowed him from the *Lawrence* to the *Niagara*. It is said that in passing from the *Lawrence* to the *Niagara*, in an open boat, the gallant commodore stood up until he received two broadsides, directed at his little barque from the enemy, and was then pulled down by the skirts of his coat, by the faithful tars, that accompanied him.

Com. Barclay certainly did himself honor by a brave and obstinate resistance. He had seen much service, having been dangerously wounded in the battle of Trafalgar, and afterwards losing an arm in another engagement with the French. In this battle, he was twice carried below, on account of his wounds, and unfortunately lost his remaining hand.

At a public dinner and ball, given to Com. Barclay, at Terrebonne, (Canada) this gallant, but unfortunate officer, gave the following toast :—"*Com. Perry, the gallant and generous enemy.*"

Gen. Harrison sent reinforcements to assist Com. Perry in the action, which terminated in the capture of the whole British fleet. In return, Com. Perry volunteered with Gen. Harrison, and assisted him in the capture of the British army.

In the following letter justice is done to the zeal of Gen. Harrison and his gallant soldiers.

SIR,   *U. S. Schooner Ariel, Sept.* 15, 1813.

The very great assistance, in the action of the 10th

inst. derived from those men you were pleased to send on board the squadron, renders it a duty to return you my sincere thanks for so timely a reinforcement.   In fact, Sir, I may say, without those men the victory could not have been achieved ; and equally to assure you, that those officers and men behaved as became good soldiers and seamen.   Those who were under my immediate observation, evinced great ardour and bravery.   Capt. Prevort, of the 2d company of Infantry, serving on board the Niagara, I beg leave to recommend particularly to your notice : he is a brave and gallant officer, and as far as I am capable of judging, an excellent one.   I am convinced you will present the merit of this officer to the view of the Hon. Secretary of War, as I shall to the Hon. Secretary of the Navy.

Very respectfully, I am, sir,

your obedient servant,

Maj. Gen. W. H. HARRISON,   O. H. PERRY.
Commander in chief of the N. W. army.

An officer on board the *Lawrence,* and a volunteer on board the same vessel, having circulated a report, that the Niagara, commanded by Capt. Jesse D. Elliott, had not taken an active part in the battle, the following notes of Captains Perry and Elliott are inserted, which prove the report to have been totally false.

United States Brig Niagara,

SIR,   *Put-in-Bay, September* 18, 1813.

I am informed a report has been circulated by some malicious person, prejudicial to my vessel, when engaged with the enemy's fleet.   I will thank you, if you will, with candour, state to me the conduct of myself, officers and crew.

Respectfully your obedient servant,

Capt. O. H. PERRY.   JESSE D. ELLIOTT.

United States Schooner Ariel,

MY DEAR SIR,   *Put-in-Bay, September* 18, 1813.

I received your note last evening after I had turned in, or I should have answered it immediately.   I am

indignant that any report should be circulated, prejudicial to your character, as respects the action of the
10th instant.   It affords me great pleasure that I have
it in my power to assure you, that the conduct of yourself, officers, and crew was such as to meet my warmest approbation.   And I consider the circumstance of
your volunteering and bringing the small vessels into
close action, as contributing largely to our victory.
I shall ever believe it a premeditated plan to destroy
our commanding vessel.   I have no doubt had not the
Queen Charlotte run from the *Niagara*, from the superior order I observed her in, you would have taken
her in twenty minutes.

  With sentiments of esteem I am, dear Sir,
     your friend and obedient servant
Capt. J. D. Elliott.   O. H. PERRY.

  The following is the opinion of the court of inquiry,
held on board the United States sloop of war *Ontario*,
in the harbor of New York, in pursuance of the follow-
orders.

Sir   *Navy Department, April 20, 1815,*
 It has been stated to this department, that by the
proceedings of a court of inquiry, in Great Britain,
ordered to investigate the causes of the loss of the
British fleet on Lake Erie, on the 10th of September
1813, the conduct of Capt. Jesse D. Elliott, of the
United States navy, who commanded the brig *Niagara* on that day, is misrepresented ; justice to the reputation of Capt Elliott, and to the navy of the United States, requires that a true statement of the facts
in relation to his conduct on that occasion, be exibited
to the world.   The court therefore, of which you are
president, will immediately proceed to inquire into the
same, to ascertain the part he sustained in the action
of that day, and report its opinion thereon to this department.

  I am very respectively, your obedient servant,
Com. A. Murray, B. W. CROWNINGSHIELD.
 New York,

The court of inquiry, convened at the request of Capt. Jesse D. Elliott, having deliberately examined all the evidences produced before them, for the purpose of investigating his conduct in the glorious battle on Lake Erie, on the 10th of September 1813, in which he bore so conspicuous a part, sincerely regret, that there should have been any diversity of opinion respecting the events of that day; and imperious duty compels the court to promulgate testimony that appears materially to vary in some of its important points. The court however feel convinced, that the attempts to wrest from Capt. Elliott the laurels he gained in that splendid victory, as second in command under that gallant and highly meritorious officer, Capt. Perry ought in no wise to lesson him in the opinion of his fellow citizens, as a brave and skilful officer, and that the charge made in the proceedings of the British court martial, by which Capt. Barclay was tried, of his attempting to withdraw from the battle, is malicious, and unfounded in fact. On the contrary, it has been proved to the satisfaction of this court, that the enemy's ship, *Queen Charlotte*, bore off from the fire of the *Niagara*, commanded by Capt. Elliott.

ALEXANDER MURRAY, *Pres.*
HENRY WHEATON *Judge Adv.*
Approved, B. W. Crowningshield.

LOSS OF THE ESSEX.

COPY OF A LETTER FROM CAPT. PORTER, TO THE SECRETARY OF THE NAVY.

Sir, *Essex Junior, at sea, July 3, 1814.*

I have done myself the honor to address you repeatedly, since I left the Delaware; but have scarcely a hope that one of my letters has reached you; therefore consider it necessary to give a brief history of my proceeding since that period.

I sailed from the Delaware on the 27th of October 1812, and repaired, with all dilligence, (agreeably to instruction from Com. Bainbridge) to Port Praya,

13

Fernando de Noronho, and Cape Frio; and arrived at each place on the day appointed to meet him. On my passage from Port Praya to Fernando de Noronho, I captured H. B. M. packet *Nocton*; and after taking out about 11,000*l.* sterling in specie, sent her under command of Lieut. Finch, for America. I cruised off Rio de Janeiro, and about Cape Frio, until the 12th January 1813, hearing frequently of the Commodore, by vessels from Bahia. I here captured but one schooner, with hides and tallow. I sent her into Rio. The *Montague,* the admiral's ship being in pursuit of me, my provisions now getting short, and finding it necessary to look out for a supply, to enable, me to meet the commodore by the 1st of April off St. Helena, I proceed to the Island of St. Catharines, (the last place of rendezvous on the coast of Brazil) as the most likely to supply my wants, and at the same time afford me that secrecy necessary to enable me to allude the British ships of war on the coast, and expected there. I here could procure only wood, water and rum, and a few bags of flour; and hearing of the commodore's action with the *Java,* the capture of the *Hornet* by the *Montague,* and a considerable augmentation of the British force on the coast, and of several being in pursuit of me, I found it necessary to get to sea as soon as possible. I now, agreeably to the commodore's plan, stretched to the southward, scouring the coast as far as Rio de la Plata. I heard that Buenos Ayres was in a state of starvation, and could not supply our wants; and that the government of Montevideo was very inimical to us. The commodore's instructions now left it discretionary with me what course to pursue, and I determined on following that which had not only met his approbation, but the approbation of the then secretary of the navy. I accordingly shaped my course for the Pacific; and after suffering greatly from short allowance of provision and heavy gales off Cape Horn (for which my ship and men were illy provided) I arrived at Valparaiso on the 14th March 1813. I here took in as much jerked beef, and other provisions, as my ship would conveniently stow, and run down the coast of Chili and Peru ; in this track, I fell in with a Paruvian corsair, which had on board 24 Americans as prisoners, the crews of two whale ships, which she had taken on the coast of Chili. The captain informed me, that as the allies of Great Britain, they would capture all they should meet with, in expectation of a war between Spain and the United States. I consequently threw all his guns and ammunition into the sea, liberated the Americans, wrote a respectful letter to the Vice Roy, explaining the cause of my proceedings, which I delivered to her captain. I then proceeded from Lima and re-captured one of the vessels as she was entering the port. From thence I proceeded for the Gallapagos islands, where I cruised from the 17th April, until the 3d of October, 1813 ; during which time I touched only once on the coast of America, which was for the purpose of procuring a supply of fresh water, as none is to be found among those islands ; which are perhaps the most barren and desolate of any known.

While among this group I captured the following British ships, employed chiefly in the spermaceti whale fishery—viz.

LETTERS OF MARQUE.

	Tons.	Men.	Guns.	Pierced for
Montezuma,	270	21	2	
Policy,	175	26	10	18
Georgiana,	280	25	6	18
Greenwich,	338	25	10	20
Atlantic,	353	24	8	20
Rose,	220	21	8	20
Hector,	270	25	11	20
Catharine,	270	29	8	18
Seringapatam,	357	31	14	26
Charlton,	274	21	10	18
New Zealander,	259	23	8	13
Sir A. Hammond,	301	31	12	18
	3369	302	107	

As some of those ships were captured by boats, and others by prizes, my officers and men had several opportunities of shewing their gallantry.

The *Rose* and *Charlton* were given up to the prisoners ; the *Hector*, *Catharine*, and *Montezuma*, I sent to Valparaiso, where they were laid up ; the *Policy*, *Georgiana*, and *New-Zealander* I sent for America ; the *Greenwich* I kept as a store ship, to contain the stores of my other prizes, necessary for us ; and the *Atlantic*, now called the *Essex-Junior*, I equipped with 20 guns, and gave command of her to Lieut. Downes.

Lieut. Downes had convoyed prizes to Valparaiso, and on his return brought me letters informing me, that a squadron under the command of Com. James Hillyar, consisting of the frigate *Phœbe*, of 36 guns, the *Racoon* and *Cherub* sloop of war, and a store ship of 20 guns, had sailed on the 6th of July for this sea. The *Racoon* and *Cherub* had been seeking me for some time on the coast of Brazil, and on their return from their cruise, joined the squadron sent in search of me to the Pacific. My ship, as it may be supposed, after being near a year at sea, required some repairs to put her in a state to meet them ; which I determined to do, and to bring them to action, if I could meet them on nearly equal terms. I proceeded now, in company with the remainder of my prizes, to the island of Nooaheevah, or Madison Island, lying in the Washington groupe, discovered by Capt. Ingraham of Boston : here I caulked and completely overhauled my ship, made for her a new set of water casks, her old ones being entirely decayed, and took on board from my prizes provisions and stores for upwards of four months, and sailed for the coast of Chili on the 12th December, 1813. Previous to sailing, I secured the *Serengapatam*, *Greenwich* and *Sir Andrew Hammond* under the guns of a battery, which I erected for their protection. After taking possession of this fine island for the United States, and establishing the most friendly intercourse with the natives, I left them under the charge of Lieut. Gamble of the marines, with twenty-one men, with orders to repair to Valparaiso, after a certain period.

I arrived on the coast of Chili on the 12th January, 1814; looked into Conception and Valparaiso, found at both places only three English vessels, and learned that the squadron, which sailed from Rio de Janeiro for that sea, had not been heard of since their departure; and were supposed to be lost in endeavoring to double Cape-Horn.

I had completely broken up the British navigation in the Pacific; the vessels which had not been captured by me, were laid up, and dare not venture out. I had afforded the most ample protection to our own vessels, which were on my arrival, very numerous and unprotected. The valuable whale fishery there is entirely destroyed, and the actual injury we have done them may be estimated at two and a half millions of dollars independent of the expense of vessels in search of me. They have furnished me amply with sales, cordage, cables, anchors, provisions, medicines and stores of every discription; and the slops on board them have furnished clothing for the seamen. We have in fact lived on the enemy since I have' been in that sea, every prize having proved a well found store-ship for me. I had not yet been under, the necessity of drawing bills on the department for any object, and had been enabled to make considerable advances to my officers and crew on account of pay.

For the unexampled time we had kept the sea, my crew had been remarkably healthy; I had but one case of the scurvy; and had lost only the following men by death, viz, John S. Cowan, lieutenant; Robert Miller, surgeon; Levi Holmes, Edward Sweeney, ord. seamen; Samuel Groce, seaman; James Spafford, gunner's mate; Benjamin Geers, John Rodgers, quarter-gunners; Andrew Mahan, corporal of marines; Lewis Price, private marine.

I had done all the injury that could be done the British commerce in the Pacific, and still hoped to

the west side of the bay ; but on opening them, I saw
a prospect of passing to windward, when I took in my
top-gallant sails, which were set over single-reefed
top-sails, and braced up for this purpose ; but on
rounding the point, a heavy squall struck the ship and
carried away her main top mast, precipitating the men
who were aloft into the sea, who were drowned.   Both
ships now gave chase to me, and I endeavoured in my
disabled state to regain the port ; but finding I could
not recover the common anchorage, I ran close into a
small bay about three quarters of a mile to leeward of
the battery on the east side of the harbor, and let go
my anchor within pistol shot of the shore, where I intended to repair my damages as soon as possible.

The enemy continued to approach, and shewed an
evident intention of attacking, regardless of the neutrality of the place where I was anchored ; and the
caution observed in their approach to the attack of the
crippled *Essex*, was truly rediculous, as was their display of their motto flags, and the number of jacks at
their mast heads.   I, with as much expedition as circumstances would admit of, got my ship ready for action, and endeavoured to get a spring on my cable,
but had not succeeded when the enemy, at 54 minutes
after 3, P. M. made his attack, the *Phœbe* placing
herself under my stern, and the *Cherub* on my starboard bow ; but the *Cherub* soon finding her situation a hot one, bore up and ran under my stern also,
where both ships kept up a hot raking fire.   I had got
three long 12 pounders out of the stern ports, which
were worked with so much bravery and skill, that in
half an hour we so disabled both as to compel them
to haul off to repair damages.   In the course of this
firing, I had by the great exertions of Mr. Edward
Barnewell, the acting sailing master, assisted by Mr.
Linscott, the boatswain, succeeded in getting springs
on our cable three different times ; but the fire of the
enemy was so excessive, that before we could get our
broadside to bear, they were shot away, and thus rendered useless to us.   My ship had received many in-

CAPTURE OF THE ESSEX.

juries, and several had been killed and wounded ; but my brave officers and men, notwithstanding the unfavorable circumstances under which we were brought to action, and the powerful force opposed to us, were no ways discouraged ; and all appeared determined to defend their ship to the last extremity, and to die in preference to a shameful surrender. Our gaff, with the ensign, and the motto flag at the mizen, had been shot away, but "free trade and sailors' rights" continued to fly at the fore. Our ensign was replaced by another ; and to guard against a similar event, an ensign was made fast in the mizen rigging, and several jacks were hoisted in different parts of the ship. The enemy soon repaired his damages for a fresh attack : he now placed himself with both his ships, on my starboard quarter, out of the reach of my carronades, and where my stern guns could not be brought to bear : he there kept up a most galling fire, which it was out of my power to return, when I saw no prospect of injuring him without getting under way and becoming the assailant. My top-sail sheets and haliards were all shot away, as well as the jib and fore-top mast stay-sail haliards. The only rope not cut away was the flying-jib haliards ; and that being the only sail I could set, I caused it to be hoisted, my cable to be cut, and ran down on both ships, with an intention of laying the *Phœbe* on board. The firing on both sides was now tremendous ; I had let fall my fore-top-sail and fore-sail, but the want of tack and sheets rendered them almost useless to us—yet we were enabled, for a short time, to close with the enemy ; and although our decks were now strewed with dead, and our cock-pit filled with wounded—although our ship had been several times on fire, and was rendered a perfect wreck, we were still encouraged to hope to save her, from the circumstance of the *Cherub*, from her crippled state, being compelled to haul off. She did not return to close action again, although she apparently had it in her power to do so, but kept up a distant firing with her long guns. The *Phœbe*,

14

from our disabled state, was enabled, however, by
edging off, to choose the distance which best suited her
long guns, and kept up a tremendous fire on us, which
mowed down my brave companions by the dozen.
Many of my guns had been rendered useless by the
enemy's shot, and many of them had their whole crews
destroyed. We manned them again from those which
were disabled, and one gun in particular was three
times manned—fifteen men were slain at it, in the
course of the action! But, strange as it may appear, the captain of it escaped with only a slight
wound. Finding that the enemy had it in his power
to choose his distance, I now gave up all hopes of
closing with him, and, as the wind, for the moment,
seemed to favor the design, I determined to endeavour
to run her on shore, land my men, and destroy her.
Every thing seemed to favor my wishes.

We had aproached the shore within musket shot,
and I had no doubt of succeeding, when, in an instant, the wind shifted from the land (as is very common in this port in the latter part of the day) and pay-
ed our head down on the *Phœbe*, where we were again
exposed to a dreadful raking fire. My ship was now
totally unmanageable ; yet as her head was toward
the enemy, and he to leeward of me, I still hoped to
be able to board him. At this moment, Lieut. Commandant Downes came on board to receive my orders,
under the impression that I should soon be a prisoner.
He could be of no use to me in the then wretched
state of the *Essex*—and finding (from the enemy's
putting his helm up) that my attempt at boarding
would not succeed, I directed him, after he had been
about ten minutes on board, to return to his own ship,
to be prepared for defending and destroying her in
case of an attack. He took with him several of my
wounded, leaving three of his boat's crew on board to
make room for them. The *Cherub* now had an opportunity of distinguishing herself, by keeping up a
hot fire on him during his return. The slaughter on
board my ship had now become horrible, the enemy

continuing to rake us and we unable to bring a gun to bear. I therefore directed, a hawser to be bent to the sheet anchor, and the anchor to be cut from the bows to bring her head round : this succeeded. We again got our broadside to bear, and as the enemy was much crippled and unable to hold his own, I have no doubt he would soon have drifted out of gun shot before he discovered we had anchored, had not the hawser unfortunately parted. My ship had taken fire several times during the action, but alarmingly so foreward and aft at this moment—flames were bursting up each hatchway, and no hopes were entertained of saving her. Our distance from the shore did not exceed three quarters of a mile, and I hoped many of my brave crew would be able to save themselves, should the ship blow up, as I was informed the fire was near the magazine, and the explosion of a large quantity of powder below served to increase the horrors of our situation—our boats were destroyed by the enemy's shot ; I therefore directed those who could swim to jump overboard, and endeavour to gain the shore—some reached it—some were taken by the enemy, and some perished in the attempt ; but most preferred sharing with me the fate of the ship. We, who remained, now turned our attention wholly to extinguishing the flames : and when we had succeeded, went again to our guns where the firing was kept up for some minutes, but the crew had by this time become so weakened, that they all declared to me the impossibility of making further resistance, and entreated me to surrender my ship to save the wounded, as all further attempt at opposition must prove ineffectual, almost every gun being disabled by the destruction of their crews. I now sent for the officers of division to consult them ; but what was my surprise to find only acting Lieutenant Stephen Decatur M'Knight remaining, (who confirmed the report respecting the condition of the guns on the gun-deck—those on the spar-deck were not in a better state.) Lieut. Wilmer, after fighting most gallantry throughout the action, had

been knocked overboard by a splinter while getting
the sheet anchor from the bows, and was drowned.
Acting Lieutenant John G. Cowell had lost a leg;
Edward Barnewell, acting sailing master, had been
carried below, after receiving two severe wounds, one
in the breast and one in the face; and acting Lieutenant William H. Odenheimer had been knocked over
board from the quarter an instant before, and did not
regain the ship until after the surrender.   I was informed that the cockpit, the steerage, the ward room,
and the birth deck could contain no more wounded;
that the wounded were killed while the surgeons
were dressing them; and that unless something was
speedily done to prevent it, the ship would soon sink
from the number of shot holes in her bottom.   On
sending for the carpenter, he informed me that all his
crew had been killed or wounded, and that he had
once been over the side to stop the leaks, when his
slings had been shot away, and it was with difficulty
he was saved from drowning.   The enemy, from the
smootheness of the water, and the impossibility of our
reaching him with our carronades, and the little apprehension that was excited by our fire, which had now
become much slackened, was enabled to take aim at us
as at a target: his shot never missed our hull, and my
ship was cut up in a manner, which was, perhaps,
never before witnessed—in fine, I saw no hopes of saving her, and at 20 minutes after 6 P. M. gave the
painful order to strike the colours.   Seventy-five men,
including officers, were all that remained of my whole
crew, after the action, capable of doing duty, and
many of them severely wounded, some of whom have
since died.   The enemy still continued his fire, and
my brave, though unfortunate companions, were still
falling about me.   I directed an opposite gun to be
fired, to show them we intended no farther resistance;
but they did not desist; four men were killed at my
side and others at different parts of the ship.   I now
believe he intended to show us no quarter, and that
it would be as well to die with my flag flying as

struck, and was on the point of again hoisting it, when about 10 minutes after hauling the colours down he ceased firing.

I cannot speak in sufficiently high terms of the conduct of those engaged for such an unparalled length of time (under such circumstances) with me in the arduous and unequal contest. Let it suffice to say, that more bravery, skill, patriotism and zeal were never displayed on any occasion. Every one seemed determined to die in defence of their much loved country's cause, and nothing but views of humanity could ever have reconciled them to the surrender of the ship; they remembered their wounded and helpless shipmates below. To acting Lieutenants M'Knight and Odenheimer, I feel much indebted for their great exertions and bravery throughout the action, in fighting and encouraging the men at their divisions, for the dexterous management of the long guns, and for their promptness in remanning their guns as their crews were slaughtered. The conduct of that brave and heroic officer, acting Lieutenant John G. Cowell, who lost his leg in the latter part of the action, excited the admiration of every man in the ship, and after being wounded, would not consent to be taken below, until loss of blood had rendered him insensible. Mr. Barnewell, acting sailing-master, whose activity and courage were equally conspicuous, returned on deck after receiving his first wound, and remained after receiving his second, until fainting with the loss of blood. Mr. Samuel B. Johnston, who had joined me the day before, and acted as marine officer, conducted himself with great bravery, and exerted himself in assisting at the long guns ; the musketry after the first half hour being useless from our long distance.

Mr. M.W. Bostwick, whom I had appointed acting purser of the *Essex-Junior*, and who was on board my ship, did the duties of aid in a manner which reflects on him the highest honor : and Midshipmen Isaacs, Farrugut, and Ogden, as well as acting Midshipmen James Terry, James R. Lyman and Samuel

Duzenbury, and Master's Mate William Pierce, exerted themselves in the performance of their respective duties, and gave an earnest of their value to the service ; the three first are too young to recommend for promotion ; the latter I beg leave to recommend for confirmation, as well as the acting lieutenants and Messrs. Barnewell, Johnston and Bostwick.

We have been unfortunate, but not disgraced—the defence of the *Essex* has not been less honorable to her officers and her crew, than the capture of an equal force ; and I now consider my situation less unpleasant, than that of Com. Hillyar, who, in violation of every principal of honor and generosity, and regardless of the rights of nations, attacked the *Essex* in her crippled state, within pistol shot of a neutral shore, when for six weeks I had daily offered him fair and honorable combat, on terms greatly to his advantage. The blood of the slain must rest on his head.; and he has yet to reconcile his conduct to heaven, to his conscience, and to the world. The annexed extracts of a letter from Com. Hillyar, which was written previous to his returning me my sword, will shew his opinion of our conduct.

My loss has been dreadfully severe, 58 killed, or have since died of their wounds, and among them Lieut. Cowell ; 39 were severely wounded, 27 slightly, and 31 are missing ; making in all 154 killed, wounded, and missing, a list of whose names is annexed.

The professional knowledge of Dr. Richard Hoffman, acting surgeon, and Dr. Alexander Montgomery, acting as surgeon's mate, added to their assiduity and the benevolent attentions and assistance of Mr. D. P. Adams, the chaplain, saved the lives of many of the wounded ; those gentlemen have been indefatigable in their attentions to them ; the two first I beg leave to recommend for confirmation, and the latter to the notice of the department.

I must in justification of myself observe, that with our six 12 pounders only, we fought this action—our caronades being almost useless.

The lost in killed and wounded has been great with the enemy; among the former is the first lieutenant of the *Phœbe*, and of the latter Capt Tucker of the *Cherub*, whose wounds are severe. Both the *Essex* and the *Phœbe* were in a sinking state, and it was with difficulty they could be kept afloat until they anchored in Valparaiso next morning. The battered state of the *Essex* will, I believe, prevent her ever reaching England, and I also think it will be out of their power to repair the damages of the *Phœbe*, so as to enable her to double Cape Horn. All the masts and yards of the *Phœbe* and *Cherub* are badly crippled, and their hulls much cut up; the former had eighteen 12 pound shot through her, below her water line, some three feet under water. Nothing but the smoothness of the water saved both the *Phœbe* and *Essex.*

I hope, Sir, that our conduct may prove satisfactory to our country, and that it will testify it by obtaining our speedy exchange, that we may again have it in our power to prove our zeal.

Com. Hillyar, I am informed, has thought proper to state to his government that the action lasted only 45 minutes; should he have done so, the motive may be easily discovered—but the thousand of disinterested witnesses who covered the surrounding hills, can testify that we fought his ships near two hours and a half; upwards of fifty broadsides were fired by the enemy agreeably to their own accounts, and upwards of seventy-five by ours; except the few minutes they were repairing damages, the firing was incessant.

Soon after my capture I entered into an agreement with Com. Hillyar to disarm my prize, the *Essex-Junior*, and proceed with the survivors of my officers and crew in her to the United States, taking with me all her officers and crew. He consented to grant her a passport to secure her from recapture. The ship was small, and we knew we had much to suffer, yet we hoped soon to reach our country in safety, that we might again have it in our power to serve it. This arrangement was attended with no additional expense, as she was abundantly supplied with provisions and stores for the voyage.

In justice to Com. Hillyar, I must observe, that, although I can never be reconciled to the manner of his attack on the *Essex*, or to his conduct before the action, he has, since our capture, shown the greatest humanity to my wounded, whom he permitted me to land, on condition that the United States should bear their expenses, and has endeavored as much as lay in his power to alleviate the distresses of war by the most generous and delicate deportment towards myself, my officers and crew; he gave orders that the property of every person should be respected—his orders, however, were not so strictly attended to as might have been expected; besides being deprived of books, charts, &c. &c. both myself and officers lost many articles of our clothing, some to a considerable amount. I should not have considered this last circumstance of sufficient importance to notice, did it not mark a striking difference between the navy of Great Britian and that of the United States, highly creditable to the latter.

By the arrival of the *Tagus*, a few days after my capture, I was informed that besides the ships which had arrived in the Pacific in pursuit of me, and those still expected, others were sent to cruise for me in the China seas, off New Zealand, Timour, and New Holland, and that another frigate was sent to the river La Plata.

To possess the *Essex*, it has cost the British government near six millions of dollars; and yet, Sir, her capture was owing entirely to accident; and if we consider the expedition with which naval contests are now decided, the action is a dishonor to them. Had they brought their ships boldly to action with a force so very superior, and having the choice of position, they should either have captured or destroyed us in one fourth of the time they were about it.

During the action, our Consul General, Mr. Poinsett, called on the governor of Valparaiso, and requested that the batteries might protect the *Essex.* The request was refused, but he promised that if she should succeed in fighting her way to the common anchorage, he would send an officer to the British commander and request him to cease firing, but declined using force under any circumstances, and there is no doubt a perfect understanding existed between them. This conduct added to the assistance given to the British, and their friendly reception after the action, and the strong bias of the faction which governs Chili in favor of the English, as well as their hostility to the Americans, induced Mr. Poinsett to leave that country. Under such circumstances, I did not conceive that it would be proper for me to claim the restoration of my ship, confident that the claim would be made by my government to more effect. Finding some difficulty in the sale of my prizes, I had taken the *Hector* and *Catharine* to sea, and burnt them with their cargoes.

I exchanged Lieut. M,Knight, Mr. Lyman, and eleven seaman, for part of the crew of the Sir Andrew Hammond, and sailed from Valparaiso on the 27th April, where the enemy were still patching up their ships to put them in a state for proceeding to Rio de Janeiro, previous to going to England.

Annexed is a list of the remains of my crew to be exchanged, as also a copy of the correspondance between Com. Hillyar and myself on that subject. I also send you a list of the prisoners I have taken during my cruise, amounting to 343.

I have the honor to be, &c.

Hon. Secr'y of the navy **D. PORTER,**
of the United States, Washington.

P. S. To give you a correct idea of the state of the *Essex* at the time of surrender, I send you the boatswain's and carpenters report of damages; I also send you a report of the divisions.

A return of the killed, wounded and missing on board
15

of the late United States frigaté *Essex*, of 32 guns, 255 men, David Porter, Esq. commander, in an action fought on the 28th March, 1814, Valparaiso Bay, with the British frigate *Phœbe*, of 36 guns, 320 men, James Hillyar, Esq. commander, and the sloop of war *Cherub*, mounting 28 guns, 180 men, commanded by T. Tucker, Esq.

Killed in action and have since died of their wounds.——James P Wilmer, 1st lieutenant ; John G. Cowell, 3d do.; Henry Kennedy, boatswain's mate ; William Smith, do.; Francis Bland, quarter master ; Reuben Marshal, quarter gunner ; Thomas Bailey, boatswain's yeoman ; and fifty-three seamen, marines, &c.

SEVERELY WOUNDED——Edward Barnewell, sailingmaster ; Edward Linscott, boatswain ; William Kingsbury, boatswain ; *Essex* jun. and twenty two others.

SLIGHTLY WOUNDED——Only twenty-five.

MISSING——Thirty-one.

RECAPITULATION.

Killed,	-	-	-	-	-	60
Severely wounded,		-	-	-	37
Slightly wounded,		-	-	-	25
Missing,	-	-	-	-	-	31
Total	-	-	--	-	153

During the action, the *Essex-Junior* lay in the port of Valparaiso, under the guns of a Spanish fort, unable to take any part in the contest. After the action, Capt. Porter and his crew were paroled, and by arrangement permitted to come home in the *Essex-Junior*, and a cartel with his crew. Off the Hook they were detained 24 hours by the British razee *Saturn*, in company with the frigate *Narcissus*. Capt. Porter left the *Essex-Junior* on the 6th of July, in one of her yawls, with six men, about thirty miles outside of the Hook, and landed on the 7th at Babylon on Long-Island, where he procured a waggon, took on board his yawl and jolly tars, and reached Brooklyn about five o'clock P. M.

The *Essex* had landed all her specie, amounting to two millions, at Valparaiso previous to her being captured.

EXTRACT OF A LETTER FROM COM. HILLYAR TO ME.

MY DEAR SIR,   *Phœbe, April 4, 1814.*

Neither in my conversations nor the accompanying letter, have I mentioned you sword. Ascribe my remissness in the first instance to forgetfulness ; I consider it only in my servant's possession with my own, until the master may please to call for it ; and although I omitted, at the moment of presentation, from my mind being much engrossed in attending to professional duties, to offer its restoration, the hand that received will be most gladly extended, to put it in possession of him who wore it so honorably in defending his country's cause.

Believe me, my dear Sir,
very faithfully yours,
JAMES HILLYAR.

Capt. PORTER.

After some conversation on the subject the following correspondence took place.

SIR,   *Valparaiso, April 4, 1814.*

Taking into consideration the immense distance we are from our respective countries, the uncertainty of the future movements of his majesty's ships under my command, which precludes the possibility of my making a permanent arrangement for transporting the officers and crew, late of the *Essex*, to Europe ; and the fast approaching season which renders a passage round Cape Horn in some degree dangerous : I have the honor to propose for your approbation the following articles, which, I hope, the government of the United States, as well as that of Great Britain, will deem satisfactory ; and to request, that should you conceive them so, you will favor me with the necessary bond for fulfillment.

First. The *Essex-Junior* to be deprived of all her armament and perfectly neutralized ; to be equiped for the voyage solely and wholy at the expense of the American government ; and to proceed with a proper American officer and crew (of which I wish to be furnished with a list, for the purpose of giving the necessary passport) to any port of the United States of America that you may deem most proper.

Second. Yourself, the officers, petty officers, seamen, marines, &c. composing your crew, to be exchanged immediately on their arrival in America, for an equal number of British prisoners of similar rank. Yourself and officers to be considered on their parole of honor until your and their exchange shall be effected.

In case of the foregoing articles being accepted, the *Essex-Junior*, will be expected to prepare immediately for the voyage, and to proceed on it before the expiration of the present month : should any of the wounded at that period be found incapable of removal, from not being sufficiently advanced in their recovery, the most humane attention shall be paid them ; and they shall be forwarded home by the first favorable conveyance that may offer.

I have the honor to be, &c.

Cap. DAVID PORTER,   JAMES HILLYAR.
Late commander of the U. S. frigate Essex.

SIR,   *Valparaiso, 5 April, 1814.*

I have the honor to acknowledge the receipt of your several favors of yesterday's date.

The conditions offered by you for our return to the United States are perfectly satisfactory to me, and I entertain no doubts of their being equally so to my country ; I therefore do not hesitate to pledge my honor (the strongest bond I can give) that every article of the arrangement shall on our part be fully complied with. A list of the *Essex-Junior's* crew shall be furnished you as soon as it can be made out, and her disarmament affected with all possible dispatch.

I have the honor to be, &c.

Com. JAMES HILLYAR,   D. PORTER.
Commanding H. B. M. frigate Phœbe.

Com. Hillyar sent me a paper, certifying that he had exchanged certain indivïduals therein named, making part of the crew of the *Sir Andrew Hammond,* for an equal number of the most severely wounded of my crew : this occasioned the following letters.

SIR, *Valparaiso*, 4 *April*, 1814.

I have received a paper signed by you, dated yesterday, stating, that you had exchanged certain wounded prisoners, making part of my crew, for the captain and crew of the prize ship *Sir Andrew Hammond ;* which paper I have taken the liberty to return to you, and protest in the strongest terms against such an arrangement.

In the first place the wounded and helpless individuals, therein named, do not wish such exchange : one died last night, and several others expect to share his fate.

Secondly, should I from any circumstances be separated from them, which would be more likely to be the case than if they remained prisoners, their situation would be more deplorable then it is at present. Thirdly, this arrangement has been made without my consent and on terms far from offering equal advantages to the United States.

I have the honor to be, &c.

Com. JAMES HILLYAR, D. PORTER.
Commanding H. B. M. Phœbe.

SIR, *H. B. M. Ship, Valparaiso, April* 4, 1814.

I have the honor to acknowledge the receipt of your letter of this day's date, protesting against the arrangement made in the paper you returned, and to express a regret that my wish, which was to alleviate and not increase the afflictions of your wounded officers and crew, has failed of being gratified. I am sorry you have thought proper to mention the dead and dying, as I so fully explained to you this morning, that in the event of the loss of any, other names should be added to the list. I shall now direct Capt. William

Porter to consider himself still a prisoner of war on his parole ; but as I have ordered the people to go on board the *Essex* to work, under the impression that no difficulty would arise, will liberate in exchange for them an equal number of prisoners, as their names, being seamen, shall be found to follow each other on your late ship's book, and give up also two mates or midshipmen for the two mates which are of the English party.   I hope this may prove satisfactory to your government and self.

I am yours, &c.

Capt. D. PORTER.   JAMES HILLYAR.

SIR,   *Valparaiso, 5 April,* 1814.

The arrangement which you have suggested respecting the exchange of the seamen of the *Sir Andrew Hammond* for an equal number of seamen of the late United States frigate *Essex*, as they stand on the list furnished you, is perfectly satisfactory. It will be great satisfaction to the three officers, who accompany the *Essex*, to know, that after your object in taking them with you shall be effected, there will be no dificulty in their proceeding immediately for the United States. I take the liberty therefore to suggest, that they might be exchanged here for Capt. William Porter and his three mates.   This will be an accomodation to all parties, and reconcile the officers so exchanged to a separation from their friends.

I have the honor to be, &c.

Com. JAMES HILLYAR,   D. PORTER.
Commanding H. M. frigate Phœbe.

COPY OF A LETTER FROM CAPTAIN PORTER TO THE SECRETARY OF THE NAVY.

SIR,   *New-York, July* 13, 1814.

There are some facts relating to our enemy, and although not connected with the action, serve to show his perfidy, and should be known.

On Com. Hillyar's arrival at Valparaiso, he ran the *Phœbe* close alongside of the *Essex*, and inquired politely after my health, observing, that his ship was cleared for action, and his men prepared for boarding, I observed, "Sir, if you by any accident, get on board of me, I assure you that great confusion will take place,; I am prepared to receive you, but shall only act on the defensive." He observed, cooly and indifferently, "Oh, Sir, I have no such intention;" at this instant his ship took aback on my starboard bow, her yards nearly locking with those of the *Essex*. I called all hands to board the enemy; and in an instant my crew were ready to spring on her decks. Com. Hillyar exclaimed, with great agitation, "I had no intention of getting on board of you;—I had no intention of coming so near you; I am sorry I come so near you." His ship fell off with her jib-boom over my decks; her bows exposed to my broadside, her stern to the fire of the *Essex-Junior*, her crew in the greatest confusion, and in fifteen minutes, I could have taken or destroyed her. After he had brought his ship to anchor, Com. Hillyar and Capt. Tucker of the *Cherub*, visited me on shore; when I asked him if he intended to respect the neutrality of the port; "Sir," said he," you have paid such respect to the neutrality of this port, that I feel myself bound, in honor, to do the same.

I have the honor to be, &c.

DAVID·PORTER.

After the capture of the *Essex*, Capt. Porter entered into an arrangement with Com. Hillyar, to transport the survivors of his crew to the U. States in the *Essex-Junior* on parole, on condition that she should receive a passport to secure her from recapture and detention. On the 5th of July, fell in with H. B. M. ship *Saturn*, Capt. Nash, who examined the papers of the *Essex-Junior*, treated Capt. Porter with great civility, furnished him with late newspapers, and sent him on board some oranges; and at the same time made him an offer of services. The boarding officer endorsed the passport, and permitted the ship to proceed. She stood on the same tack with the *Saturn;* and about 2 hours aftewards was again brought to, the papers examined, and the ship's hold overhauled by the boat's crew and an officer. Capt. Porter expressed his astonishment at such proceedings, and was inform- ed that Capt. Nash had his motives. It was stated that Com. Hillyar had no authority to make such ar- rangement ; that the passport must go on board of the *Saturn* again, and the *Essex-Junior* be detained. Capt. Porter then insisted that the smallest detention would be a violation of the contract on the part of the British, and that he should consider himself as the prisoner of Capt. Nash, and no longer on his parole ; at the same time offering his sword, which was refus- ed, assuring the officer he would deliver it up with the same feelings he had presented it to Com. Hillyar. The officer went on board, returned and informed Capt. Porter, that the *Essex-Junior* must remain all night under the lee of the *Saturn*. Then, said Capt. Porter, I am your prisoner ; I do not feel myself bound by any contract with Com. Hillyar, and I shall act accordingly.

At 7 o'clock next morning, the wind being light from the southward, the ships being about 30 or 40 miles from the land off the eastern part of Long Is- land, and about musket shot from each other, there appearing no disposition on the part of the enemy to liberate the *Essex-Junior*, Capt. Porter determined to attempt his escape. A boat was lowered down, man- ned and armed ; he desired Capt. Downes to inform Capt. Nash, that he was now satisfied that most Brit- ish naval officers were not only destitue of honor, but regardless of the honor of each other ; that he was armed and prepared to defend himself against their boats, if sent in pursuit of him ; and that they must hereafter meet him as an enemy. He now pulled off from the ship, keeping the *Essex-Junior* in a direct line between him and the *Saturn*, and got near gun-shot from them before he was discovered ; at this instant a fresh breeze sprung up, and the *Saturn* made all sail in pursuit of him, but fortunately a thick fog set in and concealed him, when he changed his course, and eluded them. During the fog he heard a firing, and on its clearing up discovered the *Saturn* in chase of the *Essex-Junior*, who soon brought her to. After rowing and sailing about 60 miles, Capt. Porter succeeded, with great difficulty and hazard, in reaching the town of Babylon, (Long Island) where, being strongly suspected to be an English officer, he was closely interrogated, and his story appearing so extraordinary, none gave credit ; but on showing his commission all doubts were removed, and he met from all the inhabitants the most friendly and hospitable reception.

The following is a copy of the arrangement, concluded between Capt. Porter, in behalf of himself and crew, with Capt. Hillyar.

By James Hillyar Esq. captain of H. B. M. Ship Phœbe, and senior officer of his majesty's ships in Valparaiso Bay.

I hereby certify, that I have on the part of his Britannic Majesty, entered into an agreement with Capt. David Porter, of the United States navy, and late commander of the frigate *Essex*, who, on the part of his government, engages as follows, to wit : That himself, his officers and crew will proceed to the United States, in the ship called the *Essex-Junior*, as a cartel, commanded by Lieut. John Downes, of the United States navy, and having a crew, consisting of the officers and men, named in the annexed list.

The said Capt. Porter, his officers and crew, a list of which is subjoined, will remain as prisoners of war on parole, not to take arms against Great Britain until regularly exchanged, and that he pledges his honor to fulfil the foregoing conditions. I therefore request, that said ship, the *Essex-Junior*, may be permitted to pass freely to the United States without any impediment, and that the officers commanding the ships of war of his Britannic Majesty, as well as those of private armed vessels, and all others in authority under the British government, also those in alliance with his said majesty, will give the said David Porter, his offi-

16

cers and crew, and the crew of the aforesaid ship called the *Essex-Junior*, every aid and assistance to enable them to arrive at the place of their destination.

And as it may become necessary for the *Essex-Junior* to touch at one or more places for the purpose of obtaining refreshment and supplies, it is requested, that in such case all, to whom this passport may be presented, will give the persons on board said ship every facility in supplying their wants, and permit them to depart with her without hindrance.

Given under my hand, on board his majesty's ship *Phœbe*, at Valparaiso, April, 1814.

A gentleman, who took part in the engagement, has related the following anecdotes exemplary of that fearless and patriotic spirit which animated the whole crew of the *Essex*, and which has characterized our hardy sailors in all their combats with the enemy. To the memory of these brave fellows their publicity is due ; and we doubt not many more instances of chivalrous heroism, resulting from a noble love of country, might be obtained and recorded, to the lasting honor of the American name.

John Ripley, after losing his leg, said "farewell, boys ; I can be of no use to you ;" and leaped out of the bow port.

John Alvinson received a cannon ball (18 pounder) through the body ; in the agony of death he exclaimed, "never mind, shipmates ; I die in defence of 'Free trade and sailors' r-i-g-h-t-s ; '" and expired with the word *rights* quivering on his lips.

James Anderson had his left leg shot off, and died animating his shipmates to fight bravely in defence of liberty.

After the engagement, Benjamin Hazen, having dressed himself in a clean shirt and jerkin, addressed his remaining messmates, and telling them he never could submit to be a prisoner to the English, threw himself into the sea.

LETTER FROM CAPT. HILLYAR TO COM. BROWN, STATIONED
AT JAMAICA.

His Majesty's Ship Phœbe,
SIR,   *Valparaiso Bay*, 30 *March*, 1814.

I have the honor to acquaint you that, at 3 o'clock,
in the afternoon of the 28th instant, after nearly four
months, anxious watching with his majesty's brig
Cherub, for the United States frigate *Essex* and her
companion to quit the port of Valparaiso, we saw the
former under way, and immediately the two ships
made sail to close with her.

On rounding the outer point of the bay, and hauling her wind, for the purpose of endeavoring to weather us and escape, she lost her main top-mast, and afterwards, not succeeding in an effort to regain the limits of the port, she bore up and anchored so near the
shore (a few miles to leeward of it) as to preclude the
possibility of either of his majesty's ships passing a-
head of her without risk. As we drew near, my intention of going close under his stern was frustrated,
from the ship's broaching off, and from the wind blowing extremely fresh. Our first fire commenced a little
past 4, and continued about 10 minutes, but produced
no visible effect ; our second, a few random shot only,
from having increased our distance by wearing, was
not apparently more successful ; and having lost the
use of our main-sail, jib, and main-stay appearances
were a little inauspicious, in standing again towards
her. I hailed the *Cherub*, and signified my intention
of anchoring, to Capt. Tucker, for which we were not
ready before with springs, directing him to keep under sail, and take a convenient station for annoying our
opponent.

On closing the *Essex*, at 35 minutes past 5, the firing
commenced, and before I gained my intended position,
her cables were cut, and a serious conflict ensued, the
guns of his majesty's ship becoming gradually more
destructive ; and when it pleased the Almighty to
bless the effort of my gallant companions, and my per-

sonal, very humble ones, with victory. My friend, Capt. Tucker, an officer worthy of their lordship's best attention, was most severely wounded at the commencement of the action, but remained on deck till it terminated ; he also informs me that his officers and crew, of whose loyalty, zeal, and discipline I entertain the highest opinion, conducted themselves to his satisfaction. I have to lament the death of four of my brave companions, and one of his, and my first lieutenant among the number : he fell early. Our list of wounded is small. The conduct of my officers, &c. was such as became good and loyal subjects.

The defence of the *Essex*, taking into consideration our great superiority of force, the very discouraging circumstances of having lost her main top-mast, and being twice on fire, did honor to her defender, and must fully prove the courage of Capt. Porter.

I was much hurt on hearing that her men had been encouraged, when the result of the action was evidently decided, some to take to their boats, and others to swim to the shore, many of whom were drowned in the latter attempt : sixteen were saved by the exertions of our people, and others, I believe between thirty and forty, effected their landing. I informed Capt. Porter, that I considered the latter, in point of honor, as my prisoners. He said the encouragement was given when the ship was in danger from fire, and I have not pressed the point.

The *Essex* is completely stored and provisioned for six months, and although much injured in her upper works, masts and rigging, is not in such a state as to give the slightest cause of alarm respecting her being able to perform a voyage to Euorpe with perfect safety.

I have the honor to be, &c.
JAMES HILLYAR, *Captain.*

SEQUEL OF CAPTAIN PORTER'S EXPEDITION IN THE
SOUTH SEA.

On the 19th November, 1813, Capt. Porter took

formal possession of the island, called by the natives Nooaheevah, generally known by the name of Sir Henry Martin's island, but now called Madison Island. It is situated between lat. 9° and 10° S. and in long. 140° W. from Greenwich.

The following is a letter from Capt. Gamble to Capt. Porter.

Capt. Gamble, the reader will recollect, was left by Capt. Porter with a few men, in charge of two or three vessels and some public property, when he sailed from Madison Island for Valparaiso, previous to his ever memorable battle in the *Essex.* The following letter comprises all the subsequent occurrances :

SIR, *New-York, August 30, 1815.*

With regret I have to inform you, the frigate had not got clear of the Marqueses, before we discovered in the natives a hostile disposition towards us, who in a few days became so insolent, that I found it absolutely necessary, not only for the security of the ships, and property on shore, but for our personal safety, to land my men, and regain by force of arms the many things they had, in the most daring manner, stolen from the encampment ; and what was of still greater importance, to prevent, if possible, their putting threats into execution, which might have been attended with the most serious consequences on our part from duty requiring my men to be so much seperated.

I however had the satisfaction to accomplish my wish without firing a musket, and from that time lived in the most perfect amity with them, until the 7th May following, when my destressed situation placed me in their power.

Before mentioning the lamentable events of that day, and the two succeeding ones, I shall give you a brief account of a few preceding occurrences, which were sources of great uneasiness to me. The first was the death of John Wetter, marine, who was unfortunately drowned in the surf, on the afternoon of the 28th February, and the desertion of four of my men. They took the advantage of a dark night, and left the bay unobserved by any person, all excepting one, a prisoner, having the watch on deck. They took with them several muskets, a supply of ammunition, and many articles of but little value. My attempt to pursue them was prevented by their destroying partially the only boat (near the beach) at that time sea-worthy.

On the 12th April, began to rig the ships *Seringapatam* and *Sir Andrew Hammond*, which, as I calculated, employed the men until the 1st of May. All hands were then engaged in getting the remainder of the property from the *Greenwich* to the *Seringapatam*, as I began to despair of your rejoining me at that place.

The work went on well, and the men were obedient to my orders, though I discovered an evident change in their countenances, which led me to suppose there was something wrong in agitation, and under that impression, had all the muskets, ammunition, and small arms of every description, taken to the *Greenwich*, the ship I lived on board, from the other ships, as a necessary precaution against a surprize from my own men.

On the 7th May, while on board the *Seringapatam*, on duty, which required my being present, a mutiny took place, in which I was wounded, and the mutineers succeeded in getting the *Seringapatam* out of the bay. Two days after, when making the necessary preparations to depart for Valparaiso, we were attacked by the savages, and I have, with the deepest regret, to inform you, sir, that Midshipman, William Felters, John Thomas, Thomas Gibbs, and William Brudinell, were massacred, and Peter Coddington, marine dangerously wounded. After bending the jib and spanker we cut our moorings, and fortunately had a light breeze, that carried the ship clear of the bay, with six cartridges remaining out of the only barrel left us by the mutineers.

After getting out of the bay, we found our situation

most distressing. In attempting to run the boat up, it broke in two parts, and we were compelled to cut away from the bows the only anchor, not being able to cat it. We mustered altogether eight souls, out of which there was one cripple, one dangerously wounded, one sick, one just recovering from the scurvy, and myself confined to the bed with a high fever, produced by my wound.

In that state, destitute of charts, and almost of every means of navigating the ship, I reached the Sandwich Islands, after a passage of seventeen days, and suffering much from fatigue and hardships. I was there unfortunately captured by the English ship *Cherub*, remained a prisoner on board of her seven months, during which time my men were treated in a most shameful manner. We were then put on shore at Rio de Janeiro, without the possibility of getting away until after hearing of the peace. I then, by the advice of the physician who attended me, embarked on board a Swedish ship bound to Havre de Grace, (there being no other means of my getting away at that time,) leaving behind Midshipman Clapp and five men, having lost one soon after my arrival in that place with the small pox.

On the 1st inst. lat. 47° N. long. 18° W. we fell in with the American ship *Oliver Ellsworth*, from Havre, bound to this port. I took a passage on board of her, and arrived here two days since, after being upwards of an hundred days at sea. I am at present unable to travel, and shall therefore await either your orders, or the orders of the commandant of the marine corps at this place.

I have the honor to remain,
> with the highest respect and esteem,
>> sir, your obed't serv't,
>>> **JOHN M. GAMBLE**

PEACOCK AND EPERVIER.

EXTRACT OF A LETTER FROM CAPT. CHARLES MORRIS, COMMANDING THE U. S. SHIP ADAMS AT SAVANNAH, TO THE SECRETARY OF THE NAVY.

SIR,　　　　　　　　　　*Savannah, May 2, 1814.*

I have the honor to inform you, that a fine brig of 18 guns, prize to the United States sloop *Peacock,* anchored here this morning. She is much shattered in her hull, and damaged in her rigging, having fought 45 minutes—her loss 8 killed and 15 wounded. The *Peacock,* 2 slightly wounded. She was chased on the 30th April, by a frigate, but escaped by running close in the shore in the night. Lieut. Nicholson, prize master, will forward you a more detailed account of this handsome affair. I am &c.

Hon. W. JONES &c.　　　　　　**C. MORRIS.**

LETTER FROM LIEUT. NICHOLSON TO THE SECRETARY OF THE NAVY.

SIR,　　　　　　　　　　*Savannah, May 1, 1814.*

I have the honor to inform you of my arrival here in late his Britannic majesty's brig *Epervier,* of eighteen 32 pound carronades, Capt. Wales, captured by the sloop *Peacock,* on Friday morning, the 29th, off Cape Carnaveral, after an action of 45 minutes, in which time she was much cut up in hull, spars, rigging and sails, with upwards of five feet of water in her hold, having the weathergage.

She has lost 8 killed and 15 wounded ; among the latter her first lieutenant, who has lost his arm. I am happy to say, the *Peacock* received no material injury—her fore-yard and two men slightly wounded—she received not one shot in her hull. The brig had upwards of one hundred thousand dollars on board.

I have the honor to be &c.

JOHN B. NICHOLSON.

Hon. WILLIM JONES,
　Sec'y of the navy.

THE PEACOCK AND EPERVIER.

COPIES OF LETTERS FROM CAPT. WARRINGTON TO THE
SECRETARY OF THE NAVY.

U. S. Sloop Peacock, at sea, lat 27° 47', *long.* 80° 9',
29 *April,* 1814.

I have the honor to inform you that we have this
morning captured, after an action of 45 minutes, his
majesty's brig *Epervier*, rating and mounting 18 thirty-two pound carronades, with 128 men, of whom 8
were killed and 15 wounded (according to the best information we could obtain :) among the latter is her 1st
lieutenant, who has lost an arm, and received a severe splinter wound on the hip. Not a man in the
Peacock was killed, and only two wounded; neither
dangerously so. The fate of the *Epervier* would have
been determined in much less time, but for the circumstance of our foreyard being totally disabled by two
round shot in the starboard quarter from her first
broadside, which entirely deprived us of the use of
our fore and fore-top sail, and compelled us to keep
the ship large throughout the remainder of the action.
This, with a few top-mast and top-gallant back-stays
cut away, a few shot through our sails, is the only injury the *Peacock* has sustained. Not a round shot
touched her hull; our masts and spars are as sound
as ever. When the enemy struck, he had five feet
water in his hold, his main top-mast was over the side,
his main-boom shot away, fore-mast cut nearly in two
and tottering, his fore rigging and stays shot away,
his bowsprit badly wounded, and 45 shot holes in his
hull, 20 of which were within a foot of his water line.
By great exertion we got her in sailing order just as
dark came on.

In fifteen minutes after the enemy struck, the *Peacock* was ready for another action, in every respect but
her fore-yard, which was sent down, fished, and had
the fore-sail set again in 45 minutes—such were the
spirit and activity of our gallant crew. The *Epervier*
had under convoy an English hermaphrodite brig, a
Russian and a Spanish ship, all which hauled their

17

wind and stood to the E. N. E. I had determined
upon pursuing the former, but found that it would not
answer to leave our prize, in her then crippled state
and the more particularly so, as we found she had in
$ 120,000 in specie, which we soon transferred to this
sloop. Every officer, seaman, and marine did his duty, which is the highest compliment I can pay them.
                I am respectfully,
                        L. WARRINGTON.
    P. S. From Lieut. Nicholson's report, who was
counting up the *Epervier's* crew, there were 11 killed
and 15 wounded.   L. W.

SIR,   *Savannah, May 4,* 1814.
    I have great satisfaction in being able to report to
you the arrival of the *Peacock* at this anchorage today, and also the arrival of the *Epervier* on Monday
last. I have now to detail to you the reason of our
separation. We made sail as mentioned in my last,
on the evening of the 29th of April. The next afternoon we were, at ½ past 5, abreast the centre of Amelia
Island, with the vessels in sight over the land, when
two large ships, which had been seen sometime previous a little to the northward of the Island, were
clearly ascertained to be frigates in chase of us. In
this situation, at the suggestion of Lieut. Nicholson,
I took out all but himself and sixteen officers and
men, and stood to the southward along shore, on a
wind, leaving him to make the best of his way for St.
Mary's; which place I felt confident he would reach,
as the weather frigate was in chase of the *Peacock,*
and the other was too far to the leeward to fetch him:
at 9 we lost sight of the chaser, but continued standing all night to the southward, in hopes to get entirely
clear of him. At day light we shortened sail and
stood to the northward, and again made the frigate,
who gave chase the second time, which he continued
until 2 P. M. when finding he could not come up, he
desisted. In the evening we resumed our course, and
saw nothing until day light on Tuesday morning, when

a large ship, supposed to be the same, was again seen in chase of us, and again run out of sight.

This morning, at ¼ past 3, we made Tybee light, and at half past 8 anchored near the United States ship Adams. As the enemy is hovering near to St. Mary's, I concluded he had received information of, and was waiting to intercept us. Accordingly we steered for this place, where we received intelligence of the *Epervier's* arrival, after frightening off a launch which was sent from the enemy's ship to leeward on Saturday evening to cut him off from the land.

From the 18th of April to the 24th we saw but one neutral, and two privateers, both which were chased without overhauling although we ran one among the shoals of Cape Carnaveral, and followed him into four fathoms water. We have been to the southward as far as the Great Isaacs, and have cruised from them to Maranilla reef, and along the Florida shore to Cape Carnaveral. Not a single running vessel has been through the gulf in all this time. The fleet sailed from Jamaica under convoy of a 74, two frigates, and two sloops, from the 1st to the 10th of May. They are so much afraid of our cruisers, that several ships in the Havanna ready for sea, which intended to *run it* (as it is called) were forced to wait the arrival of the convoy from Jamaica.

The *Epervier* and her convoy were the first English vessels we had seen.

We shall proceed in the execution of your further instructions, as soon as we can get a fore yard, provisions, and water.

The *Epervier* is one of their finest brigs, and is well calculated for our service. She sails extremely fast, and will require but little to send her to sea, as her armament and stores are complete.

I enclose you a list of the brig's crew, as accurately as we can get it.

I am respectfully,

L. WARRINGTON.

U. S. Sloop Peacock, Savannah,

SIR,   *5 May, 1814.*

As my letter of yesterday was too late for the mail, I address you again in the performance of a duty which is pleasing and gratifying to me in a high degree, and is but doing justice to the merits of the deserving officers under my command, of whom I have hitherto refrained from speaking, as I considered it most correct to make it the subject of a particular communication.

To the unwearied and indefatigable attention of Lieut. Nicholson (1st) in organizing and training the crew, the success of this action is in a great measure to be attributed. I have confided greatly in him, and have never found my confidence misplaced. For judgment, coolness, and decision in times of difficulty, few can surpass him. This is the second action in which he has been engaged in this war, and in both he has been successful. His greatest pride is to earn a commander's commission by fighting for, instead of *heiring* it.

From Lieut. Henly (2d,) and Lieut. Voorhees, (acting 3d, who has also been twice successfully engaged,) I received every assistance that zeal, ardor, and experience could afford. The fire from their two divisions was terrible, and directed with the greatest precision and coolness.

In Sailing Master Percival, whose great wish and pride it is to obtain a lieutenant's commission, and whose unremitting and constant attention to duty, added to his professional knowledge, entitles him to it in my opinion, I found an able, as well as willing assistant. He handled the ship, as if he had been working her into a roadstead. Mr. David Cole, acting Carpenter, I have also found such an able and valuable man in his occupation, that I must request in the most earnest manner, that he may receive a warrant; for I feel confident, that to his uncommon exertion, we in a great measure owe the getting our prize into port. From 11 A. M. until 6 P. M. he was over her side,

THE WASP AND REINDEER.

stopping shot holes, on a grating, and, when the ordinary resources failed of success, his skill soon supplied him with efficient ones. Mr. Philip Myers, master's mate, has also conducted himself in such a manner as to warrant my recommendation of him as a master. He is a seaman, navigator, and officer; his family in New-York is respected, and he would prove an acquisition to the service. My clerk, Mr. John S. Townsend is anxious to obtain through my means a midshipman's warrant, and has taken pains to qualify himself for it by volunteering, and constantly performing a midshipman's duty—indeed, I have but little use for a clerk, and he is as great a proficient as any of the young midshipmen, the whole of whom behaved in a manner that was pleasing to me, and must be gratifying to you, as it gives an earnest of what they will make in time—3 only have been to sea before, and 1 only in a man of war, yet they were as much at home, and as much disposed to exert themselves as any officer in the ship. Lieut. Nicholson speaks in high terms of the conduct of Messrs Greeves and Rodgers, midshipmen, who were in the prize with him.

I have the honor to be,
sir, very respectfully, your obe't serv't,
L. WARRINGTON.
Hon. WILLIAM JONES, &c.

UNOFFICIAL PARTICULARS.

The *Epervier*, being to windward, gallantly met the *Peacock*; but the battle would have ended very soon, had not Capt. Warrington hailed, to ascertain whether she had struck, (her colors being shot away,) by the time spent in which he lost a commanding position; for the action appeared to have ceased for the moment, and the brave Warrington would not shed blood wantonly. The force of the vessels in guns and weight of metal is the same, each rating 18, and carrying 22; but in men we had some superiority, the British having only 128, and we about 160; but the disparity of the execution done excites anew our wonder. The hull of the *Peacock* was not struck by a round shot, whereas on the larboard side of the *Epervier* between 50 and 60 took effect, many of them within a foot of the water line, and she was otherwise dreadfully mauled, and had one of her guns dismounted, with 5 feet water in her hold.   She is one of the finest vessels of her class in the British navy, built in 1812.   It is said that "when she left London, bets were three to one, that she would take an American sloop of war or small frigate."

The *Peacock's* length is 118 ft.—breadth of beam 32 ft.—depth of hold 14 ft.—tonnage 509—she mounts 20 guns—had 160 men—killed *none*, wounded 2, shots in her hull, *none*.   The *Epervier's* length 107 ft.— breadth of beam 32 ft.—depth of hold 14 ft.—tonnage 477.   She mounted 18 guns, same calibre with those of the *Peacock*—had 128 men—killed 11, wounded 15, shots in her hull 45 !

The *Epervier* was sold at Savannah and purchased by government for *fifty five thousand dollars.*

WASP AND REINDEER.

LETTER FROM JOHNSTON BLAKELEY, TO THE SECRETARY OF THE NAVY.

SIR,   *U. S. Sloop Wasp, L'Orient,* 8 *July,* 1814.

On Tuesday, the 28th ult. being then in lat. 48° 36' N. and long. 11° 15' W. we fell in with, engaged, and after an action of 19 minutes, captured, his Britannic Majesty's sloop of war the *Reindeer,* William Manners Esq. commander.   Annexed are the minutes of our proceedings prior to, and during the continuance of the action.

Where all did their duty, and each appeared anxious to excel, it is very difficult to discriminate.   It is, however, only rendering them their merited due, when it is declared of Lieuts. Reilly and Bury, 1st and 3d of this vessel, and whose names will be among those of the conquerors of the *Guerriere* and *Java ;* and of Mr. Tillinghast, 2d lieutenant, who was greatly instrumental in the capture of the *Boxer*; that their conduct and courage on this occasion fulfilled the highest expectation and gratified every wish.   Sailing Master Carr is also entitled to great credit for the zeal and ability with which he discharged his various duties.

The cool and patient conduct of every officer and man, while exposed to the fire of the shifting guns of the enemy, and without an opportunity of returning it, could only be equalled by the animation and ardor exhibited, when actually engaged, or by the promptitude and firmness with which every attempt of the enemy to board was met and successfully repelled. Such conduct may be seen but cannot well be described.

The *Reindeer* mounted sixteen 24lb. carronades, two long 6 or 9 pounders, and a shifting 12 pound carronade, with a complement on board of 118 men. Her crew were said to be the pride of Plymouth.

Our loss in men has been severe, owing in part to the proximity of the two vessels and the extreme smoothness of sea, but chiefly in repelling boarders. That of the enemy, however, was infinitely more so, as will be seen by the list of killed and wounded on both sides.

Six round shot struck our hull, and many grape which did not penetrate far.   The fore-mast received a 24lb. shot which passed through its centre, and our rigging and sails were a good deal injured.

The *Reindeer* was literally cut to pieces in a line with her ports; her upper works, boats, and spare spars were one complete wreck.   A breeze springing up next afternoon, her fore-mast went by the board.

Having received all the prisoners on board, which from the number of wounded occupied much time, together with their baggage, the *Reindeer* was on the evening of the 29th set on fire, and in a few hours blew up.

I have the honor to be,
    very respectfully, your most obe't serv't,
                                        J. BLAKELEY

Hon. WILLIAM JONES, &c.

*Minutes of the action between the U. S. Sloop Wasp,
and H. B. M. Sloop Reindeer on the 28th of June
1814, in lat. 48° 36′ N. and long. 11° 15′ W.*

At 4 A. M. light breezes and cloudy ; at ¼ after 4,
discovered two sails, two points before the lee-beam,
kept away in chase ; shortly after discovered one sail
on the weather beam ; altered the course and hauled
by in chase of the sail to windward ; at 8, sailed to
windward, bore E, N. E. wind very light ; at 10, the
stranger sail, bearing E. by N. hoisted an English
ensign and pendant, and displayed a signal at the
main (blue and yellow diagonally,) Meridian, light
airs and cloudy ; at ¼ past 12, the enemy showed a
blue and white flag diagonally at the fore, and fired a
gun ; 15 minutes after 1, called all hands to quarters
and prepared for action ; 22 minutes after 1, believing we could weather the enemy, tacked ship and
stood for him ; 50 minutes after 1, hoisted our colors
and fired a gun to windward, which was answered by
the enemy with another to windward ; 20 minutes after 2, the enemy still standing from us, set the royals ;
25 minutes after 2, set the flying gib ; 29 minutes after 2, set the upper stay-sails ; 32 minutes after 2, the
enemy having tacked for us, took in the stay-sails ; 37
minutes after 2, furled the royals : 51 minutes after 2,
seeing that the enemy would be able to weather us,
tacked ship ; 3 minutes after 3, the enemy hoisted his
flying gib ; brailed up our mizen ; 15 minutes after 3,
the enemy on our weather quarter, distant about sixty
yards, fired his shifting gun, a 12lb. carronade, at us,
loaded with round and grape shot, from his top-gallant fore-castle ; 17 minutes after 3, fired the same
gun a second time ; 19 minutes after 3, fired it a third
time ; 21 minutes after 3, fired it a fourth time, 24
minutes after 3, a fifth shot, all from the same gun.
Finding the enemy did not get sufficiently on the beam
to enable us to bring our guns to bear, put the helm
a-lee, and at 26 minutes after 3, commenced the action with the after carronade on the starboard side,
and fired in succession ; 34 minutes after 3, hauled up

the main-sail; 40 minutes after 3, the enemy having his bow in contact with our larboard quarter, endeavored to board us, but was repulsed in every attempt; at 44 minutes after 3, orders were given to board in turn, which were promptly executed, when all resistance immediately ceased; and at 45 minutes after 3, the enemy hauled down his flag.

J. BLAKELY.

List of killed and wounded on board the United States sloop of war Wasp, in the action with the Reindeer.

KILLED——Five seamen.
WOUNDED——Twenty one.

RECAPITULATION.

Killed	-	-	-	5
Wounded	-	-	-	21

List of the killed and wounded on board his B. M. sloop of war Reindeer.

KILLED——William Manners, Esq. commander; John Thos. Barton, and 23 petty officers and seamen.

WOUNDED——Thos. Chambets, 1st lieutenant: Richard Jones, master, and 40 petty officers and seamen.

RECAPITULATION.

Killed	-	-	-	35
Wounded—dangerously		-	10
Severely		-	17
Slightly		-	15
Whole number wounded			42

N. B. More than half the wounded were, in consequence of the severity and extent of their wounds, put on board a Portuguese brig, called the *Lisbon Packet*, on the third day after action, to wit, 1st July, bound to plymouth, England.

18

COPY OF A LETTER FROM CAPTAIN J. BLAKELEY TO THE SECRETARY OF THE NAVY.

SIR,   *U. S. Sloop Wasp, L'Orient, 8 July,* 1814.

I have the honor to announce to you the arrival of this ship to day at this place.——By the pilot who carried us out of Portsmouth N. H. I had the satisfaction to make you acquainted with our having left that place, and again had the pleasure of addressing you by the French national brig *Olive,* and which was the first vessel we had spoken since our departure from the United States. From the time of our sailing I continued the rout pointed out in your instructions, until our arrival at this place, during which we have been so fortunate as to make several captures ; a list of which will accompany this.——These with their cargoes were wholly destroyed, with one exception. This was the *Galliott Henrietta,* which was permitted to return with prisoners, 38 in number, after throwing overboard the greater part of her cargo, leaving only sufficient to ballast her. When arrived on our crusing ground, I found it impossible to maintain any thing like a station, and was led, in chase, farther up the English channel then was intended. After arriving on soundings, the number of neutrals, which are now passing, kept us almost constantly in pursuit. It gives me much pleasure to state to you the very healthy condition of the crew of the *Wasp* during the cruise : sometimes without one on the sick list, and at no time any who remained there more than a few days. Great praise is due to Dr. Clark for his skill and attention at all times ; but particularly after the action with the *Reindeer,* his unweared assiduity to the necessities of the wounded was highly conspicious.

The ship is at present under quarantine, but we expect to be released from it tomorrow, when the wounded will be sent to the hospital, and every exertion made to prepare the *Wasp* for sea.

I have the honor to be, very respectfully,
              your most obedient servant,
Hon. WM. JONES,   J. BLAKELEY.
Secretary of the navy.

LETTER FROM CAPTAIN BLAKELEY TO THE SECRETARY OF THE NAVY

SIR,   *U. S. Sloop Wasp, L' Orient,* 10 *July,* 1814.

After the capture of his B. M. sloop of war, the *Reindeer,*it was my wish to have continued the cruise, as directed by you.   I was however necessitated to relinquish this desire after a few days, from a consideration of the wounded of our crew, whose wounds had at this season become offensive, and aggravated by the number of prisoners on board at the time, being seventy-seven in number.   Fearing, from the crowded state of the *Wasp,* that some valuable lives might be lost, if retained on board, was compelled, though with reluctance, to make the first neutral port.   Those belonging to the *Reindeer,* who were dangerously wounded, were put on board a Portuguese brig bound to England three days after the action, and from the winds which prevailed, arrived probably in two or three days after their departure. Their surgeon, the captain's clerk, and officers' servants, and the crew of the *Orange Boven,* were put on board of the same vessel to attend upon them.   Since our arrival at this place we have experienced every civility from the public authorities.   Our quarantine was only for a few hours, and our wounded, fourteen in number, were carried yesterday to the hospital, where they were comfortably situated.   Our fore-mast, although badly wounded, can be repaired, and will be taken on shore as soon as possible.   All other damages sustained can be repaired by ourselves.

I have the honor to be, very respectfully,
                    your most obedient servant,
Hon. W. JONES, &c.   J. BLAKELY.

LETTER FROM J. BLAKELEY ESQ. TO THE SECRETARY OF THE NAVY.

U. S. Sloop of war Wasp, at sea, off Belle Isle,
SIR,   27 *August,* 1814.

It is with sincere sorrow that I have to announce to you the decease of Midshipmen Henry S. Langdon and Frank Toscan. They were wounded in the rencontre with the *Reindeer*, and all our efforts to save them, after our arrival, proved unavailing. It was their first essay, and although wounded, remained at their posts until the contest terminated. The constancy and courage with which they bore their sufferings leads to the melancholy, though proud reflection, of what they might have been, had providence ordained otherwise. Every respect due to worth was shown to their memory.

It is with regret that I have to inform you of the delays we have experienced at this place, but had they been of shorter duration, we could not possibly have sailed, as one continued westerly wind has prevailed from the hour of our arrival up to the present day.

The course pointed out in your instructions having been interrupted, I shall endeavor to fulfil your further intentions as far as possibly be in my power.

With great satisfaction, I add, that every aid in the power of Mr. Crawford has been promptly afforded, and that I feel under many obligations to him for his attention and assistance.

We are now off this place with a fair wind and favorable prospects.

I have the honor to be, very respectfully,

your most obedient servant,

Hon. W. JONES, &c.   J. BLAKELY.

WASP AND AVON.

LETTER FROM CAPT. BLAKELEY TO THE SECRETARY OF THE NAVY.

U. S. Sloop Wasp, at sea, lat. 41° *N. long.* 11° *W*
SIR,   *11th Sept.* 1814.

AFTER a protracted and tedious stay at L'Orient, had at last the pleasure of leaving that place on Saturday, 27th of August. On the 30th, captured the British brig *Lettice*, Henry Cockbain master; and on

THE WASP AND AVON

and with the expectation of drawing the second brig from his companions; but in this last we were disappointed. The second brigcontinued to approach us until she came close to our stern, when she haulted by the wind, fired her broadside, which cut our rigging and sails considerably, and shot away a lower main cross tree, and retraced her steps to join her consorts ; when we were necessitated to abandon the prize. He appeared in every respect a total wreck. He continued for some time firing guns of distress, until probably delivered by the two last vessels who made their appearance.

The second brig could have engaged us if he thought proper, as he neared us fast : but contented himself with firing a broadside, and immediately returned to his companions.

It is with real satisfaction I have again the pleasure of bearing testimony to the merits of Lieut. Reilly, Tillinghast, Baury and Sailing Master Carr : and to the good conduct of every officer and man on board the *Wasp.* Their divisions and departments were attended and supplied with the utmost regularity and abundance, which, with the good order maintained, together with the vivacity and precision of their fire, reflects on them the greatest credit. Our loss is two killed, and one slighily wounded with a wad. The hull received four round shot, and the fore-mast many grape shot. Our rigging and sails suffered a great deal. Every damage has been repaired the day after, with the exception of our sails.

Of the vessels with whom we were engaged, nothing positive can be said with regard to her name or force. While hailing him previous to his being fired into, it was blowing fresh (then going ten knots) and the name was not distinctly understood. Of her force, the four shot which struck us are all 32 pounds in weight, being a pound and three quarters heavier than any belonging to this vessel. From this circumstance, the number of men in her tops, her general appearance and great length, she is believed to be one of the largest brigs in the British navy.

I have the honor to be, very respectfully,

your most obedient servant,

Hon. W. JONES, &c.   J. BLAKELEY.

P. S. I am told the enemy, after his surrender, asked for assistance, and said he was sinking—the probability of this is confirmed by his firing single guns for some time after his capture.

List of Killed and wounded on board the U. S. Sloop of war the Wasp Johnston Blakeley, Esq. commander, in the action with his Britannic Majesty,s Sloop of war————,on the 1st of September 1814.

KILLED—Joseph Martin, boatswain ; Henry Staples, quarter gunner.

WOUNDED—One. seaman.

RECAPITULATION.

Killed	-	-	-	-	2
Wounded	-	-	-	-	1
		Total		3

Extract of a private letter from an officer of the United States Sloop Wasp.

At sea, September 23, 1814.

" Capt. Blakely, I believe, sends official accounts up to this date, doubtless for publication. To his letters therefore I refer you for correct particulars regarding our cruise.

" The *Wasp* has been one of the most successful cruisers out of the United States. She has been the favorite of Fortune, and we offer thanks to divine Providence for its support and protection.

" She has now been three months and five days at sea, with a complement of 173 men, whose ages average only 23 years. The greatest part so green, that is, unaccustomed to the sea, that they were sick for a week. In that time however she has destroyed twelve

British merchant vessels and their cargoes, the whole value of which, I presume, was not less than 200,000 pounds sterling.   The thirteenth merchantman we are now despatching to the United States.   She is the first we have attempted to send in but being an uncommon fast sailer, we have great hopes of her safe arrival ; and for my part, with judicious management, I have no doubt of it.   She is a very beautiful brig of 253 tons, coppered to the bends and copper fastened, and has a very valuable cargo on board, consisting of brandy, wines, cambrics, &c.   She was from Liverpool bound to Bordeaux, thence to Pensacola.

" The *Wasp* is a beautiful ship, and the finest sea boat, I believe in the world ; our officers and crew, young and ambitious—they fight with more cheerfulness than they do any other duty.   Capt. Blakeley is a brave and discreet officer ; as cool and collected in action as at table."

BRITISH ACCOUNT.

Cork, September 7, 1814.

On Thursday last, his Majesty's ships *Castillian,* Lieut. Lloyd, (acting) and *Avon* Hon. Capt. Arbuthnot, having sailed hence about a month ago, gave chase to an American schooner privateer, (having previously recaptured a vessel taken by her,) but owing to the superior sailing of the *Castillian,* she left the *Avon* a considerable distance behind, who, after a short time, found herself in sight of a vessel, which she hailed and demanded who she was ; upon which she replied, " heave to, and I'll let you know who I am ; (this was about 9 at night,) and fired a gun at the *Avon,* when a most sanguinary action commenced, which continued until 11 o'clock ; she then sheared off, and said, "this is the *Wasp.*"   She appeared in a sinking state, and glad to get off.   The *Avon* then fired signal guns to the *Castillian.*   Upon the *Castillian* coming to the *Avon,* she fell in with the *Wasp,* and demanded who she was ; to which she made no answer.   The *Castillian* luffed under her lee quarter and gave her a broad-

ENGRAVED FOR THE NAVAL MONUMENT

Com: Macdonough's Victory on Lake Champlain Sep: 11th 1814.

side, and then hailed again—but no answer, nor yet a single musket fired. The *Castillian* finding the sinking state of the *Avon*, made every effort to save the lives of her brave crew : fortunately the whole were saved. As the last boat with the wounded had got about half way to the *Castillian*, the *Avon* went down head foremost.

We lament to say, that between the second and third broadside, Lieut. Prendergast, the gallant first lieutenant of the *Avon* received a mortal wound across the belly, from a grape shot, while in the act of cheering the crew. The *Avon* had nine killed and thirty three wounded. As soon as the *Castillian* had discharged the duties of humanity, in taking on board the *Avon's* crew, she made all sail for the *Wasp*, who appeared so cut up, as to be in a sinking state ; but could not make out any trace whatever of her.

Names of the superior officers on board the *Avon* : Hon. John James Arbuthnot, captain ; John Harvey, first lieutenant ; John Prendergast, second do. ; and James Allen, master.

The *Tartarus* sloop of war, joined the *Castilian* as the *Avon* was sinking, and took on board forty of her men.

VICTORY ON LAKE CHAMPLAIN.

COPIES OF LETTERS FROM COM. MACDONOUGH TO THE SECRETARY OF THE NAVY.

U. S. Ship Saratoga, off Plattsburg,
September 11, 1814.

SIR,

THE Almighty has been pleased to grant us a signal victory on Lake Champlain, in the capture of 1 frigate, 1 brig, and 2 sloops of war of the enemy.

I have the honor to be, very respectfully,
Sir, your most obedient servant,

Hon WILLIAM JONES,   T. MACDONOUGH.
Sec'y of the navy.
19

Sir,   *September* 13, 1814.

By Lieut. Commandant Cassin, I have the honor to convey to you the flags of his Britannic Majesty's late squadron, captured on the 11th inst. by the United States squadron under my command. Also my despatches relating to that occurance, which should have been in your possession at an earlier period, but for the difficulty in arranging different statements.

The squadron under my command now lies at Plattsburg. It will bear considerable diminution, and still leave a force sufficient to repel any attempt of the enemy in this quarter. I shall wait your order what to do with the whole or any part thereof.

I have the honor to be, &c.

Hon W. JONES,   T. MACDONOUGH.
Secretary of the navy.

Sir,   *September* 13, 1814.

I have the honor to give you the particulars of the action which took place on the 11th instant on this lake.

For several days the enemy were on their way to Plattsburg, by land and water, and it being well understood that an attack would be made at the same time by their land and naval forces, I determined to await at anchor the approach of the latter.

At 8 A. M. the look-out boat announced the approach of the enemy. At 9 he anchored in a line ahead, at about 300 yards distance from my line; his ship opposed to the *Saratoga*, his brig to the *Eagle*, Capt. Robert Henly his galleys, 13 in number, to the schooner, sloop, and a division of our galleys; 1 of his sloops assisting their ship and brig, the other assisting their galleys : our remaining galleys with the *Saratoga* and *Eagle.*

In this situation the whole force on both sides became engaged, the *Saratoga* suffering much from the heavy fire of the *Confiance.* I could perceive at the same time, however, that our fire was very destructive to her. The *Ticonderoga*, Lieut. Com. Cassin, gallantly sustained her full share of the action. At $\frac{1}{2}$ past

10 o'clock, the *Eagle*, not being able to bring her guns to bear, cut her cable and anchored in a more eligible position, between my ship and the *Ticonderoga*, where she was much annoyed by the enemy, but unfortunately leaving me exposed to a galling fire from the enemy's brig. Our guns on the starboard side being nearly all dismounted, or not manageable, a stern anchor was let go, the bow cable cut, and the ship winded with a fresh broadside on the enemy's ship, which soon after surrendered. Our broadside was then sprung to bear on the brig, which surrendered in 15 minutes after.

The sloop that was opposed to the *Eagle* had struck some time before and drifted down the line, the sloop which was with their galleys having struck also.

Three of their galleys are said to be sunk; the others pulled off. Our galleys were about obeying with alacrity the signal to follow them, when all the vessels were reported to me to be in a sinking state; it then became necessary to annul the signal to the galleys and order their men to the pumps.

I could only look at the enemy's galleys going off in a shattered condition, for there was not a mast in either squadron that could stand to make sail on; the lower rigging being nearly all shot away, hung down as though it had been just placed over the mast heads.

The *Saratoga* had 55 round shot in her hull, the *Confiance* 105. The enemy's shot passed principally just over our heads, as there were not 20 whole hammocks in the nettings at the close of the action, which lasted without intermission 2 hours and 20 minutes.

The absence and sickness of Lieut. Raymond Perry, left me without the services of that excellent officer; much ought fairly to be attributed to him for his great care and attention in disciplining the ship's crew as her 1st Lieutenant. His place was filled by a gallant young officer, Lieut. Peter Gamble, who, I regret to inform you was killed early in the action. Acting Lieut. Valette worked the 1st and 2d divisions of guns with able effect. Sailing-Master Brum's attention to the springs, and in the execution of the order to wind the ship, and occasionally at the guns, meets with my entire approbation, also Capt. Youngs, commanding the acting marines, who took his men to the guns. Mr. Beale, purser, was of great service at the guns, and in carrying my orders throughout the ship, with Midshipman Montgomery. Master's Mate Joshua Justin, had command of the 3d division : his conduct during the action was that of a brave and correct officer. Midshipmen Monteath, Graham, Williamson, Platt, Thwing, and acting Midshipman Baldwin, all behaved well, and gave evidence of their making valuable officers.

The *Saratoga* was twice set on fire by hot shot from the enemy's ship.

I close, sir, this communication with feelings of gratitude for the able support I received from every officer and man attached to the squadron which I have the honor to command.

I have the honor to be, with great respect,
Sir your most obedient servant,
Hon. W. Jones,   T. MACDONOUGH.
Secretary of the navy.

P. S. Accompanying this is a list of killed and wounded, a list of prisoners, and a precise statement of both forces engaged. Also letters from Capt. Henley and Lieut. Com. Cassin.   T. M.

Return of killed and wounded on board the United States squadron on Lake Champlain, in the engagement with the British fleet on the 11th September, 1814.

Ship Saratoga. KILLED—Peter Gamble, lieutenant ; Thomas Butler, quarter gunner ; James Norberry, boatswain's mate ; Abraham Davis, quarter master ; William Wyer, sail maker ; and twenty-three seamen.

WOUNDED—Twenty-nine.
Brig Eagle. KILLED—Thirteen.

WOUNDED—Joseph Smith, lieutenant; William A. Spencer, acting lieutenant; Francis Breeze, master's mate; Abraham Walters, pilot; and sixteen seamen.

Schooner Ticonderoga. KILLED—John Stansbury, lieutenant; John Fisher and John Atkinson, boatswain's mates; and three seamen.

WOUNDED—Six.

Sloop Preble. KILLED—Two.

WOUNDED—None.

Gun-boat Borer. KILLED—Three.

WOUNDED—One.

Gun-boat Centipede. WOUNDED—One.

Gun-boat Wilmer. WOUNDED—One.

RECAPITULATION.

	Killed.	Wounded.
Saratoga	28	29
Eagle	13	20
Ticonderoga	6	6
Preble	2	0
Borer	3	1
Centipede	0	1
Wilmer	0	1
Total	52	58

Gun-boats *Nettle, Allen, Viper, Burrows, Ludlow, Alwyn, Ballard*—None killed or wounded.

GEORGE BEALE, jr. *Purser.*

Statement of the American force engaged on the 11th September, 1814.

Saratoga, eight long 24 pounders, six 42 pound carronades, and twelve 32 pound carronades - 26

Eagle, twelve 23 pound carronades, and eight long 18s - - - - - 20

Ticonderoga, eight long 12 pounders, four long 18 pounders, and five 32 pound carronades - 17

Preble seven long 9 pounders - - - 7

Ten galleys, viz.—*Allen, Burrows, Borer, Net-*

tle, Viper, Centipede, one long 24 pounder
and one 18 pound columbiad each   -   -   12
Ludlow, Wilmer, Alwin, Ballard, 1 long 12
pounder each   -   ·   -   -   -   -   -   4
                                                  ——
                           Guns,   86

Recapitulation—fourteen long 24 pounders, six 42
pound carronades, twenty-nine 32 pound carronades,
twelve long 18 pounders, twelve long 12 pounders,
seven long 9 pounders, six 18 pound columbiads.
Total 86 guns.

T. MACDONOUGH

*Statement of the Enemy's force engaged on the 11th
of September, 1814.*

Frigate *Confiance,* twenty-seven long 24 pounders,
four 32 pound carronades, six 24 pound carronades, and two long 18 pounders on the birth
deck   -   -   -   -   -   39
Brig *Linnet,* Sixteen long twelve pounders   -   16
Sloop *Chub,* * ten 18 pound carronades, one long
6 pounder   -   -   -   -   11
Sloop *Finch,* * six 18 pound carronades, one 18
pound columbiad, and four long 6 pounders   -   11
Thirteen galleys, viz.--*Sir James Yeo, Sir George
Prevost, Sir Sidney Beckwith,* one long 24
pounder, and one 32 lb. carronade each   -   6
Broke, one 18 pounder, and one 32 lb. carronade   -   2
Murry, one 18 pounder, and one 18 lb. carronade   -   2
Wellington, Tecumseh, and one other, name un-
known, one 18 pounder each   -   -   ·-   3
Drummond, Simcoe and 3 others, names un-
known, one 32 lb carronade each   -   -   5
                                                  ——
                    Total, guns,   95

Recapitulation—thirty long 24 pounders, seven 18
pounders, sixteen 12 pounders, five 6 pounders, thirteen 32 pound carronades, six 24 pound carronades,

---

* These sloops were formerly the U. S. Growler and Eagle.

seventeen 18 pound carronades, one 18 pound columbiad.　Total 95 guns.

T. MACDONOUGH

COPY OF A LETTER FROM LIEUT. CASSIN TO COM. MACDONOUGH.

U. S. Schooner Ticonderoga, Plattsburg Bay,
SIR,　　　　　　　　　　　*September 12, 1814.*

It is with pleasure I state, that every officer and man under my command did their duty yesterday.

Your's respectfully,

Com. T. MACDONOUGH.　STEPHEN CASSIN,
Lieut. commanding.

COPY OF A LETTER FROM LIEUT. HENLEY TO COM. MACDONOUGH.

SIR,　*U. S. Brig Eagle, Plattsburg, Sept.* 12, 1814.

I am happy to inform you that all my officers and men acted bravely, and did their duty in the battle of yesterday with the enemy.

I shall have the pleasure of making a more particular representation of the respective merits of my gallant officers to the honorable the secretary of the navy.

I have the honor to be, respectfully,

Sir, your most obedient servant,

R. HENLEY.

P. S. We had 39 round shot in our hull (mostly 24 pounders) 4 in our lower masts—and we were well peppered with grape. I enclosed my boatswain's report.　　　　　　　　　　　R. H.

COPY OF A LETTER FROM GEORGE BEALE, JR. TO COM. MACDONOUGH.

SIR,　　　　*U. S. Ship Saratoga Sept.* 13, 1814.

I have the honor to enclose you a list of the killed and wounded on board the different vessels of the squadron under your command, in the action of the 11th inst.

It is impossible to ascertain correctly the loss of the enemy. From the best information received from the British officers, from my own observations, and from various lists found on board the *Confiance*, I calculate the number of men on board that ship at the commencement of the action at 270, of whom at least 180 were killed and wounded, and on board the other captured vessels at least 80 more, making in the whole, killed and wounded, 260. This is doubtless short of the real number, as many were thrown overboard from the *Confiance* during the engagement.

The muster books must have been thrown overboard, or otherwise disposed of, as they are not to be found.

I am, sir, very respectfully,
your obedient servant,
GEORGE BEALE, jr. *Purser.*
Com. T. MACDONOUGH.

List of British officers captured on the 11th September, on Lake Champlain, and sent to Greenbush.

Capt. Daniel Pring, on parole ; Lieutenants Hicks, Creswick, Robinson, M'Glie, Drew, Hornby, Child, and Fitzpatrick ; Sailing Master Bryden ; Masters' Mates Clark and Simmonds ; Surgeon Todd ; Purser Gile ; Captain's Clerk Guy ; Midshipmen Aire, Boudell, Toorke, Kewstra ; Davidson, boatswain ; Elvin, gunner ; Mickell, gunner ; Cox, carpenter ; Parker, purser ; Martin, surgeon ; M'Cabe, assistant surgeon.

COPY OF A LETTER FROM COM. MACDONOUGH TO BRIG. GEN. MACOMB.

U. S. Ship Saratoga, off Plattsburg,
DEAR SIR,   *September* 13, 1814.

Enclosed is a copy of a letter from Capt. White Youngs, and a list of killed and wounded attached to his command.

I beg leave to recommend Capt. Youngs to your particular notice ; during the action his conduct was such as to meet with my warmest approbation. I feel much indebted to him for his personal valor and example of coolness and intrepidity to his own men, as well as to the sailors. He volunteered in a sinking boat to carry my order to the gallies, for close action, in the hottest part of it ; and supplied the guns with his men as fast as the sailors were disabled.

I am with much respect and esteem,
your obedient servant,
Brig. Gen. MACOMB,   T. MACDONOUGH.
of U. S. army.

LETTER FROM GEN. MACOMB TO THE SEC'Y OF WAR.

Capt. Youngs of the 15th, is an officer of distinguished merit, and has conducted himself with the greatest propriety on board the fleet. By his example and attention we have been able to keep the fleet manned from the line, which has been the means of contributing to the result of the naval engagement ; I therefore recommend him to the particular notice of the war department.
September 18, 1814.   ALEX. MACOMB.

COPY OF A LETTER FROM GAPT. YOUNGS TO COM. MACDO-
NOUGH.

United States Ship Saratoga Lake Champlain,
SIR,   *September* 14, 1814.

I have the honor of encloseing to you a list of killed and wounded troops of the line (acting marines on board the squadron, Lake Champlain) in the action of the 11th instant.

In attempting to do justice to the brave officers and men I have had the honor to command, my feeble abilities fall far short of my wishes—First Lieut. Morrison, 33d infantry, stationed on board the U. S brig *Eagle,* was wounded, but remained on deck during the action, animating his men by his honorable conduct. Second Lieut. James Young, 6th infantry, on board the U. S. schooner, *Ticonderoga,* merits my warmest thanks : I would particularly recommend him to your notice. Second Lieut. William B. Howell, 15th infantry in the U. S. ship, *Saratoga,* rendered me every
20

assistance; notwithstanding his having been confined for ten days of a fever, yet, at the commencement of the action, he was found on deck, and continued until the enemy had struck, when he was borne to his bed. I would also recommend him to your notice.

The conduct of the non-commissioned officers and privates was so highly honorable to their country and themselves, it would be superfluous to particularize them.

I have the honor to be,
Sir, your obedient servant,
Com. T. MACDONOUGH, &c. WHITE YOUNGS,
Capt. 15th Inf. com'ing detach.
of acting marines.

COPY OF A LETTER FROM LIEUT. HENLEY TO THE SECRETARY OF THE NAVY.

SIR, *U. S. Ship Eagle, off Plattsburg, Sept.* 10, 1814.
Permit me to make you acquainted with that part of the action of yesterday, which was particularly borne by the vessel which I have the honor to command, as it may not appear in the official report of Capt. Macdonough, whose duty it is to make a true and impartial statement of facts.

Being at anchor in the harbor of Plattsburg, in a line north and south, at the distance of about 100 yards the *Eagle* north, the *Saratoga* in the centre, and the *Ticonteroga* south, the enemy approached, in a line a breast, with a favorable wind, which enabled him to choose his position; his brig taking her station on the stabord bow of the *Eagle,* at the distance of about a mile, his ship about one point abaft her [the *Eagle's*] beam, and the sloop *Linnet,* of 11 guns, making an effort to obtain a raking position under our stern. Perceiving the object of the sloop, I ordered her a broadside, which compelled her immediately to strike her colours.

At the moment when the enemy's ship had approached within point-blank distance, the *Eagle* commenced upon her a most destructive fire of her whole broadside, excepting the two long 18s forward, which were occasionally discharged at the enemy's brig, who frequently relieved her position and kept up a raking and most destructive fire upon this vessel.

I was confident that it was of the highest importance, in order to insure success, to endeavour first to carry the enemy's ship. For a great length of time after the commencement of the action, the ship levelled her whole force upon the *Eagle*, dealing forth destruction.

After having sustained the severest of the action for more than one hour—having my springs shot away—many of my starboard guns disabled, and not being in a situation to bring one of them to bear upon either the enemy's ship or brig, I ordered the cable cut and cast the brig, taking an advantageous position a little south of the *Saratoga*, bringing my larboard broadside to bear upon the ship, which was very soon compelled to haul down her colours. Our fire was now directed at the brig, which struck in the space of eight minutes, and our contest terminated in victory. We now turned our attention toward the gallies, some of which, it is believed, sunk, and the residue made their escape. The *Eagle*, was in too shattered a condition to pursue them.

I have the honor to enclose the surgeon's report of the killed and wounded on board the *Eagle*, by which you will perceive there were 13 killed and 27 wounded, most of them severely : also a copy of the report of the meritorious conduct of my officers and men, which I made to Capt. Macdonough, for your information, and which he has since informed me he had lost.

I have the honor to be,
Sir, with high respect, your obe't serv't.
ROBERT HENLEY.

Another letter from Capt. Henley to the Secretary of war, of the above date, encloses his report of killed and wounded, and recommends Lieut. Joseph Smith, Acting Lieut. Spencer, Acting Sailing-master

Record, Acting Lieut. Loomis, Midshipmen Chamberlain, Machesny and Tardy, Surgeon Stoddard, Volunteer Loomis, Mr. Smith the gunner, Mr. Johnson the carpenter, Mr. Willson the boatswain, as having discharged their duties as became Americans.

PARTICULARS.

Com. Macdonough is the son of Dr. Macdonough, late of New-Castle county, state of Delaware. He was a midshipman under Com. Decatur, at Tripoli, and one of the gallant band that destroyed the *Philadelphian.* At the time of the battle on Lake Champlain, he was about 28 years of age. He is a religious man, as well as a hero, and prayed with his brave men on the morning of the victory. All the officers on board the commodore's ship were either killed or wounded. He was asked how he escaped amid such carnage, and replied, pointing to heaven, "There was a power above which determined the fate of man."

He had repeatedly to work his own guns, when his men at them were shot and three times he was driven across the deck by splinters.

At one time during the battle, Macdonough had all his guns on one side but two dismounted, when he wore his ship. The enemy endeavouring to do the same, failed and gave us an opportunity to rake him. Our superior gunnery is again provided, as the enemy had two to one of ours killed or wounded; and they had locks to their guns, which we had not

The gallies did but little, and the enemy's gallies, which were distant spectators, pulled off when they saw their fleet was beaten.

The battle was exceedingly obstinate; the enemy fought gallantly; but the superiority of our gunnery was irresistible. We fired much oftener than they did. All the vessels were much wrecked.

The killed on both sides have a very unusual proportion to the wounded—on ours 52 to 58! This is perhaps unprecedented, and may serve to shew the warmth and closeness of the action.

Despatch   *Majestic*   *Endymion*   *Tenedos*   *President*   *Pomone*

THE PRESIDENT ENGAGING THE ENDYMION, WHILE PURSUED BY THE BRITISH SQUADRON.

In the hottest of the action, a cock in the commodore's ship flew into the shrouds, and crowed three times! The crew seized the happy omen, and shouted *victory!* This little incident must have had a powerful effect on the seamen.

A sailor, who had been hard at work from the commencement until the conclusion of the fight, seeing the British flag lowered, with a smile on his countenance, addressed a companion, "Well, Jack, this is all the fun I have had this war," at the same time very leisurely wiping the sweat from his face. "I am more lucky," said the other, "for this is the *second Frolic** I have had!"

The schooners *Growler* and *Tigress*, captured from us the year preceding, were desperately defended. When the former was towed into Plattsburg, she had only five men on board on their legs.

The British loss was immense. On board the *Confiance* alone 160 were killed. Com. Downie fell in the early part of the action. Capt. Preng, who had been censured by Sir George Prevost, fought his brig 15 minutes after the other vessels had struck.

The British certainly supposed that the battle would have terminated in their favor. It appears evident, that they expected to defeat our squadron, to proceed to the upper end of the lake, and to establish themselves on shore. For this purpose they had provided heavy cannon for mounting, and put them on board their vessels to be landed and stationed after the engagement. Com. Macdonough found, on examining the prizes, concealed under the platform of the vessels where they served for ballast, 25 pieces, 6, 9, 12, and long 18 pounders, and a large quantity of grape and cannister shot—so happily diverted from their original purpose by the glorious victory of the 11th of September.

---

*He was with Capt. Jones at the taking of the *Frolic.*

LOSS OF THE PRESIDENT.

**COPY OF A LETTER FROM COM. DECATUR TO THE SEC-
RETARY OF THE NAVY.**

H. B. M. Ship Endymion, at sea,
SIR,　　　　　　　　　　　*January* 18, 1814.

THE painful duty of detailing to you the particular causes which preceded and led to the capture of the late United States frigate *President*, by a squadron of his Britannic Majesty's ships (as per margin) has devolved upon me. In my communication of the 14th, I made known to you my intention of proceeding to sea on the evening. Owing to some mistake of the pilot, the ship in going out grounded on the bar, where she continued to strike heavily for an hour and a half: although she had broken several of her rudder braces, and had received such other material injury as to render her return into port desirable, I was unable to, do so from the strong westerly wind which was then blowing. It being now high water, it became necessary to force her over the bar before the tide fell; in this we succeeded by 10 o'clock, when we shaped our course along the shore of Long-Island for 50 miles, and then steered S. E. by E. At 5 o'clock, three ships were discovered ahead: we immediately hauled up the ship, and passed two miles to the northward of them. At daylight we discovered four ships in chase, one on each quarter, and two astern, the leading ship of the enemy a razee. She commenced a fire upon us, but without effect. At meridian the wind became light and baffling; we had increased our distance from the razee, but the next ship astern, which was also a large ship, had gained and continued to gain upon us considerable; we immediately occupied all hands to lighten ship, by starting water, cutting away the anchors, throwing overboard provisions, cables, spare spars, boats, and every article that could be got at, keeping the sails wet from the royals down. At 3, we had the wind quite light ; the enemy, who had now been joined by a brig, had a strong breeze, and were coming up with us rapidly. The *Endymion* (mounting 50 guns, 24 pounders on the main deck) had now approached us within gun-shot, and had commenced a fire with her bow guns, which we returned from our stern. At 5 o'clock, she had obtained a position on our starboard quarter, within half point-blank shot, on which neither our stern nor quarter guns would bear ; we were now steering E. by N. the wind N. W. I remained with her in this position for half an hour, in the hope that she would close with us on our broadside, in which case I had prepared my crew to board ; but from his continuing to yaw his ship to maintain his position, it became evident that to close was not his intention. Every fire now cut some of our sails or rigging. To have continued our course under these circumstances, would have been placing it in his power to cripple us, without being subject to injury himself ; and to have hauled up more to the northward to bring our stern guns to bear, would have exposed us to his raking fire. It was now dusk, when I determined to alter my course south, for the purpose of bringing the enemy abeam, and although their ships astern were drawing up fast, I felt satisfied I should be enabled to throw him out of the combat before they could come up, and was not without hopes, if the night proved dark, (of which there was every appearance) that I might still be enable to effect my escape. Our opponent kept off at the same instant we did, and our fire commenced at the same time. We continued engaged, steering south, with steering sails set, two hours and a half, when we completely succeeded in dismantling her. Previously to her dropping entirely out of the action, there were intervals of minutes, when the ships were broadside and broadside, in which she did not fire a gun. At this period, (half past 8 o'clock) although dark, the other ships of the squadron were in sight, and almost within gun-shot. We were of course compelled to abandon her. In resu-

ming our former course for the purpose of avoiding
the squadron, we were compelled to present our stern
to our antagonist—but such was his state, though we
were thus exposed and within range of his guns for
half an hour, that he did not avail himself of this favorable opportunity of raking us.   We continued this
course until 11 o'clock when two fresh ships of the enemy (the *Pomone* and *Tenedos*) had come up.   The
Pomone had opened her fire on the larboard bow, within musket shot ; the other about two cables' length
astern, taking a raking position on our quarter ; and
the rest (with the exception of the *Endymion*) within
gun-shot. . Thus situated, with about one fifth of my
crew killed and wounded, my ship crippled, and a
more than four-fold force opposed to me, without a
chance of escape left, I deemed it my duty to surrender.

It is with emotions of pride I bear testimony to the
gallantry and steadiness of every officer and man I
had the honor to command on this occasion ; and I
feel satisfied that the fact of their having beaten a
force equal to themselves, in the presence and almost
under the guns of so vastly a superior force, when, too,
it was almost self-evident, that whatever their exertions might be, they must ultimately be captured, will
be taken as evidence of what they would have performed, had the force opposed to them been in any degree equal.

It is with extreme pain I have to inform you that
Lieutenants Babbit, Hamilton, and Howell fell in the
action.   They have left no officers of superior merit
behind them.

If, Sir, the issue of this affair had been fortunate, I
should have felt it my duty to have recommended to
your attention Lieutenants Shubric and Gallagher.
They maintained throughout the day the reputation
they had acquired in former actions.

Lieut. Twiggs, of the marines, displayed great zeal,
his men were well supplied and their fire incompara-

ble, so long as the enemy continued within musket range.

Midshipman Randolph, who had charge of the forecastle division, managed it to my entire satisfaction.

From Mr. Robinson, who was serving as a volunteer, I received essential aid, particularly after I was deprived of the services of the master, and the severe loss I had sustained in my officers on the quarter deck.

Of our loss in killed and wounded, I am unable at present to give you a correct statement.; the attention of the surgeon being so entirely occupied with the wounded, that he was unable to make out a correct return when I left the *President ;* nor shall I be able to make it until our arrival in port, we having parted company with the squadron yesterday. The enclosed list, with the exception, I fear, of its being short of the number, will be found correct.

For 24 hours after the action, it was nearly calm ; and the squadron were occupied in repairing the crippled ships. Such of the crew of the *President* as were not badly wounded, were put on board the different ships : myself and a part of my crew were put on board this ship. On the 17th we had a gale from the eastward, when this ship lost her bowsprit, fore and main-masts and mizen top-mast, all of which were badly wounded, and was in consequence of her disabled condition, obliged to throw overboard all her upper deck guns. Her loss in killed and wounded must have been very great. I have not been able to ascertain the extent. Ten were buried after I came on board (36 hours after the action) ; the badly wounded, such as are obliged to keep their cots, occupy the starboard side of the gun deck from the cabin bulk-head to the main-mast. From the crippled state of the *President's* spars, I feel satisfied she could not have saved her masts, and I feel serious apprehensions for the safety of our wounded left on board.

It is due to Capt. Hope to state, that every atten

tion has been paid by him to myself and officers who have been placed on board his ship, that delicacy and humanity could dictate.

I have the honor to be, with much respect,
Sir, your obedient servant,
STEPHEN DECATUR.

Hon. B. W. CROWNINGSHIELD,
Secretary of the navy.

British squadron referred to in the letter.

Majestic (razee,) *Endymion, Pomone, Tenedos, Despatch* (brig).

List of killed and wounded on board the United States Frigate President.

KILLED—Lieutenants F. H. Babbit, and twenty two seamen.

WOUNDED—Sailing-Master Rogere, Mr. Robinson, Midshipmen Dale and Brewster, Master's Mate Parker, and fifty seamen.

FURTHER PARTICULARS.

When the President first saw the British ships at day light, directly astern of her, and knowing them of course to be enemies, crowded all sail to escape— but owing to the misfortune which she sustained the night before of beating on the bar, off New-York, being deeply laden with water and provisions for a long cruise, and not having her proper trim, the enemy's leading ship the *Endymion*, succeeded in getting close along side of her, and brought her to action about sun-set. Both ships were under a press of sail. The *Endymion* was disabled and silenced, and the *President*, when she finally struck to the *Pomone* and *Tenedos*, was carrying royal studding sails, still endeavoring to effect her escape.

Remaining two hours on the bar was the primary cause of the lost of this noble ship—for had she passed over without difficulty, she would have been out of sight of the British ships before day-light.

The *President*, after her capture, lost all her masts by the board in a violent gale of wind, and arrived at Bermuda under jury masts, on the 28th of January, just a fortnight from the date of her sailing from New-York. The *Endymion* arrived two days before, with the loss of her fore and main-masts, (considerably above deck by wounds) and bowsprit.

The *Endymion's* loss, according to the report of the British officers, was 11 killed and 14 wounded.

Our brave commodore received a severe contusion on the breast, which knocked him down, but he soon recovered.

The lamented Lieut. Babbit, 1st of the *President*, was from Brookfield, Mass. He was mortally wounded early in the action by a round shot in the thigh, which shattered it so dreadfully, that he expired in about an hour. He was in his 25th year, and was justly esteemed one of the best officers in the service.

Lieut. Hamilton, 4th, served on the gun-deck, and was instantaneously killed towards the close of the action, by a 24lb. shot, which struck him in the abdomen, and cut him in pieces. He was the son of Paul Hamilton, Esq. of South Carolina, late secretary of the navy, and was a youth of such gentlemanly deportment, and amiable manners, as to win and retain the esteem of all who knew him. He was a great favorite in the navy, and will be long affectionately remembered by many, both in and out of the service. Mr. Hamilton was a midshipman on board the *United States*, when that ship took the *Macedonian*, and was the officer, who had the honor of bearing her colors to the city of Washington.

Lieut. Howell, 5th, lost his life by a splinter, which struck him on the head and fractured his scull. He was from New-Jersey, and was, like Hamilton, a most excellent and exemplary youth.

In that trying engagement, the crew of the *President* behaved most nobly. The marines in particular, under Lieut. Twigs, acquitted themselves with the highest honor.

However we may lament the loss of the brave men, who fell in this contest, the services of those wounded or carried into captivity, or of the vessel herself, we rejoice that our naval glory remains untarnished, and that this capture of Decatur, like Porter's, will add to his own fame, and the renown of his country.

In the Bermuda paper of the 3d of April, is inserted a corespondence between the governor of those islands, and Mr. Ward, the editor of the Royal Gazette, which closes on the part of the governer by withdrawing from that paper its title of Royal Gazette, and from Mr. Ward the office of his Majesty;s printer. The governor appears to have been determined in this course by the pertinacious adherance of Mr. Ward to a false statement, published in his paper, of the circumstances attending the capture of the United States frigate *President*, which statement was at first corrected by him, but afterwards re-asserted and adhered to.

The Editor, in giving the reports of the capture, stated, among other things, that the *President* struck to the *Endymion;* and that after the *President* struck, Com. Decatur concealed 68 men in the hold of the *President*, for the purpose of rising on the prize crew, and recapturing her. On the appearance of this account, Capt. Hope, of the *Endymion*, immediately sent an officer to Com. Decatur, disclaiming any participation in the article ; and the governor of the island demanded of the editor of the Gazette, that he should immediately contradict the statement ; which was complied with.

The editor then repeats, that the retraction spoken of was inserted merely as an act of generosity, and a palliative for the irritated feelings of prisoners of war. He had previously declared that he had, "subsequently to the publication of the retracting article, ascertained, that the original statement was correct ; and we do not (he says) hesitate unequivocally to declare, upon the best authority, that 68 men were concealed on board the *President*, and from other information we have obtained, we are convinced the act was authorized by Com. Decatur."

Immediately on the appearance of the above remarks, the governor of Bermuda directed a letter, of which the following are extracts, to be sent to the editor.

EXTRACTS FROM AN OFFICIAL LETTER FROM C. COOPER ESQ. PRIVATE SECRETARY TO THE GOVERNOR AND COMMANDER IN CHIEF.

SIR, *Government-House, Bermuda, April* 15, 1815.

In your paper of Thursday last, which calls for his excellency's animadversion, you have ventured to assert, that your publication in contradiction to your original paragraph above alluded to, was issued in consequence of your having been " requested to smooth it over ;" and you go on to insinuate that the statement contradicted was " founded in truth." It is impossible for his excellency to permit such a direct and positive misrepresentation to stand uncontradicted, and more especially as his excellency himself communicated to you Capt. Hope's pointed declaration, that there was not the slightest foundation whatsoever for the assertion which you had published, and that he himself and every officer in his majesty's service, felt the utmost indignation and regret at the wanton insult offered thereby to an enemy, who then being a prisoner under the protection of the British flag, was entitled to peculiar marks of delicacy and attention, of which Capt. Hope, with the nicety of honourable feeling, natural to an officer of the British navy, had felt so truly sensible, as to have sent a brother officer the moment the indecorous paragraph referred to met his eye, to express to Com. Decatur his indignation and regret at its having appeared.

His excellency at the same time stated to you his own opinion, and that of the officers of his majesty's service, that the reprehensible paragraph should be instantly and unequivocally contradicted, and not merely "smoothed over," as you have now thought proper to

declare ; though at the time you seem fully impressed
with the propriety of contradicting a statement, which
you had erroneously put forth, and of thereby making
the only retrebution which it was then in your power to
offer to those, whose characters had been so unjustly
defamed.   His excellency felt anxious that the disa-
vowal to be published should be couched in terms the
least disagreeable to your own feelings, or hurtful to
the paper, of which you are the editor.

His excellency has since seen with pain and regret,
that you have subsequently, on more than one occasion, endeavored to retract the correction then made
by you of your prior mis-statement, and to impress
the readers of the Gazette with a belief, that your
original statement was established in fact, though you
had the highest authority, (that of Capt. Hope himself,) for knowing it to be completely unfounded.
These attempts his excellency has hither to passed
over—but your publication of Thursday imposes it
upon him as a duty to himself, to Capt. Hope, and to
the British nation, and in common justice to Com.
Decatur, who is not present to defend himself from
the aspersion which you have cast upon him, of " uttering with reference to yourselves as base a falsehood
as ever was imposed upon the world," not to admit of
such a document standing uncontradicted in a paper,
professed to be published under the immediate authority of his majesty's government.

His excellency is thoroughly aware of the great importance of preserving to the utmost extent perfect
freedom of dicussion, and the fullest liberty of the
press, in every part of the British dominions, and undoubtedly therefore nothing could be further from his
intentions than the most distant desire to " compel a
British editor to retract a statement founded in
truth"—but when a statement is founded in falsehood,
his excellency conceives it to be incumbent upon him,
equally in duty to the British public and in support of
the true character of the British press, to demand that
that falsehood, whether directed against friend or foe,

should be instantly contradicted, or that the paper which thinks fit to disgrace its columns by persevering in error, should no longer be distinguished by the royal protection—and I am therefore commanded to signify to you his excellency's desire, that your ensuing publication may contain a due and respectful contradiction of those parts of your comments upon Com. Decatur's letter, which have now called for his excellency's censure, or his excellency will feel it his bounden duty to remove you from the office of his majesty's printer, which now gives a degree of weight to observations contained in your paper, to which otherwise they might not be entitled.

I have the honor to be,
Sir, your obedient servant,
C. COOPER, *Private Sec'y*
EDMUND WARD, Esq.
Editor of the Royal Gazette, Bermuda.

EXTRACT OF A LETTER FROM COM. DECATUR TO THE SECRETARY OF THE NAVY.

New York, March 6, 1815.

In my official letter of January 18, I omitted to state, that a considerable number of my killed and wounded was from the fire of the *Pomone*, and that the *Endymion* had on board, in addition to her own crew, 1 lieutenant, 1 master's mate, and 50 seamen, belonging to the *Saturn*, and when the action ceased, was left motionless and unmanageable until she bent new sails, rove new rigging, and fished her spars ; nor did she join the squadron until six hours after the action, and three hours after the surrender of the *President.* My sword was delivered to Capt. Hays, of the *Majestic*, the senior officer of the squadron, on his quarter deck, which he with great politeness immediately returned. I have the honor to enclose to you my parole, by which you will perceive the British admit the *President* was captured by the squadron. I should have deemed it unnecessary to have drawn your attention to this document, had not the fact been stated differently in the Bermuda Gazette, on our arrival there ; which statement, however, the editor was compelled to retract, through the interference of the governor and some of the British officers of the squadron.

The great assiduity of Dr. Trevett and Surgeon's Mates Dix and Wickes to the wounded, merits the highest approbation. The only officer badly wounded is Midshipman Richard Dale, who lost a leg, a circumstance to be particularly regretted, as he is a young man possessed of every quality to make a distinguished officer.

I have the honor to be, &c.

STEPHEN DECATUR.

The following extract from a Bermuda paper was republished at New York, in the Commercial Advertiser.

"On Wednesday evening last, Mr. Randolph, of the United States navy, late of the *President* frigate, in company with some other officers of the ship, attacked the editor of the Royal Gazette in a most violent and unprovoked manner, with a stick, while he was walking unarmed. The timely arrival of some British officers prevented his proceeding to further acts of violence. A guard shortly after came up, when the offender had decamped ; and the next morning, we understand, he was hoisted into a boat at the crane, from the market wharf, and absconded—an honourable way truly for an officer to quit a place, where he had been treated with civility and politeness."

The following is a letter from Mr. Randolph to the editors of the Commercial Advertiser.

New York, April 3, 1815.

Messrs. LEWIS & HALL,

Having observed in your paper of Saturday last, an extract from the Bermuda Gazette, containing a false and scandalous account of an affair in which I had an agency, I send you for publication the subjoined statement, which I declare to be correct.

As soon as I read the scurrilous remarks in the Royal Gazette of the 15th ult. in relation to the capture of the late U. S. frigate *President,* I walked to the King's Square, with a determination to chastise the editor. I soon fell in with him and executed my purpose, in the most ample and satisfactory manner.

There was no American officer in company, except Midshipman Emmet. Mr. Ward, the editor, was attended by Lieut. Sammon, of the royal navy ; but by neither of these officers was I interrupted or assisted in the operation.

Having previously obtained my passport, and being advised that the editor of the Royal Gazette was taking measures to employ the civil authority against me, I left the Island the next day, for the United States.

I am gentlemen, &c. &c.
R. B. RANDOLPH, *Midshipman,*
Late of the United States frigate President.

Copy of a letter from Com. Alexander Murray, president of a court of inquiry, held at New York, to investigate the causes of the capture of the United States frigate President, to the Secretary of the navy.

"Sir, *New York, April 17, 1815.*

"I herewith transmit to you the result of the court of inquiry, respecting the capture of the frigate *President,* with the opinion of the court.

"We have been more minute in our investigation than might, at first view, have been deemed necessary ; but as there has been a diversity of opinion prevailing among the British commanders, concerned in her capture, it was desirable in our view, to lay before the world, in the most correct manner, every circumstance, that led to that event ; which has afforded another high proof of American heroism, and so highly honorable to her commander, officers and crew,

22

that every American citizen must feel a pride in knowing that our flag has been so nobly defended."

The minutes of the court having been read and approved, the court was cleared, and after due deliberation, resolved to express the sentiments and opinions of the members, on the matters submitted to them, as follows:

" In the execution of the orders of honorable the secretary of the navy, we have (with the exception of two very young midshipmen) examined every officer belonging to the *President*, within the reach of the court, who survived the late glorious contest between the frigate *President* and a squadron of his Britannic majesty.

" We are of opinion, that the primary cause of the loss of the *President* was her running on the bar, as she was leaving this port. The violence and the continuance of the shocks she received for an hour and a half or more, considering that she was laden with stores and provisions for a very long cruise, could not but have injured her greatly, and must have impeded her sailing. Her hogged and twisted appearance after she arrived at Bermuda, must have been the effects of this unfortunate accident. We are convinced, that it was owing to this that the enemy were able to overtake her.

" The striking of the *President* on the bar cannot be imputed to the fault of any officer who was attached to her. On the contrary, we think every possible precaution was taken, and the utmost exertions were used by her commander and officers, to insure her safe passage over the bar, and to relieve her after she had struck. The accident was occasioned by some mistake in placing the boats, which were to serve as beacons to the *President*, through a channel always dangerous for a vessel of her draught, but particularly so at such a time as she was obliged to select for passing it, when the land marks could not be distinguished.

" From the time that the superiority of the enemy's

force was ascertained, and it became the duty of the *President* to evade it, we are convinced, that the most proper measures were pursued, and that she made every possible effort to escape. No means, in our opinion, were so likely to be attended with success, as those which were adopted by Com. Decatur. Any suggestion, that different measures would have been more proper or more likely to accomplish the object, we think, are without foundation, and may be the result of ignorance or the dictates of a culpable ambition, or of envy.

We consider the management of the *President*, from the time the chase commenced till her surrender, as the highest evidence of the experience, skill, and resources of her commander, and of the ability and seamanship of her officers and crew. We fear that we cannot express, in a manner that will do justice to our feelings, our admiration of the conduct of Com. Decatur, and his officers and crew, while engaged with the enemy, threatened with a force so superior, posessing advantages, which must have appeared to render all opposition unavailing, otherwise than might affect the honor of our navy, and the character of our seamen. They fought with a spirit, which no prospect of success could have heightened, and if victory had met its common reward, the *Endymion's* name would have been added to our list of naval conquests. In this unequal conflict the enemy gained a ship, but the victory was ours. When the *President* was obliged to leave the *Endymion* to avoid the other ships, which were fast coming up, the *Endymion* was subdued; and if her friends had not been at hand to rescue her, she was so entirely disabled, that she soon must have struck her flag. A proof of this is, that she made no attempt to pursue the *President*, or to annoy her by a single shot, while the *President* was within her reach, when, with the hope of escape from the overwhelming force, which was nearly upon her, the *President* presented her stern to the *Endymion's* broadside. A farther proof that the *Endymion* was conquered is, the shattered condition in which she appeared, while the *President*, in the contest with her, had sustained but little injury ; and the fact, that the *Endymion* did not join her squadron till many hours after the *President* had been surrounded by the other four enemy ships, and had surrendered to them, is strong corroborative evidence of the disabled state in which the *President* left the *Endymion*.

" We think it due to Com. Decatur and his heroic officers and crew, to notice the proposition he made to board the *Endymion*, when he found she was coming up, and the manner in which this position was received by his gallant crew.

" Such a design, at such a time, could only be conceived by a soul without fear, and approved with enthusiastic cheering by men regardless of danger. Had not the enemy perceived the attempt, and availed himself of the power he had in the early part of the action to shun the approach of the *President*, the American stars might now be shining on the *Endymion*. In the subsequent part of the engagement, the enemy's squadron was too near to permit the execution of this design, and the disabled state of the *Endymion* would have frustrated the principal object which Com. Decatur had in making so bold an attempt, which was to avail himself of the *Endymion's* superior sailing to escape with his crew from his pursuers.

" We conclude by expressing our opinion, that Com. Decatur, as well during the chase, as through his contest with the enemy, evinced great judgment and skill, perfect coolness, the most determined resolution and heroic courage—that his conduct, and the conduct of his officers and crew, are highly honorable to them, and to the American navy, and deserve the warmest gratitude of their country—that they did not give up their ship till she was surrounded and overpowered by a force so superior, that further resistance would have been unjustifiable, and a useless sacrifice of the lives of brave men.

" The order of the secretary of the navy requires us

Cyane.

Constitution.

Levant.

THE CONSTITUTION TAKING THE CYANE AND LEVANT.

to express an opinion as to the conduct of the officers and crew of the *President* after the capture. The testimony of all the witnesses concurs in enabling us to give it our decided approbation.

By the Court.

"ALEX. MURRAY, *President.*
"CODWALADER D. COLDEN, *Judge Advocate.*
Approved, B. W. CROWNINGSHIELD."
"April 20, 1815.

LETTER FROM THE SECRETARY OF THE NAVY TO COM. DECATUR.

SIR, *Navy Department, April 20, 1815.*

In the course of official duty, it is my highest satisfaction to render justice to the gallantry and good conduct of the brave officers and seamen of the United States navy.

In giving an official sanction to the recent proceedings of the court of inquiry, instituted at your request, to investigate the cause of the loss by capture of the frigate *President*, late of the navy of the United States, while under your command ; and to inquire into the conduct of the commander, officers, and crew of said frigate, before and after the surrender to the enemy ; it would be equally unjust to your merit, as well as to my sentiments and feeling, to pass over this investigation with a formal approbation. I have therefore, sir, to express to you, in the fullest manner, the high sense of approbation, which the President of the United States and this department entertain for your professional character as an officer, who, in every instance has added lustre to the stars of the union ; and whose brilliant actions have raised the national honor and fame, even in the moment of surrendering your ship to an enemy's squadron of vastly superior force, over whose attack, singly, you were decidedly triumphant ; and you will be pleased to present to each of your gallant officers and crew, the thanks of your government, for their brave defence of the ship, and the flag of the United States.

The proceedings and opinions of the court of inquiry, of which Com. Alexander Murray is president, are approved.

B. W. CROWNINGSHIELD.

Com. STEPHEN DECATUR.

CONSTITUTION AND CYANE & LEVANT.

LETTER FROM LIEUT. HOFFMAN TO THE SECRETARY OF THE NAVY.

His Britannic Majesty's late ship Cyane.

SIR,   *New-York, April* 10, 1815.

I have the honor to inform you that on the evening of the 28th of February last, while cruising off Madeira, the United States frigate *Constitution* fell in with His Britannic Majesty's ships *Cyane* and *Levant*, which she captured after an action of 40 minutes.

The *Cyane* is a frigate built ship, mounting 34 carriage guns, viz. twenty-two 32lb. carronades on the main deck, eight 18lb. carronades on the quarter deck, two 18lb. carronades and two long 9s on the forecastle, and from the best information I could obtain, carrying a complement of 175 men, commanded by Gordon Falcon, Esq.; the *Levant* mounting twenty-one carriage guns, viz. eighteen 24lb. carronades, two long 6s and a shifting 12 pounder on the top-gallant forecastle, with a complement of 150 men, commanded by the Hon. George Douglas—both ships suffered severely in their spars, rigging and sails. The *Constitution* received but trifling injury, having only 4 men killed and 10 wounded. As to the loss of the enemy, I cannot possibly ascertain, but should presume it was very severe.

On the 9th of March the *Constitution*, with her two prizes in company, anchored off the Isle of May, (one of the Cape de Verd Islands.) On the 10th at 5 A. M. got under way and made sail for St. Jago, where we anchored at 45 minutes past 10. On the 12th, at half past meridian, discovered three sail in the offing—at 10 minutes past 1, made them to be frigates —at which time the *Constitution* made signal to get under way. At 20 minutes past 1, cut our cable and made sail to the southward and eastward, close on a wind. At 30 minutes past 1, the forts on shore commenced firing on us. At 2, the *Constitution* made signal to tack, which I did to the northward and westward. At 5 minutes past 2, the sternmost frigate commenced firing on us, and hoisted English colors, distance about 2 miles. At 20 minutes past 2, lost sight of the *Constitution* and *Levant*, who were standing on a wind to the southward and eastward; the frigates in chase. At 35 minutes past 2, lost sight of the enemy. At 3, heard a heavy cannonading, which continued at intervals until half past 4. At sun-down shaped my course for the United States. For the further particulars of our cruise, I beg to refer you to Capt. Stewart's official account, on his arrival in the United States.

I cannot conclude my letter without particularly recommending to your notice Midshipman Joseph Cross, for whose unremitted attention and exertions I feel myself greatly indebted; and he is a young man who, I think, would do honor to a commission.

As to Midshipmen James Delany, and James F. Curtis, and the few men I have under my command, words would be insufficient to express my gratitude towards them. Very respectfully,

I have the honor to be,
your obedient servant,
B. V. HOFFMAN.

COPY OF A LETTER FROM LIEUT. BALLARD TO THE SECRETARY OF THE NAVY.

SIR,   *Baltimore, May 2,* 1815.

I have the honor to make known to you my arrival at this place with a part of the officers and crew of the United States frigate *Constitution*, captured in a prize, the *Levant*, in the harbor of Port-Praya, in the Island of St. Jago, by a squadron of his Britannc Majesty's ships, consisting of the *Leander*, Sir George Collier ; the *Newcastle*, Lord George Stuart ; and the *Acasta*, Capt. Kerr.   For the particulars of my recapture, I beg leave to refer you to the enclosed extract from the log-book of the *Levant*.

Having caused the destruction of my own papers, as well as those of the officers with me, I can only say to you relative to the *Constitution*, that, after leaving the port of Boston, she successively cruised off the Islands of Bermuda and Madeira, in the Bay of Biscay, and for some time in sight of the Rock of Lisbon, without having met with but two of the enemy's vessels, one of which was destroyed, the other ordered in ; and that, on the evening of the 20th February, the Island of Madeira bearing W. S. W. distant 70 leagues, fell in with, engaged, and after a close action of 40 minutes, captured his Britannic Majesty's ships *Cyane*, Capt. Gordon Falcon, and *Levant*, Hon. Capt. Douglass.

It would, sir, be deemed presumption in me to attempt to give you particular details respecting the nature of this action.   I shall, therefore, only remark generally, that every officer, seaman and marine on board did their duty.   I cannot, however, deny myself the pleasure, that this opportunity affords me, of noticing the brilliant management of Capt. Charles Stewart, through whose unerring judgment every attempt of an ingenious enemy to gain a raking position was frustrated.

I have the honor to be, very respectfully,
Sir, your obedient servant,
HENRY E. BALLARD.

The *Cyane* mounted on her main deck twenty-two 32lb. carronades—on her upper decks, ten 18lb. carronades, two long 9s, and one 12lb. carronade on a travelling carriage, with a complement of 175 men. The *Levant* mounted eighteen 32lb. carronades, two long 9s, and one 12lb. carronade, with 138 men on board. The *Constitution* had 4 killed and 10 wounded—the *Cyane* 7 killed and 17 wounded—the *Levant* 9 killed and 17 wounded.

COPY OF A LETTER FROM CAPTAIN STEWART TO THE SECRETARY OF THE NAVY.

SIR, *U. S. Frigate Constitution, May* —, 1815.
On the 20th of February last, the Island of Madeira bearing about W. S. W. distant 60 leagues, we fell in with His Britannic Majesty's two ships of war, the *Cyane* and *Levant*, and brought them to action about 6 o'clock in the evening, both of which, after a spirited engagement of 40 minutes, surrendered to the ship under my command.

Considering the advantages derived by the enemy, from a divided and more active force, as also their superiority in the weight and number of guns, I deem the speedy and decisive result of this action the strongest assurance which can be given to the government, that all under my command did their duty, and gallantry supported the reputation of American seamen.

Enclosed you will receive the minutes of the action; and a list of the killed and wounded on board this ship; also enclosed you will receive for your information a statement of the actual force of the enemy, and the number killed and wounded on board their ships, as near as could be ascertained.

I have the honor to remain, very respectfully,
Sir, your most obedient servant,
CHARLES STEWART.

Statement of the actual force of His Britannic Majesty's ships Levant, Capt. the Hon. George Douglass commander—and Cyane, Capt. Gordon Falcon commander ; with the number killed and wounded on board each ship, on the 20th Feb. 1815, as near as could be ascertained, while engaged with the United States Frigate Constitution :—

Levant—Eighteen 32 pounders, carronades ; one
23

12 pounder, do.; two 9 pounders, long guns.   Total
21 guns, 156 officers, seamen, and marines.   Prisoners, 133 officers, seamen and marines.   Killed, 23;
wounded, 16.   Total killed and wounded, 39.

Cyané—Twenty-two 32 pounders, carronades ; ten
18 pounders, do.; two 12 pounders, long guns.   Total
34 guns (besides 2 brass swivels,) 180 officers, seamen, and marines.   Prisoners, 168 officers, seamen,
and marines.   Killed, 27; wounded, 26.   Total killed and wounded, 38.

Minutes of the action between the United States frig-
ate Constitution and His Majesty's ships Cyane
and Levant, on the 20th February, 1815.

Commences with light breezes from the east, and
cloudy weather.   At 1 P. M. discovered a sail two
points on the larboard bow—hauled up, and made sail
in chase.   At half past 1, made the sail to be a ship ;
at half past 1, discovered another sail ahead ; made
them out, at 2, to be both ships, standing close hauled, with their starboard tacks on board ; at 4, the
weathermost ship made signals, and bore up for her
consort, then about ten miles to leeward ; we bore up
after her, and set lower top-mast, top-gallant and
royal studding sails, in chase ; at half past 4, carried
away our main royal-mast ; took in the sails, and got
another prepared.   At 5, commenced firing on the
chase from our two larboard bow guns ; our shot falling short, ceased firing ; at half past 5, finding it
impossible to prevent their junction, cleared ship for
action, then about 4 miles from the two ships : at 40
minutes past 5, they passed within hail of each other,
and hauled by the wind on the starboard tack, hauled
up their courses, and prepared to receive us : at 45 minutes past 5, they made all sail close hauled by the wind,
in hopes of getting to windward of us : at 55 minutes
past 5, finding themselves disappointed in their object,
and we were closing with them fast, they shortened
sail, and formed on a line of wind, about half a cable's
length of each other : at 6, having them under com-

mand of our battery, hoisted our colors, which was answered by both ships hoisting English ensigns : at 5 minutes past 6, ranged up on the starboard side of the sternmost ship, about 300 yards distant, and commenced the action by broadsides, both ships returning our fire with great spirit for about 15 minutes ; then the fire of the enemy beginning to slacken, and the great column of smoke collected under our lee, induced us to cease our fire to ascertain their positions and conditions : in about three minutes, the smoke clearing away, we found ourselves abreast of the headmost ship, the sternmost ship luffed up for our larboard quarter ; we poured a broadside into the headmost ship, and then braced aback our main and mizen topsails, and backed astern under cover of the smoke, abreast the sternmost ship, when the action was continued with spirit and considerable effect, until 35 minutes past 6, when the enemy's fire again slackened, and we discovered the headmost ship bearing up ; filled our top-sails, shot ahead, and gave her two stern rakes ; we then discovered the sternmost ship wearing also ; wore ship immediately after her, and gave her a stern rake—she luffed to on our starboard bows, and gave us her larboard broadside : we ranged up on her larboard quarter, within hail, and were about to give her our starboard broadside, when she struck her colors, fired a lee gun, and yielded. At 50 minutes past 6, took possession of His Majesty's ship *Cyane*, Capt. Gordon Falcon, mounting 34 guns. At 8, filled away after her consort, which was still in sight to leeward. At ½ past 8, found her standing towards us, with her starboard tacks close hauled, with top-gallant sails set, and colors flying. At 5 minutes past 8, ranged close along side to windward of her, on opposite tacks, and exchanged broadsides—wore immediately under her stern, and raked her with a broadside : she then crowded all sail, and endeavored to escape by running--hauled on board our tacks, set spanker, and flying jib in chase. At ½ past 9, commenced firing on her from our starboard bow chaser ; gave her several shot, which

cut her spars and rigging considerably. At 10, finding she could not escape, fired a gun, struck her colors, and yielded. We immediately took possession
of His Majesty's ship *Levant*, Hon. Capt. George
Douglass, mounting 21 guns. At 1 A. M. the damages of our rigging were repaired, sails shifted, and the
ship in fighting condition.

*Minutes of the chase of the U. S. frigate Constitution,
by an English squadron of three ships, from out
the harbor af Port Praya, Island of St. Jago :—*

Commences with fresh breezes and thick foggy
weather. At 5 minutes past 12, discovered a large
ship through the fog, standing in for Port Praya. At
8 minutes past 12, discovered two other large ships
astern of her, also standing in for the port. From
their general appearance supposed them to be one of
the enemy's squadrons, and from the little respect
hitherto paid by them to neutral waters, I deemed it
most prudent to put to sea. The signal was made to
the *Cyane* and *Levant* to get under way. At 12 minutes past 12, with our topsails set, we cut our cable
and got under way, (when the Portuguese opened a
fire on us from several of their batteries on shore) the
prize ships following our motions, and stood out of the
harbor of Port Praya, close under East Point, passing
the enemy's squadron about gun shot to windward of
them ; crossed our top gallant yards, and set foresail,
mainsail, spanker, flying-jib and top-gallant sails.
The enemy seeing us under way, tacked ship and made
all sail in chase of us. As far as we could judge of
the rates, from the thickness of the weather, supposed them two ships of the line and one frigate. At ½
past 12, cut away the boats towing astern—first cutter and gig. At 1 P. M. found our sailing about
equal with the ships on our lee quarter, but the frigate
luffing up, gaining our wake and rather dropping astern of us ; finding the *Cyane* dropping astern and to
leeward, and the frigate gaining on her fast, I found
it impossible to save her if she continued on the same

course, without having the *Constitution* brought to action by their whole force. I made the signal at 10 minutes past 1, to her to tack ship, which was complied with. This manœuvre, I conceived, would detach one of the enemy's ships in pursuit of her, while at the same time, from her position, she would be enabled to reach the anchorage at Port Praya, before the detached ship could come up with her ; but if they did not tack after her, it would afford her an opportunity to double their rear, and make her escape before the wind. They all continued in full chase of the *Levant* and this ship ; the ship on our lee quarter firing broadsides, by divisions—her shot falling short of us. At 3, by our having dropped the *Levant* considerably, her situation became (from the position of the enemy's frigate) similar to the *Cyane*. It became necessary to separate also from the *Levant*, or risk this ship being brought to action to cover her. I made the signal at 5 minutes past 3, for her to tack, which was complied with. At 12 minutes past 3, the whole of the enemy's squadron tacked in pursuit of the *Levant*, and gave up the pursuit of this ship. This sacrifice of the *Levant* became necessary for the preservation of the *Constitution*. Sailing Master Hixon, Midshipman Varnum, one boatswain's mate, and 12 men, were absent on duty in the 5th cutter, to bring the cartel brig under our stern.

ANECDOTES.

The *Constitution* is so deservedly a favorite with the public, that a few anecdotes of her last cruise will not be uninteresting. The modest, plain letter of Capt. Stewart, with the accompanying extracts from the log-book, have given the clearest official accounts of the action. The masterly manœuvreing of his ship so as to prevent either of the enemy's ships from raking him, and the final capture of them both, in such a neat and workmanlike manner, the prompt decision at Port Praya, when in 7 minutes after the British squadron were first discovered, the whole of the ships had cut their cables and were at sea; the judgment in the time of giving orders to the prizes to tack, which secured the *Cyane* first, and afterwards the *Constitution*, speak for themselves, and are fully appreciated by the public. It should not be forgotten, that this same *Cyane* engaged a French 44 gun frigate last year, and kept her at bay, till a ship of the line came up and captured her; and a few years since in the bay of Naples, that she engaged a frigate, a brig of 14 guns, and five gun boats, and beat them off, for which Capt. Benton, who commanded her, was knighted; yet, with the known skill of British officers, this same vessel, and a sloop of war of the largest class, with full crews of picked men, were captured by an American frigate, after a short action.

But it is not only to skilful officers that praise is due; to be successful, they must be aided by brave and excellent seamen. The crew of the *Constitution* were all yankee seamen, as docile and obedient to the ordinary discipline of the service, as they were intrepid in action. It would be easy to mention a number of anecdotes of the heroic character of our common sailors. There are two in this action that are particularly striking. A man by the name of Tobias Fernall, of Portsmouth, had his arm shattered by a ball; after the surgeon had amputated it, when he had taken up the arteries, and before the dressing was completed, the cheers on deck were heard for the surrender of the *Cyane;* the brave fellow twitched the bleeding stump from the surgeon, and waved it, joining the cheers! He is since dead. Another, John Lancey, of Cape Ann, was brought below, one thigh shattered to pieces, and the other severely wounded; the surgeon said to him, "my brave fellow, you are mortally wounded;" "yes, sir, I know it, I only want to hear, that the other ship has struck." Soon after the cheers were given for the surrender of the *Levant;* he raised his head, echoed the cheer, and expired a minute after. The wounds were generally severe; and much credit is due to the skill and humanity of Mr. Kearney, the surgeon, for saving so many of the wounded.

The *Cyane* was first discovered at the distance of three or four leagues ; the *Levant*, Cap. Douglass, the seinour, being to the leeward. The first signal from the *Cyane* was, that it was an American sloop of war ; afterwards, when they came within four miles of the *Constitution*, and the course was so altered, that she discovered her broadside, she made a signal that it was a heavy American frigate, superior to one of them but inferior to both. The signal from the *Levant* to her consort was, to join company. The *Constitution* was not able to prevent their junction. The action was invented on the part of the *Constitution*, by firing a signal shot across the bow of the *Cyane*. The two ships cheered, and fired their broadsides : after receiving both she returned it, and such was the eagernes of the men to fire, that when the word was given, they discharged the whole broadside, at the same instant. In commencing the action, there was perfect silence on board the *Constitution*—the cheers were returned when the ships surrendered. The weight shot fired by the British ships, was superior by about 90 pounds, taking their shot, at their nominal weight, though it was found, on weighing some of the English shot, that came on board, that they weighed full 32lbs. while the American of the same rate weighed only 29lbs. ; the action was so close, that their carronades had their full power. One of their shot came through the side of the ship, killed one and wounded four men, and lodged in the galley ; another killed two men in the waist, went through a boat in which two tigers were chained, and lodged in the head of a spar in the chains. In the action of the *Guerriere* the *Constitution* was hulled three times ; in that of the *Java*, four times ; and in this engagement, thirteen times. The British ships were fully officered, and manned with picked men, and fired better than they have usuly done in their engagements with our ships.

During the chase by Sir George Collier's squadron,

when the *Cyane* was ordered to tack, all the three ships kept after the *Constitution* and *Levant*. After sufficient time had been allowed to the *Cyane* to make her escape, as none of the enemy pursued her, orders were given to the *Levant* to tack. The *Leander*, Sir George Collier, who was the most astern, then made signal to the *Acasta* to tack, and the *Newcastle*, Lord George Stewart, to continue the chase. The *Acasta* sailed faster than the *Constitution*, and was gaining on her ; the *Newcastle* about the same rate of sailing, and the latter fired several broadsides, but the shot fell short from one to two hundred yards. After the other ships tacked, the *Newcastle* made a signal that her fore-top-sail yard was sprung, and tacked also. The British officers on board, who had expressed the most perfect confidence that the *Constitution* would be taken in an hour, felt the greatest vexation and disappointment, which they expressed in very emphatic terms. The *Levant* ran into port so as to run her jib-boom over the battery ; the *Acasta* and *Newcastle* came in, and though her colors were hauled down, fired at her a number of times. They were obliged to hoist and lower their colors twice ; yet not a gun was fired from the *Levant*. Lieut. Ballard, who commanded, had ordered his men to lay on the decks, by which they all escaped injury, though considerable damage was done to the town. It seemed unnecessary for two heavy frigates to fire into one sloop of war, who neither did nor could make any resistance. After the escape of the *Constitution* from this squadron, till she arrived at the Brazils, the greatest watchfulness was necessary. With a very diminished crew, she had on board 240 prisoners, and the number of British officers was more than double her own.

It is known, that sailors are apt to be superstitious. Lieut. Hoffman had a fine terrier, who was a great favorite on board the ship : when he was transferred to the *Cyane*, he took the dog with him. At Port Praya, the dog, being much attached to *Old Ironsides*, jumped over to swim to her. A boat was low-

THE HORNET AND PENGUIN.

ered down from the *Constitution* to try to save him; but the poor animal was drowned. The sailors then said, that they should have a fight, or a run, in twenty-four hours. The next morning the British squadron hove in sight. This was not likely to lessen their belief in omens.

At Maranham, all the principal people asked leave to visit the *Constitution*. They had heard much of her, and had been told by the English, that she was a ship of the line. They were requested to examine and count her guns, which they found to be 52, as she carried two less than in her former cruise. The American character was most highly respected at Porto-Rico, where a boat was sent in. The governor made the most earnest entreaties, that the ship would come into port, that he might see her, and offerered every kind of refreshment, and expressed the highest regard for our country. How much has our little navy done to elevate the character of the nation!

In a hurricane, when the ship made much water, a petty officer called on Lieut. Shubrick, who was the officer on the deck, and said, " Sir, the ship is sinking "—"well, sir," said this cool and gallant officer, " as every thing in our power is made tight, we must patiently submit to the fate of sailors, and all of us sink or swim together."

When the officer from the British squadron, which retook the *Levant*, went on board of her he advanced briskly towards the quarter deck, and observed that he presumed he had the proud satisfaction of receiving the sword of Capt. Blakeley, commander of the American sloop of war the *Wasp*. No, sir, was the reply; but if there is any pride in the case, you have the honor of receiving the sword of Capt. Ballard, 1st of the *Constitution* frigate, and now prize officer of his Britannic Majesty's ship the *Levant*.

According to the British mode of calculation, the *Constitution* ought to have been captured. The *Cyane* and *Levant* could discharge from all their can-

24

non at once, 1514lbs. of shot   The *Constitution* 1424. Difference, 90lbs.

The *Constitution* has captured, in her three victories, 154 gun carriages ; made upwards of 900 prisoners ; killed and wounded 298 of the enemy ; and the value of property captured, including the stores, provisions, &c. cannot be estimated at less than 1,500,000.

The first escape of the *Constitution* in 1812, was from a British squadron, consisting of the *African* 64, *Shannon*, 38, *Guerriere* 38, *Belvidier* 38, and *Æolus* 32. The chase continued 51 hours. Her last escape was from the *Leander* 50, *Newcastle* 50, and *Acasta* 40.

In 1804, the *Constitution* made several daring attacks on the batteries before the town Tropoli, mounting 115 pieces of heavy cannon. She repeatedly, and for hours, engaged their forts, within musket shot, and her bold movements and destructive fire most essentially assisted in wresting from captivity 300 of our countrymen, as the Bashaw was compelled to submit to terms of peace.

HORNET AND PENGUIN.

COPY OF A LETTER FROM CAPT. BIDDLE TO COM. DECATUR.

United States Sloop Hornet off Tristand' Acuna,
SIR,   *March 25, 1815.*

I have the honor to inform you, that on the morning of the 23d inst. at half past 10, when about to anchor off the north end of the Island of Tristan d' Acuna, a sail was seen to sothered and eastward steering to the westward, the wind fresh from S. S. W. In a few minutes she had passed on to the westward so far that we could not see her for the land. I immediately made sail for the westward and shortly after getting in sigh of her again perceived her to bear up before the wind.   When she had approached near, I filled the main-top-sail, and continued to yaw the ship, while she continued to come down, wearing occasionally to prevent her passing under our stern.   At 10 minutes past 1 P. M. being within nearly musket shot distance, she hauled her wind on the starboard tack, hoisted English colors and fired a gun.   We immediately luffed to, hoisted our ensign, and gave the enemy a broadside.   The action being thus commenced, a quick and well directed fire was kept up from this ship, the enemy gradually drifting nearer to us, when at 55 minutes past 1, he bore up apparently to run us on board.   As soon as I perceived he would certainly fall on board, I called the boarders so as to be ready to repel any attempt to board us.   At the instant every officer and man repaired to the quarter deck, when the two vessels were coming in contact, and eagerly pressed me to permit them to board the enemy ; but this I would not permit, as it was evident from the commencement of the action, that our fire was greatly superior both in quickness and in effect.   The enemy's bowsprit came in between our main and mizzen rigging, on our starboard side, affording him an opportunity to board us, if such was his design ; but no attempt was made.   There was a considerable swell on, and as the sea lifted us ahead, the enemy's bowsprit carried away our mizzen shrouds, stern davits, and spanker boom, and he hung upon our larboard quarter.   At this moment an officer who was afterwards recognized to be Mr. M'Donald, the 1st lieutenant and the then commanding officer, called out that they had surrendered.   I directed the marines and musketry-men to cease firing, and while on the taffril, asking if they had surrendered, I received a wound in the neck.   The enemy just then got clear of us, and his fore-mast and bowsprit being both gone, and perceiving us wearing to give him a fresh broadside, he again called out, that he had surrendered.   It was with difficulty I could restrain my crew from firing into him again, as he had certainly fired into us after having surrendered.   From the firing of the first gun, to the last time the enemy cried out he had surrendered, was exactly twenty-two minutes by the watch.   She proved to be His Britannic Majesty's brig *Penguin*, mounting sixteen 32lb. carronades, two long 12s, a 12lb. carronade on the top-gallant fore-castle, with a swivel on the capstern in the tops.   She had a spare port forward, so as to fight both her long guns of a side.   She sailed from England in September last.   She was shorter upon deck than this ship by two feet, but she had a greater length of keel, greater breadth of beam, thicker sides, and higher bulwarks than this ship, and was in all respects a remarkably fine vessel of her class.   The enemy acknowledged a complement of 132 ; 12 of them supernumerary marines from the *Medway* 74, received on board in consequence of their being ordered to cruise for the American privateer *Young Wasp*.   They acknowledge also a loss of 14 killed and 28 wounded ; but Mr. Mayo, who was in charge of the prize, assures me, that the number of killed was certainly greater. Among the killed are Capt. Dickenson, who fell at the close of the action, and the boatswain ; among the wounded are the 2d lieutenant, purser, and two midshipmen.   Each of the midshipmen lost a leg. We received on board, in all, 118 prisoners, 4 of whom have since died of their wounds.   Having removed the prisoners, and taken on board such provisions and stores as would be useful to us I scuttled the *Penguin*, this morning, before day light, and she went down. As she was completely riddled by our shot, her foremast and bowsprit both gone, and her mainmast so crippled as to be incapable of being secured, it seemed inadvisable, at this distance from home, to attempt sending her to the United States.

This ship did not receive a single round shot in her hull, nor any material wound in her spars ; the rigging, and sails were very much cut ; but having bent a new suit of sails, and knotted and secured our rigging, we are now completely ready in all respects, for any service. We were eight men short of a complement, and had 9 upon the sick list the morning of the action.

Enclosed is a list of killed and wounded. I lament to state, that Lieut. Conner is wounded dangerously. I feel great solicitude on his account, as he is an officer of much promise, and his loss would be a serious loss to the service.

It is a most pleasing part of my duty to acquaint you, that the conduct of Lieutenants Conner and Newton, Mr. Mayo, Acting Lieut. Brownlow of the marines, Sailing Master Rommey, and the other officers, seamen, and marines, I have the honor to command, was in the highest degree creditable to them, and calls for my warmest recommendation. I cannot indeed do justice to their merits. The satisfaction which was diffused throughout the ship, when it was ascertained, that the stranger was an enemy's sloop of war, and the alacrity with which every one repaired to his quarters, fully assured me, that their conduct in action would be marked with coolness and intrepidity.

I have the honor to be,
your obedient servant,
J. BIDDLE.

Loss on board the *Hornet*, 1 killed and 11 wounded.

EXTRACT OF A LETTER FROM AN OFFICER ON BOARD THE SLOOP OF WAR PEACOCK OFF TRISTAN D'ACUNA.

April, 10, 1815.

The *Hornet* separated in chase, two days out, and we fell in, off here, a few days since. We were delighted to hear of her good fortune—so superior to our own. She had captured, two days previous, His Britannic Majesty's brig *Penguin*, after an action of 20 ½ minutes. The *Penguin* was fitted out by Admiral Tyler at the Cape of Good Hope, expressly to capture the privateer *Young Wasp*, who had captured an Indiaman in that neighborhood, and landed the prisoners ; and was supposed to have brought her prize here to strip her and to refresh. The *Penguin* was commanded by Capt. Dickenson, a distinguished young man in their chronicles : and it appears from some of his papers, of respectable connexions, and a great favorite in the navy.

Admiral Tyler loaned him 12 marines from the *Medway*, and was very minute in his instructions, and grave to a degree, in his injunctions, upon Dickenson, as to the manner of engaging the privateer : to get close enough was the great desideratum. What a man seeks earnestly he is almost sure to find, and Capt. Dickenson supposed he *had* the *Wasp*, when he only *saw* the *Hornet*, a vessel considerably smaller in all her dimensions, and decidedly inferior in her armament to the privateer. The *Hornet*, on perceiving that the brig bore up for her, laid all aback ; the brig came stern on, lest the *Hornet*, might discover her guns and be off, and brushing close along side of her, fired a gun, and run up her St. George. An entire broadside from the *Hornet*, every shot of which told, opened the eyes of John Bull upon a yankee man of war : just what they had been wishing ever since they left England. In 20 minutes the *Penguin* had her foremast over the side—-her bowsprit in two pieces—her broadside nearly driven in—20 men killed, including the captain, and one of Lord Nelson's boatswains, and 35 wounded, including the second lieutenant, 2 midshipmen, and master's mate, &c. The *Hornet*, untouched in her hull, was severely cut up in her rigging, especially about her main and fore-top-gallant masts, her mizzen being a vast deal to low for British gunnery—one marine killed, the captain and 1st Lieutenant Conner,(severally) and 9 others wounded. The officers of the *Penguin* ascribed their misfortune entirely to the superiority of the men belonging to the *Hornet ;* and have repeatedly said, they would be glad to try it again with her, if the *Penguin* were manned with such men.

Now these gentlemen left England last September, and the prisoners are as stout, fine looking fellows, as I ever saw. One fact, which is probable, is worth all speculation in such an inquiry. On examining her guns after the action, a 32lb. carronade, on the side engaged, was found with his tompion as nicely puttied and stopped in as it was the day she left Spithead!— Capt. Dickenson, towards the close of the fight, told his 1st lieutenant, M'Donald, that "the fellows are giving it to us like hell; we must get on board:" and on being asked by Biddle why he did not, as there never had been a better opportunity—he said, "he did try, but found the men rather backward—and so, you know, we concluded to give it up." After M'Donald had repeatedly called out that they had surrendered, and Biddle had ceased his fire, two fellows on board the *Penguin* fired upon him and the man at the wheel. Biddle was struck on the chin, and the ball passing round the neck, went off through the cape of his surtout, wounded him, however, severely, but not dangerously; the man escaped but the ruffians did not, for they were observed by two of Biddle's marines, who levelled and laid them dead upon the deck in an instant.

ANECDOTES.

In this action a private marine of the *Hornet*, named Michael Smith (who had served under the gallant Porter in the *Essex*) received a shot through the upper part of the thigh, which fractured the bone, and nearly at the same moment had the *same* thigh broken immediately above the knee by the spanker boom of the *Hornet*, which was carried away by the enemy's bowsprit, while afoul of her. In this situation, while bleeding upon the deck and unable to rise, he was seen to make exertions to discharge his musket at the enemy on the top-gallant forecastle of the *Penguin*— this, however the poor fellow was unable to accomplish; and was compelled to be carried below.

The officers of the *Penguin* relate, that, during the action with the *Hornet*, a 32lb. shot came in at the after port of the *Penguin*, on the larboard side, carried away *six legs*, killed the powder boy of the di-

vision, capsized the opposite gun on the starboard
side, passed through the port, and " sunk in sullen silence to the bottom."

ESCAPE OF THE HORNET.

COPY OF A LETTER FROM CAPT. BIDDLE . TO COM. DE-
CATUR.

Sir, *U. S. Sloop Hornet, St. Salvador, June* 10,1815.

I HAVE the honor to report, that the *Peacock* and
this ship, having continued off Tristan d' Acuna the
number of days directed by you in your letter of instructions, proceeded in company to the eastward on
the 12th of April, bound to the second place of rendezvous. Nothing of any importance occurred to us
until the 27th of April, when at 7 A. M. in lat. 38°
30' S. and lon. 33° E. we made a strange sail in the
S. E. to which we gave chase. The wind was from
the N. E. by N. and light throughout the day, and by
sundown we had neared the chase considerably. It
was calm during the night, and at day-light on the
28th, he was yet in sight. A breeze springing from
the N. W. we crowded sail with steering sails on both
sides ;- the chase standing to the northward upon a
wind. At 45 minutes past 2 P. M. the *Peacock* was
about six miles ahead of this ship ; and observing that
she appeared to be suspicious of the chase, I took in
starboard steering sails, and hauled up for the *Peacock*—I was still, however, of opinion, that the chase
was an Indiaman, though indeed the atmosphere was
quite smoky and indistinct, and I concluded, as she
was very large, that Capt. Warrington was waiting for
me to join him, that we might together go along side
of her. At 22 minutes past 3 P. M. the *Peacock*
made the signal, that the chase was a ship of the line,
and an enemy. I immediately took in all steering
sails, and hauled open a wind ; the enemy then upon
our lee-quarter, distant about 8 miles. By sun-down

THE HORNET'S ESCAPE FROM A BRITISH 74.

I had perceived, that the enemy sailed remarkably fast, and was very weatherly.

At 9 P. M. as the enemy was gaining upon us, and as there was every appearance that he would be enabled to keep sight of us during the night, I considered it necessary to lighten this ship. I therefore threw overboard 12 tons of kentledge, part of our shot, some of our heavy spars, cut away the sheet anchor and cable, and started the wedges of the masts. At 2 A. M. the enemy being rather before our lee-beam, I tacked to the westward ; the enemy also tacked, and continued in chase of us. At day light on the 29th, he was within gun-shot upon our lee-quarter. At 7 A. M. having hoisted English colors, and a rear admiral's flag, he commenced firing from his bow guns. As his shot went over us, I cut away the remaining anchor and cable, threw overboard the launch, six of our guns, more of our shot, and every heavy article that was at hand ; the enemy fired about thirty shot, not one of which took effect, though most of them passed over us. While he was firing, I had the satisfaction to perceive, that we slowly dropped him, and at 9 A. M. he ceased his fire.

At 11 A. M. the enemy was again coming up with us. I now, therefore, threw overboard all our remaining guns but one long gun nearly all our shot, all our spare spars, cut away the top-gallant fore-castle, and cleared every thing off deck, as well as from below, to lighten as much as possible. At noon the enemy again commenced firing. He fired many shot, only three of which came on board ; two striking the hull, and one passing through the jib. It is, however, extraordinary, that, every shot did not take effect ; for the enemy, the second time he commenced firing, was certainly within three quarters of a mile of the ship and the sea quite smoth.

I perceived from his sails that the effect of his fire was to deaden his wind, and at 2 P. M. the wind which had previously, and grately to our disadvantage, backed to the southeast, hulled to the westward, and freshened up. At sun-down the enemy was about

25

four miles astern. The wind was fresh, and we went at the rate of nine knots throughout the night. We saw the enemy at intervals through the squalls during the night and at day light, on the 30th, he was about 12 miles astern, still in chase of us. At 30 minutes after 9 A. M. he took in steering sails, reefed his top-sail and hulled to the eastward, and at 11 he was entirely out of sight.

During the chase the enemy appeared to be very crank, and I therefore concluded he must have been lightened while in chase of us. I did not at any time fire our stern chasers, because it was manifest that the enemy injured his sailing by his firing.

As we had now no anchor, no cable, no boat, and but one gun, there was of course an absolute necessity of relinquishing our intended cruise; and as in our then condition, it would have been extremely hazardous on account of the enemy's cruisers, to approach our own coast, I considered it most advisable to proceed for this port. I arrived here yesterday, and on my arrival I received information of the peace between the United States and Great Britain. Permit me to state, that it was with the most painful reluctance, and upon the fullest conviction that it was indispensable, in order to prevent a greater misfortune, that I could bring my mind to consent to part with my guns; and I beg leave to request, that you will be pleased to move the honorable secretary of the navy, to call a court of inquiry to investigate the loss of the arrangement of this ship. It will be very satisfactory to me to have such an investigation.

I have the honor to be,
respectfully, your obe't serv't.

Com. DECATUR. J. BIDDLE.

Narrative of the escape of the Hornet from a British 74, after a chase of 24 hours—extracted from a private journal of one of the officers on board the Hornet.

U. S. Ship Hornet, *off the Cape of Good Hope,*
May 9, 1815.

April 27, 1815. At 7 P. M. the *Peacock* made a signal for a strange sail, bearing S. E. by S. We immediately made all sail in chase. Friday 28th commenced with light breezes and pleasant weather, all sail set in chase ; at sun down we had neared the stranger considerably, when it fell perfectly calm, and remained so during the whole night ; the stranger ahead, and could discern his top-sails out of the water. At day-light the sail not to be seen from the deck ; at 5 A. M. a breeze sprung up from the N. W. we immediately crowded all sail, in order if possible to get sight of the chase again ; soon after descried him standing to the northward and eastward on a wind. Saturday 29th, at 3-4 past 2 P. M. the *Peacock* was about 10 miles ahead of the *Hornet ;* we observed Capt. Warrington approaching the stranger with much precaution ; we therefore took in all our larboard steering-sails, set the stay-sails, and hauled up for the *Peacock*, still under the impression the sail in sight was an English Indiaman, and from the apparent conduct of the commander of the *Peacock*, we were under the impression (as the ship looked very large) that Capt. W. was waiting until we came up with him in order to make a joint attack. At half past three, the *Peacock* made the signal, that the chase was a line-of-battle ship, and an enemy ; our astonishment may easily be conceived ; we took in all steering-sails and hauled upon the wind, bringing the enemy upon our lee-quarter, and about 3 leagues distant ; the *Peacock* on his weather bow and apparently not more than 3 miles from the enemy. At sun-down the enemy bore E. half S. the *Peacock* E. by N. We soon perceived the enemy sailed remarkably fast, but the *Peacock*

left him running off to the eastward. The enemy
continued by the wind and evidently in chase of us,
at 6, loosed the wedges of the lower masts ; at 8, we
discovered the enemy weathered upon us fast, and that
there was every appearance he would, if not come up
with us, continue in sight all night. It was thought
necessary to lighten the ship ; at 9 we cut away the
sheet-anchor, and hove overboard the cable, a quantity of rigging, spars, &c. At half past 9, scuttled the
ward-room deck to get at the kentledge, hove overboard 90 pieces, weighing about 50 tons. At 2 A.
M. tacked ship to the southward and westward, which
the enemy no sooner discovered, than he tacked also.
At day-light he was within shot distance, on our lee-
quarter ; at 7, he hoisted English colors and a rear
admiral's flag at his mizzen-top-gallant masthead, and
commenced firing from his bow guns, his shot over-
reaching us about a mile. We therefore commenced
again to lighten the ship, by cutting away our remaining anchors and throwing overboard the cable, cut up
the launch and hove it overboard, a quantity of provisions with more kentledge, shot, capstern, spars, all
rigging, sails, guns, and in fact every heavy article
that could possibly tend to impede the ship's sailing.
The enemy continued to fire very heavy and in quick
succession ; but his British thunder could neither ter-
rify the yankee spirit, diminish yankee skill, nor compel us to show him the yankee stripes, which must
have irritated him excessively. None of his shot as
yet had taken effect, although he had been firing for
near 4 hours incessantly, his shot generally passing
between our masts. We thought at this period we
discovered that we were dropping him, as his shot began to fall short ; this stimulated our gallant crew to
fresh exertion. At 11, his firing ceased, and the breeze
began to freshen ; we discovered the enemy was again
coming up with us fast, which induced a general belief he had made some alteration in the trim of his
ship. At meridian squally and fresh breezes, wind
from the westward. Sunday (30th) fresh breezes and

squally, the enemy still gaining on the *Hornet ;* at 1 P. M. being within gun-shot distance, he commenced a very spirited and heavy fire with round and grape, the former passing between our masts, and the latter falling all around us. The enemy fired shells, but were so ill directed as to be perfectly harmless.

From 2 to 3, threw overboard all the muskets, cutlasses, forge, &c. &c. and broke up the bell—also cut up the top-gallant fore-castle. It was now our capture seemed inevitable—the enemy 3-4 of a mile on the lee-quarter, pouring in his shot and shells in great numbers all around us—continued to lighten the ship, by heaving every thing overboard that could either be of service to the enemy, or an impediment to the *Hornet's* sailing. The men were ordered to lay down on the quarter-deck, in order to trim ship, and to facilitate the ship's sailing. At 4, one of the shot from the enemy struck the jib-boom, another struck the starboard bulwark, just forward of the gangway, and a third struck on the deck forward of the main hatch, on the larboard side, glanced off and passed through the foresail. At half past 4, we again began to leave the enemy, and to appearance, by magic—set the larboard lower steering-sail, the wind drawing more aft. At 5 the enemy's shot fell short. At 6, fresh breezes—the enemy hull down in our wake. At 7, could just see his lower steering sail above horizon—from 8 to 12, discried him at intervals, with night glasses. At daylight, discovered the enemy astern of us, distant five leagues. At 9 A. M. the enemy shortened sail, reefed his top-sail, and hauled upon a wind to the eastward, after a chase of 42 hours. During this tedious and anxious chase, the wind was variable, so as to oblige us to make a perfect circle round the enemy. Between 2 and 3 o'clock yesterday not a person on board had the most distant idea that there was a possibility of escape. We all packed up our things, and waited until the enemy's shot would compel us to heave to and surrender, which appeared certain. Never has there been so evident an interposition of the goodness

of a Divine Father—my heart with gratitude ac-
knowledges his supreme power and goodness.   On the
morning of the 28th, it was very calm, and nothing
but murmurs were heard throughout the ship, as it
was feared we should lose our anticipated prize—many
plans had been formed by us for the disposal of our
plunder.   The seamen declared they would have the
birth deck carpeted with East India silk, supposing
her an Indiaman from India ; while the officers, under
the impression she was from England, were making
arrangements how we should dispose of the money,
porter, cheese, &c. &c.   Nothing perplexed us more
than the idea that we should not be able to take out
all the good things before we should be obliged to destroy her.   We were regretting our ship did not sail
faster, as the *Peacock* would certainly capture her
first, and would take out many of the best and most
valuable articles before we should get up—(this very
circumstance of our not sailing as fast as the *Peacock*
saved us in the first instance from inevitable capture,
for when Capt. W. made the signal for the sail to be
an enemy of superior force, we were 4 leagues to
windward.)   We all calculated our fortunes were
made, but alas, "we caught a Tartar."   During the
latter part of the chase, when the shot and shells were
whistling about our ears, it was an interesting sight
to behold the varied countenances of our crew.   They
had kept the deck during all the preceding night, employed continually in lightening the ship, were excessively fatigued, and under momentary expectation of
falling into the hands of a barbarous and enraged enemy.   The shot that fell on the main deck, (as before
related) struck immediately over the head of one of
our gallant fellows, who had been wounded in our glorious action with the *Penguin*, where he was lying in
his cot, very ill with his wounds ; the shot was near
coming through the deck, and it threw innumerable
splinters all around this poor fellow, and struck down
a small paper, American Ensign, which he had hoisted over his bed—destruction apparently stared us in

the face, if we did not soon surrender, yet no officer, no man, in the ship shewed any disposition to let the enemy have the poor little *Hornet*, Many of our men had been impressed and imprisoned for years in their horrible service, and hated them and their nation with the most deadly animosity ; while the rest of the crew, horror-struck by the relation of the sufferings of their shipmates, who had been in the power of the English, and now equally flushed with rage, joined heartily in execrating the present authors of our misfortune. Capt. Biddle mustered the crew, and told them he was pleased with their conduct during the chase, and hoped still to perceive that propriety of conduct which had always marked their character, and that of the American tar generally ; that we might soon expect to be captured, &c. Not a dry eye was to be seen at this mention of capture ; the rugged hearts of the sailors, like ice before the sun, warmed by the divine power of sympathy, wept in unison with their brave commander. About 2 o'clock, the wind, which had crossed us, and put to the test all our nautical skill to steer clear of the enemy, now veered in our favor (as before stated) and we left him. This was truly a glorious victory over the horrors of banishment and terrors of a British floating dungeon. Quick as thought, every face was changed from the gloom of despair to the highest smile of delight, and we began once more to breathe the sweets of liberty —the bitter sighs of regret were now changed, and I put forth my expression of everlasting gratitude to him, the supreme Author of our being, who had thus signally delivered us from the power of a cruel and vindictive enemy.

COURT OF INQUIRY.

A naval court of inquiry was held by order of the secretary of the navy, on board the U. S. ship *Hornet*, in the harbour of New-York, on the 23d of Aug. 1815, to investigate the causes of the return of that ship into port and to inquire into the circumstances attending the loss of armament, stores, &c. during her cruise ; and the following opinion has been pronounced by the court :

The court, after mature deliberation on the testimony adduced, are of opinion, that no blame is imputable to Capt. Biddle, on account of the return of the *Hornet* into port, with the loss of her armament, stores, &c. and that the greatest applause is due to him for his persevering gallantry nautical skill, evinced in escaping, under the most disadvantageous circumstance, after a long and arduous chase by a British line-of-battle ship.

SAMUEL EVANS, *President.*
HENRY WHEATON, *Special Judge Advocate.*

FURTHER PARTICULARS OF THE LATE WAR.

PRESIDENT AND BELVIDERA.

COPY OF A LETTER FROM CAPT. HULL TO THE SECRETARY OF THE NAVY.

United States Frigate Constitution.

Sir,   *August 28,* 1812.

The enclosed account of the affair between the *President,* Com. Rodgers, and the British frigate *Belvidera,* was taken by an officer, on board the *Belvidera,* and fell into my hands by accident. It clearly proves that she only escaped the commodore by superior sailing, after having lightened her, and the *President* being very deep.

As much has been said on this subject; if Com. Rodgers has not arrived, to give you his statement of the affair, if it meet your approbation, I should be pleased to have this account published, to prevent people from making up their minds hastily, as I find them willing to do.

I am confident, could the commodore have got along side the *Belvidera,* she would have been his, in less than one hour.

I have the honor to be, with great respect,

Sir, your obedient servant,

Hon. Paul Hamilton, &c.   ISAAC HULL.

An account of the proceedings of His Majesty's ship Belvidera, Richard Byron Esq. Captain, 23d of June, 1812.

At 40 minutes past 4 A. M. off Nantucket Shoal, saw several sail bearing S. W. made sail towards them: at 30 minutes past 6, they bore S. W. by S. made them out to be three frigates, one sloop, and

26

one brig of war, standing to the S. E. under a press
of sail.   Observed them to make signals, and haul up
in chase of us, hauling down their steering-sails, in a
confused, and irregular manner.   Tacked ship, made
the private signal, which was not answered ; made all
sail possible, N. E. by E.; at 8, moderate and fine
weather, the headmost ship of the chase S. S. W. 1-3
W. apparently gaining ground on us at times, and
leaving her consort.   At 30 minutes past 11, hoisted
our colors and pendant ; the chase hoisted American
colors, two of them hoisted commodore's broad pend-
ants ; at noon the commodore and the second headmost ship of the chase S. W. 3-4 W. about 2 and
3-4 of a mile, Nantucket Shoal N. 4° E. 48 miles ;
moderate and fine weather, cleared ship for action,
commodore of chase grining, the other ships dropping;
observed the chase pointing her guns at us ; at 40
minutes past 3 P. M. the commodore fired 3 shot, one
of which struck the rudder coat, and came into the after gun room ; the other two came into the upper, or
captain's cabin, one of which struck the muzzle of the
larboard chase gun, the other went through the beam
under the skylight, killed William Gould, seaman ;
wounded John Hill, armourer, mortally ; Joseph Lee,
seaman, severely ; George Marlon, ship's corporal,
badly ; Lieut. Bruce, and James Kelly and James
Larmont, seamen, slightly.   At 45 minutes past 3,
commenced firing with our stern guns, shot away her
larboard lower steering sail, keeping our ship a steady
course N. E. by E. at 4, the chase bore up and fired
her larboard broad side, which cut our rigging and
sails much, the long bolts, breeching-hooks, and
breechings of guns and carronades frequently breaking
(by one of which Capt. Byron was severely wounded
in the left thigh) all of which was instantly replaced.
Kept up a constant fire, which was returned by our
opponent with bow-chase guns, and at times by her
broadsides, which by her superiority of sailing she
was enabled to do till 45 minutes past 6, when we cut
away our spar sheet and small bower anchors, barge,

yawl, and jolly boats, and started 14 tons of water ; we then gained on him, when he bore up and fired three broadsides, part of which fell short of us ; at 7, opponent ceased firing, and the second frigate commenced, but finding her shot fell short, ceased again. Employed fishing our cross-jack yard, and main topmast (both badly wounded,) knotting and splicing our rigging, which was much cut and damaged. At 11, altered our course to E. by S. 1-2 S. and lost sight of our opponents.

AMERICAN SQUADRON.

Boston, Sept. 1, 1812.

We with pleasure announce the safe arrival in this port on Monday last of the United States squadron commanded by Com. Rodgers, which sailed from New-York, on the 21st June, on a cruise. The squadron, composed of the *President*, of 44 guns, bearing Com. Rodgers' flag ; the *United States* 44, bearing Com. Decatur's flag ; *Congress* 36, Capt. Smith ; *Hornet* 16, Capt. Lawrence ; and brig *Argus* 16, Capt. Sinclair ; came into harbor in a handsome style. The squadron had been seventy days at sea, during which time they had been nearly to the chops of the English Channel, along the coast of France, Spain, and Portugal ; to within ten leagues of the Rock of Lisbon ; to the vicinity of the Western Islands ; and back by the Banks and Coast of Nova Scotia to Boston ; during which time they did not even see a single British national vessel, excepting the *Belvidera*, with whom the *President* had a running fight of some hours. They have captured seven English merchantmen, two of which they burnt, and sent the other five for American ports, none of which, as we have learnt, have been fortunate enough to arrive.

The running fight between the *President* and *Belvidera* is thus stated :—The latter was descried on the 23d June, when the squadron gave chase. The *President*, by superiority of sailing, got within gun-shot of the *Belvidera*, between four and five o'clock P. M. when finding the breeze, which had enabled the *President* to overhaul the chase, was moderating, and that the chase was preparing to fire on the *President*, the latter commenced firing for the purpose of crippling the spars of the *Belvidera*, in order to come up with her. The fire was kept up two hours; the *President* yawing, and firing two or three broadsides to effect her object, and keeping up a constant fire of the chase guns, which though it cut the sails and rigging, did not stop the way of the *Belvidera*, which, as the wind became light, was accelerated by her crowding all sail, starting her water, cutting away her anchors, and by staving and throwing over her boats. The chase continued until near midnight; during which the *Congress* frigate came so near the *Belvidera* as to fire three or four shot at her. The *Hornet*, as reported, had no share in the firing. Early in the chase a very serious accident occurred on board the *President*— one of the forward guns, in being fired, burst, tore up the decks, killed several seamen, and wounded 11 or 12 others—among whom was Com. Rodgers, who had stepped forward to direct the firing of the chase guns, and who was blown up, and in the fall had the bone of his leg fractured. He has since recovered. This accident also prevented the chase guns being used for some time. The loss of the *President* we have not accurately ascertained. We understand 4 were killed by the bursting of the gun, and 3 by the shot of the *Belvidera*; and 19 were wounded, mostly slightly, and by the bursting gun.

We lament to learn, that the crews of the ships are very sickly, mostly of scurvy—occasioned by short allowance of provisions and water, made necessary in consequence of the sudden departure of the squadron from New-York, and the length of her cruise. Many have died. [*Centinel.*]

FROM COM. RODGERS TO THE SECRETARY OF THE NAVY.

U. S. Frigate President, Boston, Sept. 1, 1812.

SIR—I had the honor yesterday of informing you of the arrival of the squadron, and now to state the result and particulars of our cruise.

Previous to leaving New-York on the 21st of June, I heard that a British convoy had sailed from Jamaica for England on or about the 20th of the preceding month, and on being informed of the declaration of war against Great Britain, I determined, in the event of Com. Decatur joining me with the *United States, Congress*, and *Argus*, as you had directed to go in pursuit of them.

The *United States, Congress*, and *Argus*, did join me on the 21st; with which vessels, this ship and the *Hornet* accordingly sailed in less than an hour after I received your orders of the 18th of June, accompanied by your official communication of the declaration of war.

On leaving New-York I shaped our course southeasterly in the expectation of falling in with vessels, by which I should hear of the before mentioned convoy, and the following night met with an American brig that gave me the sought-for information ; the squadron now crowded sail in pursuit, but the next morning was taken out of its course by the pursuit of a British frigate, that I since find was the *Belvidera*, relative to which I beg leave to refer you to the enclosed extract from my journal. After repairing as far as possible the injury done by the *Belvidera* to our spars and rigging, we again crowded all sail, and resumed our course in pursuit of the convoy, but did not receive further intelligence of it until the 29th of June, on the western edge of the banks of Newfoundland, where we spoke an American schooner, the master of which reported that he had two days before passed them in latitude 43°, longitude 55°, steering to the eastward. I was surprised to find that the convoy was still so far to the eastward of us, but was urged, however, as well by what I considered my duty as by inclination, to continue the pursuit.

On the 1st of July, a little to the eastward of New-foundland Bank, we fell in with quantities of cocoa nut-shells, orange-peels, which indicated that the convoy were not far distant, and we pursued it with zeal, although frequently taken out of our course by vessels it was necessary to chase, without gaining any further intelligence until the 9th of July, in lat. 45° 30' long. 23°, we captured the British private armed brig *Dolphin*, of Jersey, and were informed by some of her crew that they had seen the convoy the preceding evening ; the weather was not clear at the time, but that they had counted 85 sail, and that the force charged with its protection consisted in one two-decker, a frigate, a sloop of war, and a brig.

This was the last intelligence I received of the before-mentioned convoy, although its pursuit was continued until the 13th of July, being then within 18 or 20 hours sail of the British channel.

From this we steered for the Island of Madeira, passed close by it on the 21st of July ; thence near the Azores, and saw Corvo and Flores ; thence steered for the banks of Newfoundland ; and from the latter place, by the way of Cape Sable, to this port, it having become indispensably necessary, by the time we reached our own coast, to make the first convenient port in the United States ; owing, I am sorry to say, to that wretched disease, the scurvy, having made its appearance on board of the vessels, most generally to a degree seriously alarming.

From the western part of the banks of Newfoundland to our making the Island of Madeira the weather was such, at least six days out of seven, as to obscure from our discovery every object that we did not pass within four or five miles of, and indeed for several days together the fog was so thick as to prevent our seeing each other, even at cable's length asunder, more than twice or thrice in 24 hours.

From the time of our leaving the United States until our arrival here we chased every vessel we saw, and you will not be a little astonished when I inform you, that, although we brought to every thing we did chase, with the exception of four vessels, we only made seven captures and one recapture.

It is truly an unpleasant task to be obliged to make a communication thus barren of benefit to our country; the only consolation I individually feel on the occasion being derived from knowing, that our being at sea obliged the enemy to concentrate a considerable portion of his most active force, and thereby prevented his capturing an incalculable amount of American property that would otherwise have fallen a sacrifice.

I am aware of the anxiety you must have experienced at not hearing from me for such a length of time; but this I am sure you will not attribute in any degree to neglect, when I inform you, that not a single proper opportunity occurred from the time of leaving the United States until our return.

Mr. Newcomb, who will deliver you this, you will find to be an intelligent young man, capable of giving such further information as you may deem of any moment. He will at the same time deliver you a chart, showing the tract in which we cruised. Annexed is a list of vessels captured, recaptured, and burnt.

The four vessels we chased and did not come up with, were the *Belvidera*, a small pilot-boat schooner, supposed to be an American privateer, the hermaphrodite privateer *Yankee*, which we lost sight of in a fog, but whose character we afterwards learnt, and a frigate supposed to be British, that we chased on the 28th ult. near the shoal of George's bank, and should certainly have come up with, had we had the advantage of two hour's more day-light.

On board of the several vessels of the squadron there are between 80 and 100 prisoners, taken from the vessels we captured during our late cruise. The government not having any agent for prisoners here, I shall send them to Com. Bainbridge, to be disposed of in such a manner as best appears with the interest of the United States, and which I hope may meet your approbation.

  With the greatest respect, I have the honor
      to be, sir, your obedient servant,
Hon. PAUL HAMILTON, JOHN RODGERS.
 Sec'y of the navy.

EXTRACT FROM COM. RODGERS' JOURNAL.

Sailed from New-York June 21. The 23d, 6 A. M. discovered and gave chase to an English frigate, supposed to be the *Belvidera.* The superiority of the *President's* sailing, while the breeze continued fresh, enabled her to get within gun-shot between 4 and 5 P. M. when it had moderated so much as to give very faint hopes of getting along side. At this time perceiving she was training her guns to bear upon the *President*, the latter commenced a fire at her spars and rigging, with the view to cripple and get abreast of her, a fire was kept up about two hours. The *President* gave her two or three broadsides, and kept up a well directed fire from the chase guns, which cut her sails and rigging very much, but did not succeed in destroying any of her spars, although some of them were much wounded. The *President* all this time was exposed to a running fire from her four sternchasers ; and once the British frigate commenced a fire from her main deck, with an intention of raking the *President* with a broadside, but at that moment receiving one from the *President*, continued the course under a press of sail, and used only her stern guns. All sail was crowded in pursuit, but in vain. The chase was now throwing overboard every thing that could be spared, to increase her sailing, and escaped by lightness of the wind ; four of her boats were seen floating by the *President*, completely knocked to pieces, together with a great number of casks, spars, &c. and it was supposed most of her guns were also thrown overboard.

  The *President* received a considerable number of

shot in her sails and rigging, but was not materially injured. The chase was continued till about midnight, when it was relinquished as hopeless, and the *President* hove to for the squadron to come up. Early in the chase, one of the *President's* chase guns, on the gun-deck, burst, and injured the upper deck so much, as to prevent the use of the chase guns on that side for a considerable time. The *President* had 3 killed, and 19 wounded; most of the latter slightly; of the wounded, 16 were by the bursting of the gun. It was by the same gun Com. Rodgers had his leg fractured; but has recovered.

The squadron afterwards pursued the Jamaica fleet, but owing to uncommonly foggy weather, missed them, although at times very near.

After the rencounter above related, Capt. Byron, of the *Belvidera*, in conversation with an American gentleman, observed that, in his opinion, Com. Rodgers had done every thing on board the *President*, which could have contributed to the capture of his ship. When the squadron first gave chase to the *Belvidera*, they gained upon her very fast; and Capt. Byron considered his vessel as lost; but as a last resort, when the *President* was coming up within gun-shot of the *Belvidera*, orders were given to cut away the anchors, stave the water casks, and throw overboard the boats, and every thing moveable, which could be spared, and which could tend to lighten the ship. As soon as this had been done, it was observed that the *Belvidera* began to draw from the chase; which being discovered by Com. Rodgers, he opened his fire upon her, in hope of disabling some of her spars, and thereby enable him to come up with her. Capt. Byron declared, that the fire from the President was extremely well directed, almost every shot taking effect; and that to the circumstance above related, and the wind at the same time becoming more light, was his escape to be attributed.

A declaration, like this, coming from an enemy, is conclusive evidence of the good conduct of Com. Rodgers.

27

BRIG NAUTILUS.

The U. S. brig *Nautilus*, 12 guns, Capt. Crane, (the loss of which was mentioned on page 9,) sixteen hours from New-York, on a cruise, was captured the 16th of July by the British frigate *Shannon*, after a hard chase of six hours, during which the *Nautilus* was obliged to start her water, and throw over all her lee-guns. She was ordered to Halifax, with Lieut. Crane on board; the remainder of the officers and crew (106 in number) were sent on board the *Africa*.

LETTER FROM A WARRANT OFFICER OF THE NAUTILUS
TO HIS FATHER.

On board His Britannic Majesty's ship Africa,
at sea, lat. 37°, long. 69°, July 23, 1812.

HONORED SIR,

I have to inform you that we sailed from New York the 15th July on a cruise. On the 16th at sun-rise discovered five sail to windward, which proved to be the British ships *Africa, Shannon, Guerriere, Belvidera,* and *Æolus,* and which gave us chase, we then standing E. We immediately wore ship to the W. and made all sail, it then blowing fresh, and used every exertion to get clear by throwing overboard our anchors, part of our guns, and starting water in the hold; all which proved fruitless. At half past 12, after a chase of six hours, the *Shannon* came within half gun-shot; when we had no alternative but to strike our colors to a force so superior to ours. The officers and crew behaved like men, and would not have submitted but to a greatly superior force. Great praises are due to Capt. Crane for his officer and seamanlike conduct; and the lieutenants and other officers merit the attention of a grateful country.

Since we have been prisoners we have been treated with the utmost politeness and humanity by the officers of this ship. We have every indulgence which we could expect, and can hardly realize that we are prisoners. We expect in a few days to be sent to Halifax, to remain until we are exchanged, which we hope will be soon, and that in the mean time our country will not forget us.   I am, &c

---

ESSEX AND ALERT.

LETTER FROM CAPT. PORTER OF THE ESSEX FRIGATE TO THE SECRETARY OF THE NAVY.

SIR,   *At sea, Aug.* 17, 1812.
   I have the honor to inform you, that on the 13th his Britannic Majesty's sloop of war *Alert*, Capt. T. L. P. Laugharne, ran down on our weather quarter, gave three cheers, and commenced an action (if so trifling a skirmish deserves the name) and after eight minutes firing struck her colors, with seven feet water in her hold, much cut to pieces, and 3 men wounded.
   I need not inform you that the officers and crew of the *Essex* behaved as I trust all Americans will in such cases, and it is only to be regretted, that so much zeal and activity could not have been displayed on an occasion that would have done them more honor. The *Essex* has not received the slightest injury.
   The *Alert* was out for the purpose of taking the *Hornet !*
   I have the honor to be with great respect,
                           your obedient servant,
Hon. PAUL HAMILTON,   D. PORTER.
   Sec'y of the navy.
   The *Alert* mounted twenty 18lb. carronades, [rated in Steel's list 16] and had 130 men.

SIR,   *At sea, Aug.* 20, 1812.
   Finding myself much embarrassed by the *Alert* from the great number of prisoners we have already made (about 500) I concluded that before our arrival in America the number would be considerably augmented, and as I found my provisions and water getting short, and being well satisfied that a plan had been

organized by them for rising on the ship in the event of an engagement ; I considered it to be for the interest of my country to get clear of them as speedily as possible, particularly as I was well assured that immediately on their arrival at St. Johns, an equal number of my countrymen would be released and find a sure and immediate conveyance. I therefore drew up written stipulations corresponding with the accompanying letters ; threw all the guns of the *Alert* overboard ; withdrew from her all the men belonging to the *Essex ;* appointed Lieut. J. P. Wilmer to command her as a cartel, put all my prisoners on board her, and despatched her for St. Johns, in Newfoundland, with orders to proceed from thence to New-York with such Americans as he may receive in exchange.

At a more suitable opportunity I shall do myself the honor to lay before you copies of every paper relative to this transaction, and sincerely hope that my conduct in this affair may meet with your approbation.

As the *Essex* has been so annoying about Bermuda, Nova Scotia, and Newfoundland, I expect I shall have to run the gauntlet through their cruisers ; you may however rest assured, that all a ship of her size can do shall be done, and whatever may be our fate our country shall never blush for us.

I have the honor to be, &c.

Hon. PAUL HAMILTON,   D. PORTER.
   Sec'y of navy.

We are obliged to omit the correspondence between Captains Porter and Laugharne, in which it was finally agreed that the *Alert*, after being disarmed, should go to Newfoundland, as a cartel, with the British prisoners. The *Alert* afterwards returned to New York with American prisoners.

EXTRACT OF A LETTER FROM ADMIRAL DUCKWORTH TO THE SECRETARY OF THE NAVY.

St. Johns, Newfoundland, Aug. 31, 1812.

A vessel captured as the *Alert* has been, could not have been vested with the character of a cartel, until she had entered a port of the nation by which she had been captured, and been regularly fitted out from thence. For every prize might otherwise be provided with a flag of truce, and proposals for an exchange of prisoners; and rendered thus effectually secure against the possibility of recapture; while the cruising ship would be enabled to keep at sea with an undiminished crew; the cartels being always navigated by the prisoners of war.

It is utterly inconsistant with the laws of war to recognise the principle upon which this arrangement has been made.

Nevertheless I am willing to give a proof at once of my respect for the liberality which the captain of the *Essex* has acted, in more than one instance, towards the British subjects who have fallen into his hands; of the sacred obligation that is always felt, to fulfil the engagements of a British officer; and of my confidence in the disposition of his royal highness the Prince Regent, to allay the violence of war by encouraging a reciprocation of that courtesy by which its pressure upon individuals may be so essentially diminished.

On the 4th of this month, a midshipman of the *Essex* arrived, and presented to me a letter from his captain, proposing an exchange for 86 British prisoners. The midshipman had however been placed alone in the charge of one of the captured vessels, with 86 prisoners, to conduct them to this port. A list of 40 prisoners of the same description, disposed of in the same manner, has been sent to me by the commander of the American private armed schooner the *Rossie.*

It is incumbant upon me to protest in the strongest manner against the practice of conducting exchanges upon terms like these; and so signify, to you that it will be utterly impossible for me to incur, in future, the responsibility of assenting to them.

WASP AND FROLIC.

The capture of the *Frolic*, by the *Wasp* has been already given. See. page 14. After Capt. Jones had manned his prize, the *Wasp* and the *Frolic* had the misfortune to fall in with the *Poictiers* 74, Capt. Beresford, and both were captured and sent to Bermuda. Lieut. James Biddle was on board the *Wasp* as a volunteer, and has briefly narrated the occurrence in the following letter to his father.

His Britannic Majesty's Ship Poictiers 74, at sea,
MY DEAR FATHER, *Oct.* 21, 1812.

The fortune of war has placed us in the hand of the enemy. We have been captured by this ship, after having ourselves captured his Britannic majesty's brig *Frolic*,

The *Frolic* was superior in force to us ; she mounted eighteen 32lb carronades, and two long 9s. The *Wasp* you know has only 16 carronades. The action lasted 43 minutes; we had 5 killed, and the slaughter on board the *Frolic* was dreadful. We are bound into Bermuda. I am quite unhurt.

In haste, &c. J. BIDDLE

A court of inquiry, convened to investigate the conduct of Capt. Jones in surrendering the *Wasp*, gave the following opinion, which was approved by the secretary of the navy.

"The court, having heard the statement and evidence in this case, and having maturely considered the circumstances attending the surrender of the U. S. ship *Wasp*, of 16 guns, to his Britannic majesty,s ship of the line, the *Poictiers*, of 74 guns; particularly the crippled and disabled state of the *Wasp* from the brilliant and successful action with his Britannic majesty's ship the *Frolic*, of superior force to the *Wasp* about two hours before the *Poictiers* hove in sight, and the force and condition of the *Poictiers*, which made it useless for them to contend, and rendered them unable to escape, are unanimously of opinion, that there was no impropriety of conduct on the part of the officers and crew of the said ship *Wasp* during the chase by the *Poictiers*, or in the surrender; but that the conduct of the officers and crew of the *Wasp* on said occasion was eminently distinguished for firmness and gallantry, in making every preparation and exertion, of which their situation would admit."

VIXEN.

THE United States brig *Vixen*, Cap. Reed, was captured in November 1812, by the *Southampton* 32, commanded by Sir James Lucas Yeo, after a chase of nine hours. Both vessels were afterwards totally lost on the island of Conception (Bahama,) but the crews were saved and carried to Nassau.

COPY OF A LETTER FROM CAPT. SIR JAMES LUCAS YEO, OF HIS MAJESTY'S SHIP SOUTHAMPTON, TO VICE ADMIRAL STIRLING.

His Majesty's Ship Southampton, at sea,
SIR,   *Nov. 22, 1812.*

His Majesty's ship under my command, this day captured the United States brig *Vixen*, Capt. George Reed, mounting twelve 18 pounders, carronades, two long 9s, and 130 men. She had been out five weeks, and I am happy to say, had not made any capture.

I have, &c.
JAMES LUCAS YEO, *Capt.*
CHARLES STIRLING, Esq.
Vice Admiral of the white &c.

CAPTURE OF THE SWALLOW.

EXTRACT OF A LETTER FROM COM. RODGERS TO THE SECRETARY OF THE NAVY.

United States Frigate President, at sea,
SIR,   *October, 17, 1812.*

I have the honor to acquaint you that on the 15th inst. near the Grand Bank, this ship, the *Congress* in

company, captured the British king's packet *Swallow*,
Joseph Morphew commander, bound from Kingston,
Jamaica, to Falmouth.   The rank of the commander
of this vessel is that of a master and commander in
the navy.   She had no cargo on board except twenty
boxes of gold and silver, amounting to between one
hundred and fifty and two hundred thousand dollars.
The specie I took out of her, and had intended sending her to England in the character of a cartel with
her own crew ; but having fallen in with the American
schooner *Eleanor*, bound from Baltimore to France,
dismasted, induced me to change my determination.

With the greatest respect, &c.

JOHN RODGERS.

The *President* and *Congress* arrived at Boston on
the 31st of December, after an active cruise of between 80 and 90 days.   The *President* brought in
about 50 prisoners.   The cash taken from the packet
Swallow was carried to the bank from the navy yard,
with drums beating, and colours flying, in several
waggons, escorted by a part of the crews of the frigates, and a detachment of marines, amidst the huzzas
of a large concourse of spectators.   The specie and
gold dust deposited amounted to nearly three hundred
thousand dollars.

Richard Moss, quarter-master-gunner, died on board
the *President*, Oct. 16.   A few hours before his death,
he informed Com. Rodgers, that he had a wife and
three children in Boston, dependent on him for support ; and expressed considerable anxiety for them,
knowing he had but little time to live.   Soon after his
death, at the suggestion of Com. Rodgers, a subscription paper was opened, which he headed, and was
handed through the ship to the officers and crew for
subscription, when upwards of seven hundred dollars
were immediately subscribed by the generous officers
and tars, for the relief of the widow and children.

ESCAPE OF THE ARGUS.

THE nautical skill of the officers of our navy has often been acknowledged by the British. The following instance cannot but gratify the friends of the navy and of the officer who conducted the escape.

The United States brig *Argus*, Capt. Sinclair, sailed from Boston in company with the *United States*. After parting with her consort, she proceeded to the coast of Brazil, down the north coast of the country from St. Roquo to Surrinam; thence she passed to the windward of the island, and in every direction between the Bermudas, Halifax, and the continent. She arrived at New-York in the month of December, after a cruise of 96 days, having made five prizes, valued at $200,000. During her cruise she fell in with a squadron of the enemy, consisting of six sail, two of which were of the line, one of them a remarkably fast sailer. The favor of the moon enabled them to chase by night as well as in the day, the chase was continued for three days, without intermission, and under various circumstances, but the unremitted exertions of his officers and crew enabled him to elude the pursuit. Pressed on all sides by the number of the enemy, and the baffling and unsettled state of the weather, the *Argus* was at one time within musket shot of a 74, and at another surrounded. The determined vigilance of Capt. Sinclair rescued her from the difficulty. They had joined in the chase an armed transport, with a view no doubt of destracting the attention and deceiving the chase, which being discovery, he bore down upon her, and compelled her to clear the way. Such was the confidence of Capt. Sinclair in the sailing of the *Argus*, that during the chase, although at one time so closely pressed as to be compelled to lighten his vessel, by throwing over his spare anchors and spars and deck boats, and starting the salt water with which his casks had been filled as the fresh had been used, and reduced to the last necessity of wetting his sails; yet did he preserve all his guns,

28

and one night, during the chase, he found time to capture, man, and despatch a prize.   So close were they
upon him, that when he again made sail, two of the
ships opened their batteries upon him.

NAVAL ANECDOTE.

On board the *United States*, Capt. Decatur, was
a little boy, about nine years old.   He was not considered one of the regular crew ; but he shared the
mess of a generous sailor, who had, two years before,
taken him from his widowed mother.   The spirit of
his father, who had also been a seaman, had long since
gone aloft, and left his wife and little ones on the
shoals of poverty.

When the *Macedonian* hove in sight, and all hands
were clearing ship for action, the little fellow stepped
up to Com. Decatur,—"And it please you, Captain,"
said he, " I wish my name might be put down on the
roll."—"And what for my lad ?"—inquired the commodore.   " So that I can draw a share of the prize
money, sir," answered he.   Pleased with the spirit
and confident courage of the little hero, his name was
ordered on the list ; but the moment was to important
to say more.

After the prize was taken, Decatur thought of the
little sailor boy, and called him up—" Well, Bill,"
said he, " we have taken her, and your share of the
prize, if we get her safe in, may be about two hundred dollars ; what will you do with it ?"—"I'll send
one half to my mother, sir, and the other half shall
send me to school."   " That's noble," cried the commodore, delighted with the spirit of the lad, took him
under his immediate protection, and obtained for him
the birth of a midshipman.   Every attention has been
paid to his education, and he gives great promise of
making an accomplished officer.

EXTRACT OF A PRIVATE LETTER FROM COM. BAINBRIDGE.

At sea, January 24, 1813.

" The *Java* was exceedingly well fought and bravely defended. Poor Lambert, whose death I sincerely regret, was a distinguished, gallant officer, and worthy man. He has left a widow and two helpless children ! But his country makes provision for such events.

" We are now homeward bound. The damage the *Constitution* received in the action, and the decayed state she is in makes it necessary for me to return to the United States for repairs ; this I much regret ; my crew participate in this sentiment ; they are however consoling themselves with the hope of receiving their prize money. One says, he will buy himself a snug little ship on the highest hill he can find, that he may thence, in his old age, view all our sea-fights. Another, that now he will marry his Poll—another, that he will send his little Jack to school, &c.

" Poor fellows, I trust they will not be disappointed in their expectations. Twice have they willingly and gallantly encountered the enemy, and twice have they succeeded. To return home now, and find they have nothing but a remnant of pay coming to them, would be extremely mortifying. It would inevitably depress their spirits, and damp that noble ardor which they have hitherto felt and displayed. The officer may feel differently. For the performance of his duty he feels a reward in his own bosom, and in his country's thanks. Patriotism and a laudable thirst for renown, will lead *him* to court perils in defence of his country's rights. These feelings operate upon the sailor also : but to keep up the high tone of his ardor, he must have prize money in view.

True policy, in my humble opinion, dictates the destruction of the enemy's ships after capture ; for by manning them, even if they are left in a managable situation, our ships would be so weakened in their crews, that they would be liable to be captured by an equal, or insulted by an inferior force. The act of destruction is done by the command of the captain only—the crew who have exposed their lives equally with him, have not the right of opposition. When I ordered the *Java* to be destroyed, these considerations presented themselves to my mind with great force.—Surely justice and sound policy obviously recommend a liberal provision in their favor. In making these observations I am not influenced by any selfish motive. The applause of my countrymen has for me greater charms than all the gold that glitters. But justice to those who have bravely fought under my command, and assisted me in gaining this victory, requires at my hands an exertion in their behalf; and should it please heaven to conduct us safe to our native shores, I shall not fail to use my best endeavors, solemnly believing, as I do, that the principle is all important to the continued success of our navy. For if it is, as I hold it, the indispensable duty of the commander to destroy the capture on account of the gauntlet he would have to run with both the prize and his own ship (except he should be very near one of our own ports) and the captain to receive (which is almost always the case) all the honor, and the others no compensation—is it not natural to suppose, that the ardent desire which our seamen, at present, so strongly manifest, to get into battle, would diminish ? Let that once take place, and your naval fights will not, I prophecy, be so decisive as they would be by keeping the ardor up. And how trifling an expense the compensations would be in a national view ! The schooner that I am now despatching (a prize to the *Hornet*) will give to the public treasury upwards of one hundred thousand dollars.

In the month of February, the letter-of-marque schooner *Lottery*, Capt. Southcomb, of Baltimore, outward bound, was taken in the Chesapeake, by nine large boats, heavily armed, and having 240 men, after a gallant fight of an hour and a half. The *Lottery* carried 6 guns and had about 35 men.

The following correspondence relates to Capt. Southcomb.

Sir, *U. S. Frigate Constellation Feb.* 16, 1813.

At the solicitation of Capt. Southcomb's friends, I sent a flag down to the squadron of the enemy in Lynnhaven roads, to bring him and his two wounded men up to Norfolk where their situation could be rendered more comfortable.

Enclosed you will receive a copy of Capt. Byron's note to Capt. Gould on the subject, and also copies of my letter to Capt. Byron and his answer. The cartel returned last evening with the body of Capt. Southcomb ; he was wounded in five places, gallantly defending his vessel against a number of armed boats.

While such instances of bravery cannot but inspire the enemy with respect for the American character, I trust this instance, among many others of the humanity and generosity of Capt. Byron, will not be forgotten by our countrymen.

I have the honor to be, &c.

Hon. W. Jones, &c. CHARLES STEWART.

Sir, *February* 11, 1813.

I am glad in being able to get the little box of China for Mrs. Gould. Rest assured of every attention being paid to the unfortunate Capt. John Southcomb and his two wounded men. Whatever vessel comes for them shall be treated with due respect, for which I have the senior captain's authority.

I am your humble servant,

Capt. Gould. R. BYRON.

U. S. Frigate Constellation, Norfolk harbour,
Sir, *February* 13, 1813.

Capt. Gould has handed me a note you addressed to him of the 11th inst. in which you state, "by authority of the senior captain of his Britannic Majesty's squadron in Lynnhaven bay, that Captain Southcomb, and his two wounded men, will be delivered to any vessel that may come for them."

I send a flag down to you for the purpose of receiving those unfortunate men, and avail myself of this opportunity to thank you for your attention and humanity to the unfortunate.

I have the honor to be, &c.
CHARLES STEWART.
Capt. RICHARD BYRON, &c.

Belvidera, Lynnhaven anchorage,
SIR,   *February 13, 1813.*

I received your letter of this morning by Dr. Ray: it is with extreme concern I acquaint you, that the unfortunate and gallant Capt. Southcomb expired this morning. It will be satisfactory in some degree to his widow, to know, he had a truly religious sense of his situation, latterly delirious, without the excess of pain that might have been expected. Capt. Gould and his steward have charge of his effects. His body will be placed in the cartel so soon as the coffin can be prepared. The two wounded men at their own request went up in the former cartel, which I am sorry to hear got on shore. I am extremely flattered with the part of your letter, thanking me for attention and humanity to the unfortunate, which gives me the most perfect assurance of the generous feelings of Capt. Charles Stewart.

I have the honor to be, &c.
Capt. C. SEWART, &c.   R. BYRON.

––––

GENEROSITY.

By the humanity of Capt. Smith the officers and crew of the *Congress* frigate, lying in Boston harbour, a subscription of one hundred and fifty dollars was raised and presented to Richard Dunn, who lost his leg in bravely fighting for "free trade and sailors, rights," on board the *Constitution*, in her engagement with the British frigate *Guerriere*.

Heroism—A Card.

R. Dunn takes this method publicly to acknowledge the receipt of the above subscription, and to present his *hearty* thanks to Capt. Smith, his officers and crew, for their kind remembrance of him. He would also assure them, that *though he has lost* ONE LEG, *he is willing to fight on* THE OTHER *for the liberty of his enslaved brethren, and the honor of his country.*

March, 1813.

COM. DECATUR'S SQUADRON.

On the 11th of June, Com. Decatur and his squadron attempted to go to sea from New York, but were prevented by two 74s and a frigate, and driven into the harbour of New London, where they were blockaded until the close of the war, except the *Hornet*, which made her escape in Nov. 1814. The American squadron consisted of the *United States* 44 *Macedonian* 38, and *Hornet* 16.

REVENUE CUTTER SURVEYOR.

THE Baltimore Revenue Cutter *Surveyor* was captured by the barges of the *Narcisus* frigate, in York river, on the night of the 12th of June. The enemy was discovered when about 150 yards distant. Capt. Travis could not bring his guns to bear, and therefore furnished each of his men with two muskets. They held their fire until the British were within pistol shot; but the enemy pushed on and finally carried the vessel by boarding, with 3 men killed and a number wounded. Capt. Travis and his crew, 15 in number, were all taken on board the *Junon*, and the next day the senior officer of the *Narcissus* returned the captain his sword, with the following complimentary letter.

SIR, *His Majesty's Ship Narcissus, June* 13, 1813.

Your gallant and desperate attempt to defend your vessel against more than double your number, on the night of the 12th inst. excited such admiration on the part of your opponents, as I have seldom witnessed, and induced me to return you the sword you had so nobly used, in testimony of mine. Our poor fellows have severely suffered, occasioned chiefly, if not solely, by the precaution you had taken to prevent surprise; in short, I am at a loss which to admire most, the previous engagement on board the *Surveyor*, or the determined manner by which her deck was disputed, inch by inch.

I am, sir, with much respect, &c.
Capt. S. TRAVIS, JOHN CRERIE.
U. S. Cutter Surveyor.

ATTACK ON A BRITISH SQUADRON BY A FLOTILLA OF GUN-BOATS.

LETTER FROM COM. JOHN CASSIN TO THE SECRETARY OF THE NAVY.

SIR, *Navy Yard, Gosport, June* 21, 1813.

On Saturday at 11 P. M. Capt. Tarbell moved with the flotilla under his command, consisting of 15 gun-boats, in two divisions, Lieut. John M. Gardner 1st division, and Lieut. Robert Henley the 2d—manned from the frigate, and 50 musketeers, ordered from Craney Island by Gen. Taylor, and proceeded down the river; but adverse winds and squalls prevented his approaching the enemy until Sunday morning at 4, when the flotilla commenced a heavy galling fire on a frigate, at about three quarters of a mile distance, lying well up the roads—two other frigates lying in sight. At half past 4, a breeze sprung up from E. N. E. which enabled the two frigates to get under way—one a razee or very heavy ship, and the other a frigate—and to come nearer into action. The boats, in consequence of their approach, hauled off, though keeping up a well directed fire on the razee and the other ship, which gave us several broadsides. The frigate first engaged, supposed to be the *Junon*, was certainly severely handled—had the calm continued one half hour, that frigate must have fallen into our hands, or been destroyed. She must have slipped her mooring so as to drop nearer the razee, who had all sail set, coming up to her with the other frigate. The action continued one hour and a half with three ships. Shortly after the action, the razee got along side of the ship, and had her upon a deep careen in a little time, with a number of boats and stages round her. I am satisfied considerable damage was done to her, for she was silenced some time, until the razee opened her fire, when she commenced again. Our loss is very trifling. Mr. Allison, master's mate, on board 139, was killed early in the action, by an 18lb. ball, which passed through him and lodged in the mast. No. 154 had a shot between wind and water. No. 67 had her franklin shot away, and several of them had some of their sweeps and their stuncheons shot away —but two men slightly injured from the sweeps. On the flood tide several ships of the line and frigates came into the roads, and we did expect an attack last night. There are now in the roads 13 ships of the line and frigates, one brig and several tenders.

I cannot say too much for the officers and crews on this occasion; for every man appeared to go into action with so much cheerfulness, apparently to do their duty, resolved to conquer. I had a better opportunity of discovering their actions than any one else, being in my boat the whole of the action.

I have the honor to be, &c.

Hon. W. JONES, &c.   JOHN CASSIN.

29

LOSS OF THE ASP.

COPY OF A LETTER FROM MIDSHIPMAN M'CLINTOCK TO THE SECRETARY OF THE NAVY.

SIR,   *Kinsale, Virginia, July* 13, 1813.

I HAVE to inform you of the unfortunate event which occurred here on the 14th; the action between the British barges and the United States schooner *Asp,* commanded by Mr. Segourney. At 9 A. M. the *Scorpion* and *Asp* got under way from Yeocomico river and stood out. At 10, discovered a number of sail, which proved to be the enemy; the *Scorpion* then made signal to act at discretion, and stood up the river; the schooner being a bad sailer and the wind ahead, we were not able to get out. Finding the enemy approaching us, we thought it best to return. Immediately two of the brigs stood towards us, and anchored a short distance from the bar, where they manned their boats. Mr. Segourney thought it would be for our advantage to run further up the creek, which we did, but finding the enemy had left their vessels, we had not time to weigh anchor, therefore we were obliged to cut our cables. We were attacked by three boats, well manned and armed; we continued a well directed fire on them, and after a short time they were compelled to retreat, and obtain a reinforcement. About an hour after they retired, we were attacked by five boats; we continued doing the same as before, but having so few men, we were unable to repel the enemy. When they boarded us, they refused giving us any quarter. There were upwards of 50 men on our decks, which compelled us to leave the vessel, as the enemy had possession. They put her on fire and retreated. A short time after they left her, we went on board, and with much difficulty extinguished the flames. But it is with deep regret that I inform you of the death of Mr. Segourney, who fought most gallantly in defence of the vessel; and the utmost exertion was used by every man on board. Our crew consisted only of 21. There are ten killed, wounded and missing.

Your obedient servant,

Hon. W. Jones,   H. M. M'CLINTOCK,
Sec'y of navy.   *Midshipman in the U. S. navy.*

VIPER.

THE United States brig *Viper*, 14 guns, commanded by Lieut. Henley, was captured by the British frigate *Narcissus*. The customary court of inquiry was held in June on the conduct of Lieut. Henley. He was honorably acquitted, as having done all in his power to escape a superior force. The court gave the same opinion respecting the conduct of Cap. Reed, late commander of the *Vixen*—See page 217.

The *Viper* was captured Jan. 1813.

REPULSE OF THE BRITISH AT CRANEY ISLAND.

Extract of a letter from Com. Cassin to the Sec'ry of the navy.

SIR,   *Navy Yard, Gosport, June 23, 1813.*

I have the honor to inform you, that on the 20th the enemy got under way, in all 13 sail, and dropped up to the mouth of James' river, one ship bearing a flag at mizen. At 5, P. M. they were discovered making great preparations with troops for landing, having a number of boats for the purpose. Finding Craney island rather weakly manned, Capt. Tarbell directed Lieuts. Neal, Shubrick, and Sanders, with 100 seamen, on shore, at 11, P. M. to a small battery on the N. W. side of the Island.

Tuesday 22d, at dawn, the enemy were discovered landing round the point of Nansemond river; at 8 A. M. the barges attempted to land in front, of the island, out of reach of the shot from the gun-boats, when Lieuts. Neal, Shubrick, and Sanders with the sailors, and Lieut. Breckenridge with the marines of the *Constellation*, 150 in number, opened the fire which was so well directed, that the enemy were. glad to get off, after sinking three of their largest boats. One of them called the *Centepede*. Admiral Warren's boat, 50 feet in length, carried 75 men, the greater part of whom were lost by her sinking. Twenty soldiers and sailors were saved, and the boat hauled up.

The officers of the *Constellation* fired their 18 pounder more like riflemen than artillerists. I never saw such shooting, and seriously believe they saved the island.

I have the honor to be, &c.
Hon. W. JONES, &c.   JOHN CASSIN.

The number of the enemy engaged in the attack was nearly 3000.

On the 25th of June the British, about 2500, attacked and took possession of the town of Hampton, after a brave resistance, by 400 Americans, under the command of Maj. Crutchfield. The atrocities of the enemy at this place are well known.

SCHOONER EAGLE.

New York, June 27, 1813.

The schooner *Eagle*, which sailed from this port on the 15th, was taken by the enemy's barges at New London on the 25th. Owing to adverse winds the enemy were unable to tow the schooner along side of the squadron. While the enemy were attempting to take out the cargo, an explosion took place, which killed a considerable number of the enemy. One barge first approached to capture the *Eagle*, but she was beat off. Three others came, and the schooner was abandoned by the crew. The cask, containing

the powder had a lock, with which was connected a
string, that was fastened to some of the articles of
spoil the enemy moved. The explosion took place by
their means, and immediately the schooner and barges
disappeared!

A fishing vessel arrived at Salem with the following
endorsement on her papers.

"His Majesty's Ship La Houge, at sea,
July 8, 1812.

" I have warned the fishing boat *Sally,* of Barnsta-
ble, immediately to proceed to her own coast, in consequence of the depredations committed by the *Young
Teazer,* and other American privateers, on the British
and coasting vessels belonging to Nova Scotia; but
more particularly from the inhuman and savage proceedings of causing the American schooner *Eagle* to
be blown up after she had been taken possession of by
His Majesty's ship *Ramilies*--an act not to be justified
on the most barbarous principles of warfare.—I have
directed His Britannic Majesty's cruisers on the coast
to destroy every description of American vessels they
may fall in with, flags of truce only excepted. Given
under my hand.

" **THOMAS B. CAPEL,** *Capt.*"

EAGLE.

**LETTER FROM COM. LEWIS TO THE SECRETARY OF THE
NAVY.**

SIR,   *Off Sandy Hook July 6, 1813.*

I have the pleasure to inform you of the capture of
the British sloop tender *Eagle,* which for some time
had been employed, by Com. Beresford, for the purpose of burning the coasters, &c. Her force was two
officers and 11 men, with a 32lb. brass howitzer. This
service was performed in the most gallant and officer
like manner by Sailing Master Percival, who with volunteers from the flotilla, which I have the honor to

command, jumped on board a fishing smack, ran along side the enemy ; and carried him by a *coup de main.* I am sorry to add, that in this little affair the enemy lost the commanding officer, one midshipman mortally wounded, and two seamen badly. I am happy to say, we suffered no injury which is to be attributed to the superior management of Sailing Master Percival, and the coolness with which his men fired ; for which they all deserve well of their country.

I have the honor to be, &c.

Hon. WILLIAM JONES, &c.   J. LEWIS.

P. S. The capture was on Sunday the 4th inst.

FURTHER PARTICULARS.

The fishing smack, named the *Yankee,* was borrowed of some fishermen at Fly Market, in the city of New York, and a calf, a sheep, and a goose purchased, and secured on deck. Between 30 and 40 men, well armed with muskets, were secreted in the cabin and forepeake of the smack. Thus prepared, she stood out to sea, as if going on a fishing trip to the banks, three men only being on deck, dressed in fishemen's apparel, with buff caps on. The *Eagle,* on perceiving the smack, immediately gave chase, and after coming up with her, and finding she had live stock on deck, ordered her to go down to the commodore, then about five miles distant. The helsman answered, aye, aye, Sir, and apparantly put up the helm for the purpose, which brought him along side of the *Eagle,* not more than three yards distant. The watch-word *Lawrence* was then given, when the armed men rushed on deck from their hiding places, and poured into her a volley of musketry, which struck the crew with dismay, and drove them all down so precipitately into the hold of the vessel, that they had not time to strike their colors. The *Eagle,* with the prisoners, was carried to the city and landed at Whitehall, amidst the shouts and plaudits of thousands of spectators, assembled on the battery, celebrating the 4th of July.

Henry Morris, commander of the *Eagle,* was buried

at Sandy Hook with military honors, and in the most respectful manner. Mr. Price who died soon after, was buried in Trinity Church yard, with every testimony of regard.

TORPEDO.

Mr. E. Mix of the navy, a gentleman of ingenuity and enterprise, constructed a torpedo for the purpose of destroying some of the enemy's shipping in Lynnhaven bay. The British 74 gun ship *Plantagenet*, which for some months had been lying abreast of Cape Henry light house, appeared to Mr. Mix, as the most favorable object on which to try his experiment. Accordingly, on the night of the 18th, and the four following, accompanied by Capt. Bowman of Salem and Midshipman M'Gowan, of the U. S. navy, he made the attempt, which proved fruitless, in consequence of being discovered by the enemy, who, suspecting some mischief, changed her position every night. On the night of the 24th however, Mr. Mix succeeded in finding her out, and having taken his position 100 yards distance, in a direction with her larboard bow, he dropped the fatal machine into the water just as the centinel was crying *all's well.* It was swept along with the tide, and very nearly effected its purpose. It exploded a few seconds too soon.

The scene was awfully sublime. It was like the concussion of an earthquake, attended with a sound louder and more terrific than the heaviest peal of thunder. A pyramid of water, 50 feet in circumference, was thrown up 40 or 50 feet ; its appearance was a vivid red, tinged at the sides with beautiful purple. On ascending to its greatest height it burst at the top with a tremendous explosion, and fell in torrents on the deck of the ship, which rolled into the chasm and nearly upset. The light, occasioned by the explosion, though fleeting, enabled Mr. Mix and his companions to discover, that the fore-channel of the ship was blown off, and a boat, which lay along side with several men in her was thrown up in the convulsion.

EXPLOIT AT GARDNERS ISLAND.

On the evening of the 28th of July, two boats from the *Macedonian* and two from the *United States*, under Lieut. Gallager, made an excursion into the sound. In the night a small boat, under the direction of Midshipman Ten Eyke, being separated by a strong wind and tide from the others, landed on Gardner's Island. In the morning, finding themselves under the guns of the *Ramilies*, the boat was hauled ashore. Soon after a boat came ashore from the *Ramilies* and the officers went to a dwelling house. Midshipman Ten Eyke seized the favorable moment, made prisoners of those who were left with the English boat, and then with two men proceeded to the house, where he took two lieutenants, making in all, prisoners of two lieutenants one midshipman, one master's mate, and five seamen. Finding they were discovered by the *Ramilies*, the captives were parolled, and Mr. Ten Eyke and crew made their escape to Long Island. The succeeding night the other boat took them off.

DELAWARE FLOTILLA.—LOSS OF GUN-BOAT NO. 121.

Extract of a letter from Lieut. Angus, commanding the U. S. Delaware flotilla, to the Secr'y of the navy.

SIR,   *Cape May, July 29, 1813.*

Lying off Dennes' creek this morning, I discovered, that an enemy's sloop of war had chased a small vessel, and taken her near the overfalls. I immediately got under way, and stood down the bay. The sloop of war stood so near the overfalls, that she grounded slightly on the outer ridge of Crow's shoals. I thought proper to endeavor to bring him to action. I succeeded, and got within three quarters of a mile, and anchored the boats (consisting of 8 gun-boats and two black ships) in a line ahead. A heavy frigate had by this time anchored about half a mile further out. After a cannonade of 1 hour and 45 minutes, in which the ships kept up a constant and heavy fire, heaving their shot from a half to three quarters of a mile over us, they doing us but little damage; the sloop of war and frigate, finding our shot to tell on their hulls, manned their boats, ten in number, (2 launches, the rest large barges and cutters,) with from 30 to 40 men in each, and despatched them after gun-boat No. 121, Sailing Master Shed, which had unfortunately fell a mile and a half out of the line, although it had been my positive and express orders to anchor at half cable length apart, and not further. From the strong ebb tide they succeeded in capturing her, after a gallant resistance,) for three times did No. 121 discharge her long gun, apparently full of canister, among the whole line of boats, when at a very short distance, which must have done execution, and not till after she was boarded, did the colors come down, before any assistance could be given her. However, we got near enough to destroy 3 or 4 of their boats, and must have killed a vast number of men. It being a calm, they succeeded in getting her away by sending all their boats ahead and towing her; but they have paid dear for their temerity. They must at least have had one third of their men killed and wounded. I am happy to say, that not a man was wounded in any of our boats, except the one captured, whose fate I have not yet learnt. I feel much indebted to Lieut. Mitchel, and officers commanding gun-boats, for their spirited conduct in carrying into execution my orders; and if I may judge from the gallant resistance, made by Sailing Master Shed, in engaging when surrounded by the boats of the enemy, that every officer and man of the flotilla will do his duty in all situations.

I have the honor to be, &c.

Hon. W. Jones, &c. SAMUEL ANGUS.

30

From Lieut. Shed's official letter it appears, that 7 of our men were wounded, 5 slightly. The loss of the enemy was 7 killed and 12 wounded.

COM. RODGER'S CRUISE.

On the 26th of September, the U. S. frigate *President*, Com. Rodgers, arrived in the harbour of Newport, after a cruise of more than five months. This ship left Boston on the 30th of April, in company with the U. S. frigate *Congress* from · which she separated on the 30th of the same month. She pursued her course to the Grand Bank, the Azores, Shetland isles, and to North Bergen, where she put in for water. She left this place on the 2d of July, shaped her course towards the orkney Islands, and from thence to the north seas. July 19th off North cape, White sea, was chased 86 hours by 2 line-of-battle ships, took a circuit round Ireland, got into the latitude of Cape Clear, proceeded to the Grand Banks, and from thence to the United States.

The following is the concluding part of the commodore's official account.

"During my cruise, although I have not had it in my power to add any additional lustre to the character of our little navy, I have nevertheless rendered essential service to my country, I hope, by harassing the enemy's commerce, and employing to his disadvantage more than a dozen times the force of a single frigate.

" My officers and crew have experienced great privations since I left the United States, from being nearly five months at sea, and living the last three months of that time upon a scanty allowance of the roughest fare ; and it is with peculiar pleasure that I acquaint you, that they are all in better health than might be expected, although you may well suppose that their scanty allowance has not been of any advantage to their strength 'or appearance.

"The *High Flyer* was commanded by Lieut. Hutchinson, second of the *St. Domingo.* She is a remarkably fine vessel of her class, sails very fast, and would make an excellent light cruiser, provided the government have occasion for a vessel of her description.

"Just at the moment of closing my letter, a newspaper has been handed me, containing Capt. Broke's challenge to my late gallant friend, Capt. Lawrence, in which he mentions, with considerable emphasis, the pains he had taken to meet the *President* and *Congress,* with the *Shannon* and *Tenedos.*

"It is unnecessary at present to take further notice of Capt. Brokes observations, than to say, if that was his dispostion, his conduct was so glaringly opposite, as to authorize a very contrary belief. Relative to Capt. Broke, I have only further to say, that I hope he has not been so severely wounded as to make it a sufficient reason to prevent his reasumming the command of the *Shannon* at a future day."

Here follow the names of 11 merchantmen, and the *High Flyer* schooner of 5 guns, captured during his cruise.

The capture of the schooner *High Flyer*, of 5 guns, by Com Rodgers, was very extreordinary. On making the schooner to the southward of Nantucket Shoals, she hoisted the private British signal, which was answered by Com. Rodgers, and fortunately proved the private British signal of that day. Upon seing this, the *High Flyer* came immediately to him. Com. Rodgers ordered one of his officers to dress in a British uniform, and manned out a boat and boarded him. The lieutenant of the schooner did not wait to be boarded, but manned his own boat and boarded the *President*, supposing her to be a British frigate. The British Lieut. was on board for some time, before he discovered his mistake. The officer, that boarded the schooner from the *President,* asked the officer left in charge of the schooner for his private signals and instructions, which were immediately handed to him; by this stratagem, Com. Rodgers has obtained possession of the British private signals, and Ad. Warren's instructions. On examining Ad. Warrens, instructions, Com. Rodgers discovered the number of British squadrons, stationed on the American coast, their force, and relative position—with pointed instructions to all of them, if possible to capture the *President*.

CHALLANGE.

Copy of a letter from Lieut. Claxton to his father:
Macedonian, New London, Jan. 19, 1814.

DEAR FATHER,

For the two last days we have been all anxiety; an American captain returned on parole from the *Ramilies* 74, a few days since, and communicated to com. Decatur, a consultation he had with Capt. Hardy, in which the letter said, "that now that two frigates were off, of equal force to the *United States* and *Macedonian*, that he should have no objection to a meeting taking place, but that he could not allow the challange to come from the English commanders." The hint was embraced in a moment, and Capt. Biddle despatched with a challange from our commanders. In the mean time every preparation was made, on our side, for an immediate engagement, which we all suppose, no objection could be made to: the crews of both ships were called together, and addressed by their commanders, who made known to them the substance of the business then on foot; they were answered by three hearty cheers. Capt. Jones concluded his short and pertinent address in the following words, spoken with great modesty: "My lads, our cruise will be short, and, I trust a very profitable one." Capt Biddle went on board the 74; a signal was immediately made for the two commanders of the English frigates, and they went on board. Capt. Hardy addressed them, "gentlemen, here are two letters for you; it rests altogether with you to decide on the matter." Stackpole, of the *Statira*, answered with the greatest affection, "pon honor, sir, it is the most acceptable letter I ever received." The final answer was to be given yesterday. Capt Biddle returned, and related the circumstance as I have mentioned. For myself, I thought from the manner of Stackpole, that he would be first to flinch. I am not able to say that he did; it is enough, that the captain of the *Borer* (sloop of war,) came in yesterday, and made known that they had declined meeting us. This circumstance has made a vast deal of conversation here, much to the credit of our commanders—it will probably be distorted into a hundred different shapes before it is done with; I have therefore given you a correct though brief account of it. The *Endymion* mounts the same weight of metal with the *United States*, and three or four guns more, and the *Statira* is superior to us by one or two guns. The disappointment, is very great with us, for every soul calculated on taking her with ease. You see we must trust altogether to our heals.

Yours affectionately,
A. CLAXTON.

GALLANT DEFENCE OF THE ALLIGATOR.
The following is Mr. Bassett's report.
U. S. Schooner Alligator, Wappo, Jan. 31, 1814.
SIR,

I have the honor to inform you, that the U. S. schooner *Alligator*, under my command, was attacked on the evening of the 29th inst. then lying at anchor in Stono river and abreast of Coles' Island, by six boats from the enemy's squadron, off the mouth of the river, and succeeded in beating them off, after a warm action of 30 mintues. I have to regret on this occasion the loss of 2 men killed and 2 wounded; one of the latter, the pilot Mr. Robert Hatch severely. This brave man fell at the helm, exorting those around him to take good aim at the enemy. I hope his conduct will entitle him to your notice. It is impossible to ascertain what loss the enemy sustained; but from suddenly ceasing their fire from the two large launches, and the other boats joining them immediately, I am induced to believe they suffered severely, as the schooner grounded, and they did not renew the action. The sails and rigging of the schooner are much cut, but no damage sustained in the hull. I cannot conclude without rendering my thanks to the gallant officers and men you did me the honor to place under my command for their meritorious conduct, which alone prevented the schooner from falling into the hands of an enemy of more then treble our number.

J. H. DENT, Esq.   R. BASSETT.

Capt. Dent in communicating this report says, great credit is due to Sailing Master Bassett, his officers and crew, for defeating a force so greatly superior in numbers, as there could not have been less than 140 men opposed to 40

LOSS OF THE FERRET.

OFFICIAL ACCOUNT.

SIR,   *Folly-Island, Feb.* 3, 1814.

I AM sorry to acquaint you of the entire loss of the U. S. schooner *Ferret.* This unfortunate circumstance occurred last evening, on the North Breakers of Stony inlet.

I am happy to say, none of her officers or men were lost or injured. They have lost every thing belonging to them, and would suffer much, were it not for the kindness of Mr. Darley and Mr. Heoland, who have rendered many services.

I am making preparations to proceed to the wreck

with a vessel, to save what articles of rigging and sails I can get at. I am in hopes to get some of her guns, which I threw into the hold. Finding the vessel half full of water, I apprehended her drifting out in deep water, should she be lightened, would render our situation more hazardous.

Mr. Brailsford, whom I have sent on with a proportion of my crew, will inform you more particularly of the circumstance which the present haste I am in will not allow me to do, as fully as I could wish.

I have the honor to be,
most respectfully your obe't serv't,
LAWRANCE KEARNEY.
Lieut. Com. U. States schooner Ferret.
Com. J. H. DENT, *Com'g Naval Officer, Charleston.*

CRUISE OF THE PRESIDENT.

The United States frigate *President*, Com. Rodgers arrived at Sandy Hook, on the 18th of February 1814, after a cruise of 75 days. She passed most of the West-India islands ; lay off Charlestown 48 hours, and was chased by a 74, two frigates, and two sloops of war. During the cruise she captured three English merchantmen, which were sunk, after taking out their cargoes. She had on board 30 prisoners. A private letter from an officer on board the *President* states,

" Situations in which we have been placed this cruise, will, I think, add lustre to the well established character of Com. Rodgers.

" After passing the light, saw several sail, one large sail to the windward ; backed our main top-sail and cleared ship for action. The strange sail came down within gun-shot—hauled her wind on the larboard tack. We continued with our main top-sail to the mast three hours, and seeing no probability of the 74 gun ship's bearing down to engage the *President*, gave her a shot to windward and hoisted our colors —when she bore for us reluctantly—when within half gun shot, backed his main top-sail. At this moment, all hands were called to muster aft; and the commodore said a few, but impressive words, though it was unnecessary; for what other stimulent could true Americans want, than fighting gloriously in sight of their native shore, where hundreds were assembled to witness the engagement? Wore ship to engage, but at this moment the cutter being discovered coming off, backed again to take in the pilot; and the British 74 (strange as it must appear) making sail to the southward and eastward—orders were given to haul aboard the fore and main tacks, to run in; there being then in sight from our deck, a frigate and gunbrig.

"The commander of the 74 had it in his power for five hours to bring us at any moment to an engagement; our main top-sail to the mast during that time."

It was afterwards ascertained, that the ship which declined battle with the *President* was the *Plantagenet* 74, Capt. Lloyd for avoiding an engagement was, that his crew were in a state of mutiny.

RATTLESNAKE AND ENTERPRIZE.

The U. S. brigs, *Rattlesnake*, Lieut. Creighton, and *Enterprize*, Lieut. Renshaw, arrived at Wilmington N. C. the former on the 9th, and the latter on the 7th of March, from a cruise. Three times they were chased by a superior force of the enemy. On the 25th of February the *Enterprize* was chased 70 hours, and escaped by throwing over her guns, cutting away her anchors, and starting her water.

DEATH OF MIDSHIPMAN HALL.

Extract of a letter from Capt. C. Gorden to the Sec'ry of the navy.

Constellation, off Craney Island, March 10, 1814.

"I have to report to you the loss of one of my

midshipmen, Mr. William C. Hall. He was quite young, and the smallest on board; but a youth of great promise, who had so much•interrested himself with the offices and crew, that his loss has spread a momentary gloom over the ship. He fell from the mizzen top-mast head, to the quarter deck, yesterday evening, while we were in the act of sending down top-gallant yards, and expired instantly.

"He had been much accustomed to going aloft, and had gone up to the mast-head, on that occasion, as he said to the captain of the top, to observe how they unrigged the yard; having hold of the top-gallant shroud, the yard must have struck him in canting. He will be buried in the church yard at Northfolk this day at noon, with the ceremonies due to his grade. He is from Queen Ann county, eastern shore of Maryland; no parents and only a sister living. This family is known to Governor Wright, the representative in congress from that district.

CONSTITUTION.

On the 3d of April, U. S. frigate *Constitution*, Capt. Stewart arrived at Marblehead, having been chased in by the British frigates *Junion* and *Tenedos*, of 38 guns each, which had been in chase of her from day light. The frigates, or one of them it is said got within 2 or 3 miles of the *Constitution*, at one time, and to effect her escape she was obliged to throw overboard her provisions, &c. and every thing moveable, and started all her water. Some prize goods were likewise thrown over.

She immediately anchored above Fort Sewall, in a posture of defence, her exposed situation rendering her liable to an attack, should she remain there long. In order to the protection of the frigate and the town, a number of heavy cannon were sent over from Salem, and Maj. Gen. Hovey issued an order for the Marblehead battalion of artillery to hold itself in readiness to act. Com. Bainbridge, to whom an express had been sent, dispatched assistance from the navy yard in Charleston, and the company of New England Guards began their March from Boston, to afford such aid as might be required of them. But towards evening the *Constitution* weighed anchor and came round into this harbour, where she is considered in a state of security. The *Constitution's* cruise has been about three months. In the Mona passage, she chased a frigate, without being able to come up with her. Her crew is in fine condition, and her safe return is hailed with joy.

[*Salem Gaz.*]

ATTACK ON VESSELS AT PETIPAGUE.

At 4 o'clock in the morning of the 8th of April, six British barges, containing 300 men, entered the port of Petipague, and burnt about twenty sail of vessels. Many of them were ships worth from fifteen to twenty thousand dollars each. They did their business effectually, for the vessels were all burnt to the water's edge. They gave out word to the inhabitants, that if they made the least resistance, they would fire the town.

The property destroyed was owned in New York, Middletown, Hartford and Petipague. A fine cutter brig they attempted to get out, but failed, and she shared the fate of the others. She was from 3 to 400 tons, and was worth about 18,000 dollars. The British force is stated, by gentleman from near the scene of action, to have been about 150, which is probably as great a number as six boats could carry. It is added, that the enemy remained on shore all day, unmolested, and went off about 8 in the evening. They came from the frigate and a gun-brig lying off Saybrook.

The enemy took possession of a store, where they remained all day, part of the time amusing themselves, and at night about 1000 men had been collected, who fortified both sides of the river, just above the ferry, intending to surprize the enemy as they returned, but the British, having waited until it was dark, passed unobserved, by muffling their oars, or laying concealed in their boats, and letting them float down with the tide. A number of small vessels, which were in the rear of the enemy, were not molested.

LOSS OF THE FROLIC.

On the 21th of April, the United States sloop of war *Frolic*, J. Bainbridge commander, was captured by the *Orpheus* frigate, without firing a gun, her armament having been thrown overboard in the chase. By this event, we have lost a fine vessel and a gallant crew, but we have lost no honor,

CRUISE OF THE ADAMS.

THE U. S. ship *Adams*, Capt. Charles Morris, sailed from the Chesapeake in January 1813—passed to the southward of Bermuda, crossed the Atlantic, captured a number of prizes and arrived home in safety, in the month of April. The official account of Capt. Morris concludes thus :

" After a long chase on the 25th of March, the last four hours of which was in thick weather, we captured the English India ship *Woodbridge*, with a cargo of rice and dye wood, but had barely taken posession of her, when the weather cleared up and we discovered a fleet of 25 sail immediately to the windward of us, and two ships of war standing for us. We were compelled to abandon the prize with precipitation, and attend to our own safety."

NAVAL ARCHITECTURAL ENTERPRIZE.

Capt. Nathaniel M. Perley, late commander of the ship *Volant*, which was captured on her passage from Bayonne to Boston and carried into Halifax, has constructed and nearly completed, within eight weeks, a schooner, of about 110 tons, which for beauty, strength and utility, is not excelled in the world. She was built near Rowley Green, one mile and a half from the water. No object of this nature and magnitude has ever created more speculation of opinion, than the building of this vessel; and it was generally conceived that she could never be transported to her destined element; but to the surprize of many, and joy of all, on the 2d day of May, she was started from her building place, at about 10 o'clock, A. M. and before 5 P. M. was landed at the water's edge. The whole apparatus for the operation was prepared under Capt. Perley's immediate direction. She was borne by a set of trucks, of four wheels each, about 2 feet in hight, and 16 inches broad. These were drawn by 100 yokes of oxen, in four strings, two of which were to the forward trucks, and two attached to a cable, prepared for the purpose. The subject is rendered more interresting by the fact, that neither man, beast, nor property received any essential injury. The weight is estimated at from 100 to 120 tons. Improvements may probably be made on this invention, which will prove highly useful to the mechanic, merchant, and man of enterprize.

On the 13 and 25 of May the flotilla of gun boats, under the command of Com. Lewis, attacked a part of the British blockading squadron near New London, and opened a passage for 40 or 50 sail of coasters. This flotilla has been of essential service on the coast rescuing many vessels from the grasp of the English with the most determined courage. It is stated in a way that seems entitled to credit, that 17 were killed and 47 wounded on board the *Maidstone* frigate, in one of the engagements with the gun-boats. The vessel was much injured.

THE U. S. schooner *Nonsuch*, Lieut Kearney, stationed off Charlestown S. C. in June narrowly escaped from capture by a frigate. During the chase she threw overboard 11 of her guns.

———

ON the 26th of June a combined attack of artillery, marine corps, and flotilla, under Com. Barney, was made on two of the enemy's frigates near Pawtuxent. An officer on board the flotilla thus writes:

"We moved down with the flotilla, and joined in the chorus with the artillery. Our fire was terrible. At 6 o'clock they began to move, and made sail down the river, leaving us master of the field. Thus we have again beat them and their rockets, which they did not spare. First, we beat off a few boats, then they increased the number, then they added schooners, and now, behold the two frigates! all have shared the same fate. We next expect ships of the line. No matter, we will do our duty. Our loss was 6 killed and 4 wounded. Young Asqueth (midshipman,) who had just joined us, was killed."

———

ALLIGATOR.

ON the 1st of July the U. S. schooner *Alligator* was upset by a violent tornado, and sunk in 4 fathoms water. She was at anchor in Port Royal sound when the blast struck her: 23 were drowned. Among them were 2 promising young officers, Midshipmen Brailsford and Rogerson. The *Alligator* was afterwards got up, by the assistance of two vessels.

LOSS OF THE RATTLESNAKE.

Extract of a letter from Joseph Wilson, jun. purser of the late U. S. brig Rattlesnake to the Sec'y of the navy.

SIR, Boston, July 29, 1814.

I have the honor of making known to you the following circumstances relative to the cruise and capture of the late U. S. brig *Rattlesnake*, by order of James Renshaw Esq. commander. May 31, lat. 40° N. long. 33° W. fell in with a frigate and very narrowly escaped, by throwing over all the guns, except two long 9s. June 9th, lat. 47° N. long. 8° W. received information by a Russian brig from England of the Revolution in France, and destroyed the English brig *John*, laden with English goods.

June 22, lat. 42° N. long. 33, W. destroyed the English brig *Crown Prince*, laden with fish. July 11th at day-light, wind south, discovered a frigate, on the weather, and Cape Sable on the lee bow; the frigate proved to be the *Leander*, to which ship the *Rattlesnake* was surrendered at 8 A. M. after every exertion had been made to escape.

The *Rattlesnake* arrived in Halifax on the 13th, and the *Leander* on the 14th inst.

I have the honor to be &c.

JOSEPH WILSON jun.

BETWEEN the 16th and 20th of August, a large force of the enemy, in all about 60 sail, several of them ships of the line, arrived in the bay of Chesapeake. More than 50 of them entered the Patuxent, and landed their troops and marines about Benedict (the head of frigate navigation,) about 40 miles S. E. of Washington.—Others landed their troops at Port Tobacco, on the Potomac. Their line stretched across the country between the two rivers. On the 22d Com. Barney's flotilla, lying near Point Pleasant, at the head of the sloop navigation of the Patuxent, consisting of 1 cutter, 1 gun-boat, and 13 barges, was blown up, and the men drawn off by the gallant commodore for the protection of the city of Washington. On the same day, the British flankers approached near the "Wood yard," 12 miles from the city, where the main body of the American forces under Brig. Gen. Winder were posted. The line of battle was formed, and our advance guard offered to engage, but the enemy filed off to the left without noticing them. On the evening of the 23d, Gen. Winder's head quarters were at the "Battalion Fields," near Bladensburg, 8 miles from the city. The enemy continued their march towards the bridge, which they passed under a heavy fire from our artillery and riflemen. When the enemy approached the city on the 24th, they met with a most obstinate resistance. It was here that they came within reach of Barney and his gallant spirits, who had just gained the ground from a station near the navy yard, and from his three 18 pounders he opened an active, and most destructive fire. The fire continued till the enemy had nearly reached the muzzle of the guns. Greater exertions, or more determined courage could not have been exhibited. But resistance was vain. Under Com. Baney were about 400. The force of the enemy amounted to between 5 and 6000. The veteran commodore, who has yet all the fire and spirit that distinguished him when he captured the *General Monk*, in the early part of the revolutionary war, fell badly wounded, and many of his brave followers were killed; yet he encouraged his men, and cautioned them not to waste their powder until the last moment that it appeared possible for them to escape, when he ordered a retreat. He was taken prisoner, with some of his men, and was treated in the handsomest manner by the enemy. On the evening of the 24th, the British took possession of the capital. The public property destroyed was the capital; the president's house; the war office; the treasury office; the fort and magazine at Greenleaf's point; the public stores,

&c. at the marine barracks. The navy yard was set on fire by order of the secretary of the navy. A new frigate on the stocks, nearly ready to be launched, rating 44 guns, which was to be called the *Essex*, and to be commanded by Capt. Porter, and a new sloop of war, the *Argus*, were destroyed. The guns for the *Independance* 74, then rigging in Boston, were saved.

Alexandria capitulated on the 28th. A series of desperately daring exertions were made by Rodgers, Porter, and Perry with the men of the two former and some of the Virginia militia, to prevent the escape of the enemy's frigates from Alexandria, with their booty. All that men could do with the means they had, by fire ships, barges, and hastily erected batteries, was done; but the enemy got off, taking with him 14 of our vessels, laden with from 15 to 18000 barrels of flour, 800 hogsheads tobacco, 150 bales cotton, and a small quantity of sugar. Twelve men were killed, and several wounded at Porter's battery; at Perry's only one was wounded, at Rodgers' none were injured.— As the capture of Washington, the capitulation of Alexandria, and the repulse of the British from Baltimore belong to the military history of the war, they are here omitted, except those particulars, which are connected with the honourable deeds of our navy officers and sailors.

LOSS OF THE ADAMS.

On the 1st of September, a large British force, about 40 sail of vessels with troops, under the command of Admiral Criffith, and Sir John Sherbrooke, Governor of Nova Scotia, entered the Penobscot.— The small garrison in the fort at Castine discharged their guns and retired. The enemy then took possession without opposition. The following day they proceeded up the river to Hamden, distant 35 miles where lay the *Adams* frigate, Capt Morris, just returned from a cruise. Capt. Morris prepared himself to receive them as well as he could, by landing his guns and erecting batteries. A considerable militia force had by this time assembled ; but they fled at the approach of the enemy. -He therefore, after a few fires, spiked his guns, burnt his stores and prize goods, and blew up the ship. He and his crew escaped. Capt. Morris was the last man who left the vessel. He made his escape, after firing the train by swimming. - ·

OFFICIAL ACCOUNT.

Letter from Capt. C. Morris to the Sec'y of the navy.
SIR, *Portland Sept. 8, 1814.*

IT is with regret that I inform you, we were compelled to destroy the *Adams*, at Hamden, on the morning of the 3d inst. to prevent her falling into the hands of the enemy.

All the officers effected their escape, and I believe the crew, with the exception of a very few, who were unable to travel. Their precise number cannot be ascertained, as we were obliged to pursue different routs, for the purpose of obtaining provisions, through the woods between the Penobscot and Kennebeck.

I am now engaged collecting and forwarding the men with the utmost despatch to Portsmouth, from which place I hope soon to forward a detailed account of our proceedings.

In the mean time, I request you to believe, that the officers and crew of this ship neglected no means in their power for her defence.

Very respectfully, your obedient servant,
HON. WILLIAM JONES, **C. MORRIS.**
Secr'y of the navy.

A letter from Capt. Morris to the secretary of the navy, dated Sept. 20th, giving a more particular account of the loss of the *Adams*, concludes as follows :

" The character of my first lieutenant, Wadsworth, was already too well established to require the additional evidence he gave of richly deserving the entire confidence of the department and his country. His brother officers of the navy and marines, equally zealous and attentive, are also entitled to my thanks and their country's approbation. The bravery of the seamen and marines is unquestioned; their uncommonly good conduct upon their march, those feelings which induced them to rally round their flag, at a distance of 200 miles from the place of their dispersion, entitled them to particular approbation, and render them an example, which their brother tars may ever be proud to imitate."

LOSS OF THE SYREN.

COPY OF A LETTER FROM CAPT. BRINE, OF HIS MAJESTY'S SHIP MEDWAY 74, TO VICE ADMIRAL TYLER.

His Majesty's Ship Medway, at sea,
SIR,   *July* 12, 1814.

I have the honor to acquaint you, that crusing in the execution of your orders, I this day fell in with and captured, after a chase of 11 hours, nearly on a wind, the United States brig of war *Syren*, commanded by J. N. Nicholson, who succeeded to the command by the death of her captain (Parker) at sea. The *Syren*, is pierced for 18 guns, had 16 mounted, viz. two 42 and twelve 24lb carronades, with two long 9 pounders, and had a complement of 137 men; all her guns, boats, anchors, cables, and spars were thrown overboard during the pursuit. The *Syren* had received a most complete repair, previous to her sailing, and is newly coppered.

I have &c.
AUG. BRINE.

A court of inquiry, convened at New York on the 2d of September 1815, after mature deliberation on the evidence adduced, and on all the circumstances attending the capture, were of opinion, "that no censure can be attached to Lieut. Com. Nicholson for the loss of the *Syren ;* but, on the contrary, that his conduct was that of a cool, vigilent, zealous, and active officer. The court were also of opinion, that the conduct of the officers and crew during the chase was perfectly correct and free from censure."

SAMUEL EVANS, Prest.

SAMUEL R. MARSHALL, *Acting Judge Advocate.*

REPULSE OF THE BRITISH AT MOBILE.

Extract of a letter from Gen. Jackson to the secr'y of the navy.

SIR, September 17, 1814.

WITH lively emotions of satisfaction, I communicate, that success has crowned the efforts of our brave soldiers in resisting and repulsing a combined British naval and land force, which on the 15th inst. attacked Fort Bowyer, on the point of Mobile.

I enclose a copy of the official report of Maj. William Lawrence, of the 2d infantry, who commanded. In addition to the particulars communicated in his letter, I have learnt, that the enemy's ship which was destroyed, was the *Hermes,* of from 24 to 28 guns, Capt. the Hon. William H. Percy, senior officer in the gulf of Mexico; and the brig so considerably damaged is the *Sophie,* 18 guns, Capt. William Lockyer. The other ship was the *Carron,* of from 24 to 28 guns, Capt. Spencer, son of Earl Spencer; the other brig's name unknown. On board the *Carron,* 85 men were killed and wounded.

An acheavement so glorious in its consequences, should be appreciated by the government; and those concerned in it are entitled to and will doubtless receive, the most gratifying evidence of the approbation of their countrymen.

In the words of Major Lawrance, " where all behaved so well, it is unnecessary to discriminate." But all being, meritorious, I beg leave to annex the names of the officers, who were engaged and present, and hope they will individually, be deemed worthy of distinction.

Maj. William Lawrence, 2d infantry ; commanding ; Capt. Walsh of the artillery ; Captains Chamberlain, Brownlow, and Bradley of the 2d infantry Capt. Sands, deputy commissary of ordnance ; Lieutenants Villerd, Sturges, Conway, H. Sanders, T. R. Sanders, Brooks, Davis, and C. Sanders, all of the 2d infantry.

I am confident that you own feelings will lead you to participate in my wishes on this subject. Permit me to suggest the propriety and justice of allowing to this gallant little band the value of the vessel destroyed by them.

I have the honor, &c.
A. JACKSON.

CAPTURE OF THE PIRATES OF BARRATARIA.

Extract of a letter from Com. Patterson to the secr'y of the navy.

Sir,   *New Orleans, Oct.* 10, 1814.

I HAVE very great satisfaction in reporting to you, that the contemplated expedition against the pirates, so long and strongly established among the western islands and waters of this state, of which I had the honor to inform you in my letter of the 10th ult. has terminated in the capture and destruction of all their vessels in port—their establishments on the islands of Grand Terre, Grand Isle, and Cheniere, and the dispersion of the band themselves. The successful issue of this attack upon them will, I trust, prevent their ever collecting again, in force sufficient to injure the commerce of this state.

The force of the pirates was 20 pieces of cannon

mounted, of different calibers, and as I have learnt since my arrival, from 800 to 1000 men of all nations and colors. I have brought with me to this city six fine schooners and one felucca, cruisers and prizes of the pirates, and one armed schooner under Carthagenion colors found in company, and ready to oppose the force under my command.

I have the honor, &c.
DANIEL PATTERSON.

In another letter from Com. Patterson to the secretary of the navy, honorable mention is made of Lieut. Alexis, T. Shields, purser, J. D. Ferris, commander of vessel No. 5, Lieut. T. A. C. Jones, Acting Lieut's Spedder and M'Keever, Sailing Masters Ulrick and Johnson, and Acting Lieut. Cunningham.

On the 23d of September, by some accident, gunboat No. 140 was blown up at Ocracock. Nine persons lost their lives by this disaster.

THE United States tender, *Franklin*, commanded by Mr. Hammersley, master's mate, was captured on the 6th of November by a tender and 14 barges and boats of the enemy, off Back River point, after a very gallant defence of an hour and a half. The *Franklin* was afterwards recaptured.

LOSS OF A FLOTILLA IN LAKE BORGNE.

Letter from Acting Surgeon Marshall to Com.
Patterson.

SIR, *New Orleans, Dec.* 17, 1814.
I HAVE the honour to inform you, that on Tuesday evening, the 13th inst, at 10 o'clock A. M. the enemy landed at Pass Christianne with one hundred and six barges from the squadron off Ship Island. At 2 P.

M.got under way, and directed their course towards the U. S. gun vessels, then laying at anchor off Bay St. Louis. They did not however come up with our squadron that night, which, in the mean time retreated to the Malheraux Islands, where the wind and tide forced them to remain. Wednesday, the14th inst. the weather being calm, at 10 o'clock, A. M. an engagement ensued, which continued about 2 hours, when the enemy closed and surrounded the gun vessels in every direction, keeping up a constant fire from their great guns and musketry, and making frequent attempts to carry by boarding. In this situation, our gallant officers and men, resolving never to give up their ships, fought with the most distinguished bravery, for the incredible space of one hour, against such an overwhelming force; when the action terminated in the capture of gun vessels No. 156, 162,163, 23, 5, and despatch boat *Alligator*, which were immediately carried to the eastward. I immediately proceeded with Mr. Johnson, to the Petitte Coquilles, where I received instructions to join the enemy, and render such aid as their prisoners might require. On Friday morning I arrived at the Bay of St. Louis, and discovered that the British had succeeded, without difficulty, in getting one large ship, several brigs and schooners through Pass Mary Ann, and others rapidly following them, amounting to at least 50 in number.— Having made this discovery, I deemed it prudent to dispense with my instructions, in order to acquaint you with this circumstance. I accordingly employed a guard to convey me in the most expeditious route to New Orleans, (the direct communication being in possession of the enemy.) Friday evening I discovered 10 schooners in the mouth of Pearl river, and five gun vessels at the east entrance of the Rigolets, under way and steering towards the Petitte Coquilles.

I have no doubt the above vessels are constructed for those waters, and that in ten days the British will have from 20 to 40 sail in Lake Ponchartrain.

I have the honor &c.

GEORGE MARSHALL.

THE American flotilla carried in all 23 guns and 182 men. The British, 42 guns and 1200 men.—Capt. Lockyer received three wounds in the action. From the nature of the engagement, and the observations made by our officers while prisoners, the enemy's loss in killed and wounded may be estimated at more than 300, among whom are an unusual proportion of officers. Our loss was comparatively small.

In May 1815, a court of inquiry was held in the naval arsenal, at New Orleans, for the purpose of investigating the conduct of the officers and men, late of the late division of United States gun-vessels, under Lieut. T. A. C. Jones, captured by the enemy December 14, 1814. They were acquitted in the most honorable manner. The opinion of the court concludes as follows : '' With the clearest evidence for their guide, the court experience the most heartfelt gratification in declaring the opinion, that Lieut. Com. Jones, and his gallant supporters—Lieutenants Spedder and M'-Keever, Sailing Masters Ulrich and Ferris—their officers and men, performed their duty on this occasion, in the most able and gallant manner, and that the action has added another and distinguished honor to the naval character of our country.''

LOSS OF U. S. SCHOONER CAROLINA.

Extract of a letter from Capt. Henley to Com. Patterson.

SIR, New Orleans, Dec. 28, 1814.

I HAVE the honor to inform you, that after you left here on the 26th inst, in pursuance to your order, every possible exertion was made to move the schooner *Carolina* higher up the river, and near Gen. Jackson's camp, without success ; the wind being at N. N. W. and blowing fresh, and too scant to get under way, and the current too rapid to move her by warping, which I had endeavored to do with my crew.

At day light, on the morning of the 27th, the enemy opened upon the *Carolina* a battery of five guns, from which they threw shells and hot shot; we returned their fire with the long 12 pounder, the only gun on board, which could reach across the river. The air being light rendered it impossible to get under way. Finding the vessels in a sinking condition, expecting every minute she would blow up, at a little after sunrise I reluctantly gave orders for the crew to abandon her, which was effected with the loss of one killed and six wounded : a short time after I had succeeded in getting the crew on shore, I had the extreme mortification of seeing her blow up. It affords me great pleasure to acknowledge the able assistance I received from Lieuts. Norris and Crowley and Sailing Master Hatter, and to say that my officers and crew behaved on this occasion as well as on the 23d, when under your own eye, in a most gallant manner.

I have &c.
JOHN D. HENLEY.

The naval officers and sailors, of the New Orleans station, fought with uncommon bravery in the glorious battle of the 8th of January 1815, of which honorable notice is taken in the following letter

————

LETTER FROM W. C. C. CLAIBORNE TO COM. PATTERSON.

SIR, *New Orleans, Jan. 28*, 1815.

I HAVE been a witness of your unwearied exertions and steady firmness during the late struggle ; I am very sensible of the obligations Louisiana is under to you and to the portion of the U. S. navy, which you command, for a most zealous and effectual co-operation in the defence of its capital. Receive then yourself, and be good enough to convey to the officers and men under your orders, my warmest thanks. The misfortune which attended our gun-boats on the lakes is, on account of the many brave men who fell on the occasion, cause of sincere regret; but we know that the unequal conflict was for a length of time, gloriously maintained; nor was the flag of our country struck, until our gallant tars had added still more lustre to the naval character of America; a character, which I sincerely hope may long live to sustain, and in those conspicuous stations, which you so well deserve to occupy.

I have the honor to be &c.
WILLIAM C. C. CLAIBORNE.

PEACOCK

THE United States sloop of war *Peacock*, Capt. L. Warrington, arrived at New York on the 30th of October 1815, after a successful cruise of nine months. During her cruise she touched at the Islands of St. Paul, Amsterdam, Java, and Bourbon. From her different captures she obtained about 15,000 dollars in silver and 4 or 5,000 more in gold, besides a large quantity of valuable goods. Among the vessels captured by the *Peacock* was the ship *Nautilus*, 14 guns and 130 men, taken after a single broadside, which killed 7 and wounded 16 men.

A FACT WORTHY OF RECORD.

THE arrival of the United States sloop *Peacock*, from her last cruise against the British, and the conclusion of the war against the States of Barbary, by the squadron under the command of Com. Decatur, have given rise to the following unprecedented historical fact, to wit: The declaration, prosecution, and successful termination of one naval war, before all the cruisers of a previous naval war had come in.

LAKE HURON.

IN the summer of 1814, the squadron under Com. Sinclair, on Lake Huron, captured the British schoon

33

er *Mink*, laden with flour. The *Mink* was built on Lake Superiour, and was a new vessel; also, his Britannic Majesty's schooner *Nancy*, of 3 guns; a fine vessel and richly laden with valuable stores. The schooner *Perseverance*, laden with provisions, was captured on Lake Superiour by Com. Sinclair, and was destroyed in passing down the falls of St. Mary's.

Com. Sinclair, having destroyed all the naval force of the enemy above the size of batteaux, on the upper. lakes, in August returned to Erie, leaving the U. S. schooner *Scorpion* and *Tygress*, under the command of Lieuts. Turner and Champlin, for the purpose of blockading Nattawasauga river. On the night of the 3d of September, the *Tygress* was captured by the barges of the enemy, and on the 5th the *Scorpion* shared the same fate.

Extract from the opinion of a court of inquiry, held on board the United States Ship Independence, in Boston harbour, to investigate the causes of the capture of the Scorpion and Tygress.

"The court find, that after Lieut. Turner had proceeded to cruise off French river, on the night of the 3d of September last, the *Tygress* was attacked by the enemy in five large boats, (one of them mounting a 6 pounder, and the others a 3 pounder each,) and by 19 canoes, carrying about 300 sailors, soldiers, and Indians, under the command of an English naval officer: that owing to the extreme darkness of the night, the enemy were not perceived until they were close on board; nor were they then discovered but by the sound of their oars.

"After they were discovered, every exertion was made by Lieut. Champlin, his officers and men, to defend his schooner, that bravery and skill could suggest; and not until all the officers were cut down, did the overwhelming numbers of the enemy prevail.— The enemy, having thus captured the *Tygress*, and having mounted on her their 6 and 3 pounders, and placed on board a complement of from 70 to 100 picked men, remained at St. Joseph's until the 5th of September,. On the evening of that day the court find, that the *Scorpion* returned from cruising off French river, and to anchor within five miles of the *Tygress*, without any information having been received, or suspicion entertained by Lieut. Turner, of her capture. At the dawn of the next day, it appears that the gunner having charge of the watch, passed word to the sailing master, that the *Tygress* was bearing down under American colours. In a few minutes after, she ran along side of the *Scorpion*, fired, boarded, and carried her.

" It appears to the court, that the loss of the *Scorpion* is, in a great measure, to be attributed to the want of signals ; and owing to this deficiency, no suspicions were excited as to the real character of the *Tygress ;* and from some of the English officers and men on board of her being dressed in the clothes of her former officers and men, and the residue of the enemy's crew being concealed, a surprise was effected, which precluded the possibility of defence.

" The court are therefore of opinion, from the whole testimony before them, that the conduct of Lieut. Turner was that of a discreet and vigilant officer."

JOHN SHAW, Pres.

W. C. ALWYN, *Judge Advocate.*
Approved, B. W. CROWINSHIELD.

LAKE ERIE.

On the afternoon of the 8th of October 1812, two British armed vessels, the *Caledonia* and *Detroit* (formerly the American brig *Adams*) arived at fort Erie, from Malden, and anchored under the guns of the fort. Capt. Elliot, the naval commander on Lake Erie, immediately conceived the project of cutting these vessels out of the harbour in the course of the succeeding night : Accordingly, the necessary arrangements having been made, about 100 volunteers, consisting principally of sailors, under the command of Capt.

Elliott, armed with sabres and pistols, embarked in two boats about midnight, and rowing into the lake above the vessels, drifted down with the current till they were hailed by a sentinel from one of the vessels, when they sprang to their oars, and closing in upon the vessels, they boarded them, drove the British below the decks, cut the cables, and towed them down the lake.

The night being dark and cloudy, the vessel run aground; the *Caledonia* ran close into the ferry at Black Rock, and the *Detroit* on the upper end of Squaw Island, near the middle of Niagara river. In their passage down and while they were aground, the British opened their batteries upon them, and the Americans returned the fire from the *Detroit*; but finding they could not bring the guns to bear upon the enemy to advantage, they left her. About 10 o'clock next morning, a company of British regulars from Fort Erie boarded the *Detroit*, with an intention to destroy the military stores with which she was principally laden; but they were dislodged by a detachment of volunteers, under the command of Capt. Cyrenus Chapin, who crossed over to Squaw Island for that purpose.

About 3 o'clock in the afternoon of the same day the British boarded the *Detroit* a second time, and were again dislodged. In this second attempt three of the British were taken prisoners, and a considerable number of them wounded. During the principal part of the day the British kept up a heavy fire from their batteries, upon the vessels for the purpose of destroying them, and to prevent them from falling into our hands.

The *Caledonia*, however, with her cargo of fur, estimated at $150,000, was secured by our men, who, after removing the principal part of the military stores from the *Detroit* set her on fire and abandoned her.

In this gallant enterprize, about 50 of the British were taken prisoners, and 28 prisoners of the regiment of Gen. Hull's army, retaken. On our part, 4 were killed and 7 wounded; one killed in boarding, and the others from the batteries on the British shore. Among the killed was the brave Maj. Cuyler, aid to Gen. Hull. He was buried with the honors of war.

The *Detroit* mounted 6lb. long guns, and had 56 men. On board her were the Americans mentioned above. The *Caledonia* mounted 2 small guns, and had a crew of 12 men. The *Detroit*, formely the United States vessel of war *Adams*, was captured by the British, on the 16th of August 1812, when Gen. Hull's army, and the town of Detroit were surrendered to the enemy.

For an account of Perry's victory,* see page 85.

LAKE CHAMPLAIN.

LOSS OF THE GROWLER AND EAGLE.

ON the morning of the 2d of June 1813, the *Growler* and *Eagle* were ordered from Plattsburg to the lines, under the command of Lieut. Sidney Smith, in consequence of British gun-boats coming into our waters, and annoying our small water craft. Next morning they discovered a British gun-boat and immediately gave her chase ; she fired an alarm gun, and in fifteen minutes four others came up to her assistance, and commenced firing upon our vessels, at the lower end of Ash Island, (six miles within the province.) In an hour and a half the enemy had landed one hundred regulars from the Isle-aux-Noix, on each side of the river, opposite our vessels, within musket shot. The current being strong, and wind southerly, it was impossible for our vessels to get back. They, however, continued an incessant and heavy fire, and kept the enemy on shore at such a respectable distance, that their fire had no effect.

---

* Immediately after Com. Perry left the *Lawrence*, a sailor, who was left behind, determining not to fall into the hands of the enemy, leaped overboard and swam to the *Niagara*. The brave tar reached the *Niagara* almost as soon as the commodore. This anecdote was mentioned by the commodore himself who was an eye witness of it. The sailor is exhibited in the plate representing the battle.

The action lasted from five to half past nine o'clock, A. M. when the *Eagle*, being no longer able to support her weight of metal, (she being very old) went down on firing her last broadside; the *Growler* was at length compelled to yield to superior force.

Our loss was one killed, six wounded, and 106 taken prisoners. The loss of the enemy is not known.

The *Growler* carried ten 12lb carronades; the *Eagle* 10 guns.

In August 1813, a considerable British force landed at Plattsburg, destroying the public buildings and stores, and immediately afterwards abandoned the place.

Soon after the battle of the 11th of September, * a quantity of shells &c. were taken out of the lake of which mention is made in the following extract of a letter from Com. Macdonough to the secretary of the navy.

November, 6, 1814.

"I have the honor to inform you, that about six tons 8 inch shells have been taken out of the lake by us at this place, which were thus secreted by the enemy in his late incursion into this country.

"A transport sloop has also recently been raised at Isle La Motte, which was sunk by the enemy, loaded with their naval stores, and various instruments of war. On weighing the powder taken on board the enemy's squadron, we find 17,000lbs. with shot in proportion, besides much fixed ammunition."

LAKE ONTARIO.

On the morning of the 19th of July 1812, Capt. M. T. Woolsey, of the *Oneida*, lying in Sacket's harbour, discovered from the mast-head of his brig, five

------

* For an account of Macdonough's victory, see page 145.

British sail, viz. the *Royal George* of 24 guns, the *Prince Regent* of 22, the *Elmira* of 20, the *Seneca* of 18, and one other, about five leagues distant, beating up for the harbour, with a wind ahead. Soon after sun-rise, the *Prince Regent* brought to, and captured the custom-house boat about 7 miles from the harbour, on her return from Gravelly Point. The boat's crew were liberated and set on shore with a message to Col. Bellenger, the commandant at the harbour, demanding the surrender of the *Oneida*, and the late British schooner *Nelson*, seized of a breach for the revenue laws, and fitting for a privateer, and declaring, that in case of a refusal to surrender the vessels, the squadron would burn the village, or lay the inhabitants under contribution. Soon after this, Capt. Woolsey left the harbour in the *Onedia*, and ran down within a league of the squadron, when he returned and moored his vessel on a line with the battery. Capt. Woolsey, being the most experienced engineer present, left the *Onedia* under the command of a lieutenant, went on shore, and took the command of a 32 pounder, mounted the day before on the battery, other guns of which consisted of 9 pounders. By this the enemy had arrived within gun-shot, the *Royal George*, as a flag ship, ahead, and firing was commenced from the 32 pounder. This was returned by the squadron, which stood off and on—and a brisk cannonading was reciprocally continued for more than two hours. All our guns were well manned and served, and it was plainly discovered, that the *Royal George* and *Prince Regent* were much injured. As the flag ship was wearing to give another broadside, a ball from the 32 pounder was seen to strike her and rake her completely; after which the squadron fired a few guns, and bore away for Kingston.

On the 31st of July, the *Julia* of 3 guns was fitted out at Sacket's harbour with orders to proceed to Ogdensburg. After entering the St. Lawrence, she was attacked by the *Earl Moira* of 18 guns, and the *Duke of Gloucester* of 10 guns. The action continued 3 hours and a half, during which time the *Duke* hauled up within half a mile of the *Julia*, and seemed preparing to board her, when two well directed shots from the *Julia's* 32 pounder forced her to abandon the idea. At 8 o'clock in the evening she weighed anchor, and proceeded to Ogdensburg.

IN October 1812 Com. Chauncey took the command of the American fleet on this lake.

On the 7th of November, Com. Chauncey's squadron sailed from Sacket's harbour on a cruise; on the 8th fell in with the *Royal George*, and chased her into the Bay of Quanti; on the morning of the 9th, she was discovered lying in Kingston channel. Our vessels gave chase and pursued her into the harbour of Kingston, and fought her and the batteries for one hour and forty-five minutes. The *Royal George* being well protected and the wind blowing directly in, it was thought prudent to desist. American loss in this engagement was 1 killed and 3 wounded. On the 10th the enemy's schooner *Governor Simcoe* was chased into Kingston. She narrowly escaped under a heavy fire from the *Governor Tomkins*, the *Hamilton*, and the *Julia*, which cut her very much. The commodore returned on the 12th. In this cruise our squadron captured 3 British trading schooners, on board one of which was Capt. Brock, of the 49th British regiment, brother of the late Gen. Brock. An interesting private letter, describing the engagement at Kingston harbour, from an officer under Com. Chauncey, concludes as follows: " Just as we were going into action, Lieut. W——, taking a little packet out of his pocket, said to me, ' My good fellow, here is a cigar for you; I heard you wish for one to day; If I should be popped off, when you puff one of them, think of me:' The gift was a trifle, but the *time*, and the *manner*, and the *circumstances*, which accompanied it, and the great alterations, which a minute might produce, were all such as to excite sensations, which before I have never felt. I have a thousand similar anecdotes to tell you, when we meet again. Throughout the action this officer was as cool, brave, and gallant as Nelson. Our sailors had no grog ; they want no stimulus of that kind ; they seem to have no fear of death. I was by the side of Garnet a few minutes before he fell. He was laughing heartily, and in that act was cut in two by a nine pound shot. I afterwards saw his countenance ; it seemed as if the smile had not yet left it. This disaster only exasperated our seamen ; they prayed and entreated to be laid close aboard the *Royal George* only five minutes, ' just to revenge Garnet's death.' When I look back upon the scene, I cannot but acknowledge that a kind Providence has kept us under his special care and protection."

CAPTURE OF YORK.

THE American fleet left Sacket's harbour on the 25th of April 1813, for the purpose of Conveying Gen. Dearborn, and the expedition under his command, against the British post at York, where the fleet arrived on the 27th. The expedition was completely successful. The most important particulars relative to this event are given in the following extracts of a letter from Com. Chauncey to the secretary of the navy.

United States ship Madison, at anchor off York,
SIR, *April 28, 1813.*
The debarcation commenced about eight o'clock A. M. and was completed about 10. The wind blowing heavy from the eastward, the boats fell to leeward of the position fixed upon, and were in consequence exposed to a galling fire from the enemy, who had taken a position in a thick wood near where the first troops landed ; however, the cool intrepidity of the officers

34

and men overcame every obstacle. Their attack, upon the enemy was so vigorous, that he fled in every direction, leaving a great many of his killed and wounded upon the field. As soon as the troops were landed I directed the schooner to take a position near the fort, in order that the attack upon them by the army and navy might be simultaneous. The schooners were obliged to beat up to their position, which they did in very handsome order under a heavy fire from the enemy's batteries, and, taking a position within six hundred yards of their principal fort, opened a heavy cannonade upon the enemy, which did great execution, and very much contributed to their final reduction.

The troops as soon as landed were formed under the immediate order of Brig, Gen. Pike, who led in a most gallant manner the attack upon the forts, and after having carried two redoubts, in their approach to the principal work the enemy having previously laid a train, blew up his magazine, which in its effects upon our troops was dreadful, having killed and wounded a great many, and amongst the former, the ever to be lamented Brig. Gen. Pike, who fell at the head of his column by a contusion received by a heavy stone from the magazine. His death at this time is much to be regretted, as he had the perfect confidence of the major general ; and his known activity, zeal and experience make his loss a national one.

The enemy set fire to some of his principal stores, containing large quantities of naval and military stores, as well as a ship upon the stocks nearly finished. The only vessel found here is the *Duke of Gloucester* undergoing repairs—the *Prince Regent* left here on the 24th for Kingston.

I have to regret the death of Midshipman Thompson and Hatfield, and several seamen killed—the exact number I do not know, as the returns from the different vessels have not yet been received.

I cannot speak in too much praise of the cool intrepidity of the officers and men generally under my command, and I feel myself particularly indebted to the officers commanding vessels, for their zeal in seconding all my views.

I have the honor to be, &c.

ISAAC CHAUNCEY.

Hon. WILLIAM JONES.

———

List of killed and wounded on board Com. Chauncey's squadron in the attack on York, Canada.

KILLED—John Hatfield, midshipman; Benjamin Quereau, sailmaker; Israel Clark, seaman; Mr. Thompson, midshipman.

WOUNDED—John Campbell, seaman, badly; Richard Welsh, blackman slightly; David C. Burrill, seaman, slightly; Benjamin Hacker, seaman, badly John Ratler, do. do. Jno. Stimas, do. slightly; John Patterson, do. badly; Lemuel Bryant, do. do.

William Buckley was wounded in the attack on Fort George, (since dead;) William Wills was also wounded.

———

CAPTURE OF FORT GEORGE.

Com. Chauncey, having returned to Sacket's harbour, sailed again on the 22d of May for Fort George. Our land and naval forces united captured this place on the 28th. Com. Chauncey's official account of this expedition concludes as follows:

" Where all behaved so well, it is difficult to select any one for commendation; yet in doing justice to Lieut. M'Phersen I do not detract from the merits of others. He was fortunate in placing himself in a situation, where he rendered very important services in covering the troops so completely, that their loss was trifling.

Capt. Perry joined me from Erie on the evening of the 25th, and very gallantly volunteered his services; and I have much pleasure in acknowledging the great assistance which I received from him in arranging and superintending the debarcation of the troops—he was present at every point where he could be useful, under showers of musketry, but fortunately escaped unhurt.   We lost but 1 killed and 2 wounded, and no injury done to the vessels."

ATTACK ON SACKET'S HARBOUR.

THE British fleet, having on board 1200 men under Sir George Prevost, arrived off Sacket's harbour on the 29th of May.   At this time the American squadron were cruising in a distant part of the lake.   On the 29th, the enemy made a bold attack, but were completely repulsed by the troops under the command of Gen. Brown, with the loss of about 200, in killed and wounded.   Among the former were an adjutant general, two majors, several captains, &c.   The American loss was about 150 killed and wounded. Among the killed were two excellent officers, Col. Mills and Col. Backus.   On the evening preceeding the attack the British captured 12 of our barges.

The officers left in charge of this station, unfortunately set fire to the naval store-houses, hospital, and marine barracks, by which the valuable stores taken at York, and the stores for the use of our fleet, were consumed.   Soon after this affair, Com. Chauncey returned to Sacket's harbour.

ON the 16th of June, Lieut. Wolcott Chauncey, with the *Lady of the Lake*, fell in with and captured the schooner *Lady Murray*, from Kingston, bound to York, with an ensign (Geo. Charles Merce) and 15 non-commissioned officers and privates, belonging to the 41st and 104th regiments, loaded with provisions, powder, shot, and fixed ammunition.

On the 17th of July a small expedition, aided by 40 soldiers, lent to Com. Chauncey by Gen. Lewis, sailed from Sacket's harbour on board two small row-boats, with a 16 pounder in each, to the head of the St. Lawrence where they captured a fine gun-boat, mounting a 24 pounder 14 batteaux loaded, 4 officers and 61 men.

THE American fleet arrived at York on the 31st of July. Com. Chauncey's official account of their proceedings concludes as follows : "We run the schooner, into the upper harbour, landed the marines and soldiers under the command of Col. Scott, without opposition, found several hundred barrels of flour and provisions in the public store-house, five pieces of cannon, eleven boats, and a quantity of shot, shells and other stores, all which were either destroyed or brought away. On the 1st of August just after receiving on board all the vessels could take, I ordered the barracks and the public store-house to be burnt."

LOSS OF THE HAMILTON AND SCOURGE.

On the 7th of August the British fleet appeared off Sacket's harbour. Com. Chauncey immediately set sail with his squadron, and made every exertion to bring the enemy to action. The British however declined an engagement. The principal occurrences during this cruise are related in the following extracts from commodore's official account : "On the 8th, at 2 A. M. missed two of our schooners ; at day-light discovered the missing schooners to be the *Hamilton* and *Scourge*. Soon after spoke *Governor Tompkins*, who informed that the *Hamilton* and *Scourge* both overset and sunk in a heavy squall, about 2 o'clock, and, distressing to relate, every soul perished except sixteen. This fatal accident deprived me at once of two valuable officers, Lieut. Winter and Sailing Master Osgood, and two of my best schooners, mounting together 19 guns.

"On the 9th, about half past 10, the enemy tacked and stood after us. At 11, the rear of our line opened his fire upon the enemy ; in about 15 minutes the fire became general from the weather line, which was returned from the enemy. At half past 11,the weather line bore up and passed to the leeward, except the *Growler* and *Julia*, which soon after tacked to the southward, which brought the enemy between them and me. Filled the main top-sail and edged away two points to lead the enemy down, not only to engage him to more advantage, but to lead him from the *Growler* and *Julia*. He, however, kept his wind until he completely separated those two vessels from the rest of the squadron, exchanged a few shot with this ship (the *General Pike*) as he passed, without injury to us, and made sail after our two schooners. Tacked and stood after him. At 12 (midnight) finding that I must either separate from the rest of the squadron, or relinquished the hope of saving the two which had separated, I reluctantly gave up the pursuit. The firing was continued between our 2 schooners and the enemy's fleet until about 1 A. M. when, I presume, they were obliged to surrender to a force so much their superior.''

Extract of a letter from Com. Isaac Chauncey to the Secretary of the navy.

On board the U. S. ship Gen. Pike, off Duck Island,
SIR,   ·   *Sept.* 13, 1813.

ON the 7th, at day light, the enemy's fleet was discovered close in with Niagara river, wind from the southward. Made the signal, and weighed with the fleet (prepared for action) and stood out of the river after him ; he immediately made all sail to the northward. We made sail in chase with our heavy schooners in tow, and have continued the chase all round the lake night and day, until yesterday morning when she succeeded in getting into Amherst Bay, which is so little known to our pilots, and said to be full of shoals, that they are not willing to take me in there. I Shall however (unless driven from my station by a gale of wind) endeavour to watch him so close as to prevent his getting out upon the lake.

During our long chase we frequently got within from one to two miles of the enemy, but our heavy sailing schooners prevented our closing with him, until the 11th, off Gennessee river, we carried a breeze with us while he lay becalmed to within about three quarters of mile of him, when he took the breeze and we had a running fight of three and a half hours, but by his superior sailing he escaped me and run into Amherst Bay yesterday morning. In the course of our chase on the 11th, I got several broadsides from this ship upon the enemy, which must have done him considerable injury, as many of the shot were seen to strike him, and people were observed over the sides plugging shot holes. A few shot struck our hull, and a little rigging was cut, but nothing of importance—not a man was hurt.

I was much disappointed that Sir James refused to fight me, as he was so much superior in point of force both in guns and men—having upwards of 20 guns more than we have, and having a greater weight of shot.

This ship, the *Madison*, and the *Sylph* have each a schooner constantly in tow, yet the others cannot sail as fast as the enemy's squadron, which gave him decidedly the advantage, and puts it in his power to enengage me when and how he chooses.

I have the honor to be, &c.

Hon. WILLIAM JONES,   ISAAC CHAUNCEY.
Secr'y of the navy.

The British squadron was blockaded four days in Amherst Bay, when, by the aid of a heavy wind from the westward, they escaped and succeeded in getting into Kingstown.

Com. Chauncey, having ascertained that the British squadron was in York Bay, sailed from Niagara on the 27th of september. The most important events of this cruise are related in the following extracts from the commodore's official letter :

"On the 28th, at 10 minutes past meridian, the enemy, finding that we were closing fast with him, and that he must either risk an action, or suffer his two rear vessels to be cut off, tacked in succession, begining at the van, hoisted his colors and commenced a well directed fire at this ship, for the purpose of covering his rear, and attacking our rear as he passed to the leeward. Perceiving his intention, I was determined to disappoint him ; therefore as soon as the *Wolf* (the leading ship) passed the centre of his line, and abeam of us, I bore up in succession (preserving our line) for the enemy's centre. This manœuvre not only covered our rear, but hove him into confusion ; he immediately bore away ; we had however closed so near as to bring our guns to bear with effect, and in 20 minutes the main and mizzen top-mast and main yard of the *Wolf* were shot away. He immediately put before the wind, and set all sail upon his foremast. I made the signal for the fleet to make all sail ; the enemy, however, keeping dead before the wind, was able to outsail most of our squadron. I continued the chase until near 3 o'clock, during which time I was enabled in this ship (the *General Pike*) with the *Asp* in tow, to keep within point blank shot of the enemy, and sustained the whole of his fire during the chase.

" At 15 minutes before 3 o'clock A. M. I very reluctantly relinquished the pursuit of a beaten enemy. The reasons that led to this determination, were such as I flatter myself you will approve.

" The loss sustained by this ship was considerable, owing to her being so long exposed to the fire of the whole of the enemy's fleet ; but our most serious loss was occasioned by the bursting of one of our guns, which killed and wounded 22 men, and tore up the top-

tainl*t forecastle, which rendered the gun upon that
and *useless. We had 4 other guns cracked in the
*le, which rendered their use extremely doubtful.
* main top-gallant mast was shot away in the ear-
*art of the action, and the bowsprit, fore and main
*st wounded, rigging and sails much cut up, and a
*mber of shot in our hull, several of which were be-
*veen wind and water, and 27 men killed and wound-
*d, including those by the bursting of the gun. We
*ave repaired nearly all our damages and are ready to
meet the enemy. During our chase one, if not two,
of the enemy's small vessels were completely in our
power, if I could have been satisfied with so partial
victory, but I was so sure of the whole, that I passed
them unnoticed, by which means they finally escaped."
In this letter mention is made of the conduct of Capt.
Crane, Lieut. Brown, Lieut. Finch, Capt. Woolsey
and Capt. Sinclair.

CAPTURE OF THE HAMILTON AND CONFIANCE.

Letter from Com. Chauncey to the Secr'y of the navy.
U. S. ship Gen. Pike, Sacket's harbour.

SIR,   *Oct.* 6, 1813.

I HAVE the pleasure to inform you, that I arrived
here this morning, with 5 of the enemy's vessels, which
I fell in with and captured last evening, off the Ducks.
They were part of a fleet of seven sail, which left
York on Sunday with 234 troops on board, bound to
Kingston. Of this fleet five were captured, one burnt
and one escaped ; the prisoners amounting to nearly
300, besides having upwards of 300 of our troops on
board from Niagara, induced me to run into port for
the purpose of landing both.

I have the additional pleasure of informing you,
that amongst the captured vessels are the *Hamilton*
and *Confiance;* late U. S. schooners *Julia* and *Growler;* * the others are gun vessels.

I have the honor to be, &c.
ISAAC CHAUNCEY.

---

* See page 270.   35

LETTER FROM COM. CHAUNCEY TO THE SEC'Y OF THE NAVY.

SIR,   *Sacket's harbour, May* 1, 1814.

I AM happy to have it in my power to inform you, that the United States ship *Superiour* was launched this morning without accident. The *Superiour* is an uncommonly beautiful and well built ship, something larger than the *President*, and could mount 64 guns, if it was thought advisable to put as many upon her.—This ship has been built in the short space of 80 days, and when it is taken into view, that two brigs of 500 tons each have also been built, rigged, and completely fitted for service since the first of February, it will be acknowledged that the mechanics employed on this station have done their duty.

I have the honour to be, &c.
ISAAC CHAUNCEY.

ATTACK ON OSWEGO.

ON the 5th of May a British force appeared off Oswego from Kingston, consisting of 3 ships, 2 brigs, 2 schooners and a number of gun-boats, commanded by Com. Yeo. They were twice repulsed in attempts to land. On the 6th they succeeded in capturing the place with a considerable quantity of military stores. They evacuated the place on the 8th, after having set fire to the barracks.

LETTER FROM COM. CHAUNCEY TO THE SEC'Y OF THE NAVY.

SIR,   *Sacket's harbour, May* 11, 1814.

THE enemy has paid dearly for the little booty which he obtained at Oswego. From the best information which I can collect, both from deserters and my agents, the enemy lost 70 men killed, and 165 wounded, drowning, and missing—in all, 231 ; nearly as many as were opposed to them.   Capt. Mulcaster is certainly mortally wounded ; a captain of marines killed, and a number of other officers killed and wounded.

I have the honor &c.

ISAAC CHAUNCEY.

CAPTURE OF THE GUN-BOATS AT SANDY CREEK.

EIGHTEEN boats, under the command of Capt. Woolsey, from Oswego for Sacket's harbour, loaded with guns and naval stores put into Sandy Creek on the 29th of May. Capt. Woolsey, apprehending an attack, placed a number of riflemen and Indians (under the command of Maj. Appling) in the woods on each side of the creek, and sent a few raw militia, with a show of opposing the enemy's landing. The militia retreated on the first fire, pursued by the enemy ; but as soon as they had passed the Indians and riflemen, who were in ambush, these last attacked them in the rear, while a battery of 4 field pieces opened upon them in front. Thus cut off in their retreat, the whole force of the enemy, 137 in number, surrendered, with their gun-boats, 5 in number, after a smart action of 20 minutes, in which they lost 20 killed and 40 or 50 wounded.

Among the enemy's killed were 1 lieutenant of marines, and 1 midshipman ; among the prisoners were 2 post captains, Popham and Spelsburg, one the commander of the *Wolf*, 4 lieutenants, and 4 midshipmen.

ON the 19th of June, Lieut. Gregory, with a small force surprised and captured, on the St. Lawrence, a gun-boat, (the *Black Snake*, or No. 9) mounting one 18 pounder, and manned with 18 men, chiefly royal marines. Being discovered and pursued by the enemy, Lieut. Gregory after taking out the prisoners scuttled the prize and arrived at Sacket's harbour the next morning with his prisoners. In Com. Chauncey's official letter, honorable notice is taken of Lieut. Gregory, Sailing Master Vaughan, and Mr. Dixon.

EXTRACT OF A LETTER FROM COM. CHAUNCEY TO THE SECRETARY OF THE NAVY.

United States Ship Superior, Sacket's harbour

SIR, *July 7, 1814.*

I AM happy that I have it in my power to detail to you another brilliant achievement of Lieut. Gregory with his brave companions.

On the 29th ult. I directed Lieut. Gregory to take with him Messrs. Vaughan and Dixon—proceed with the two largest gigs to Nicholas Island, (within about seven miles of Presque Isle harbour) and there conceal his boats and wait for some transports there to take up provisions and munitions of war, which had been sent up the Bay of Quinte for the troops at York and Fort George, but if the transports did not make their appearance in three or four days, then to proceed to Presque Isle, and burn a vessel on the stocks; but with positive orders not to injure a private building or any private property. The day after Lieut. Gregory arrived on the coast he discovered a vessel beating up, but just as he shoved off to board her, a large gun-boat hove in sight a little below him. This boat made a signal to the vessel in the offing, upon which she tacked and stood for the gun-boat. Lieut. Gregory secreted his boats as well as he could, but was apprehensive that he had been discovered. The gun-boat and her convoy (which was full of troops) stood into Presque Isle. Lieut. Gregory was determined to ascertain whether he had been discovered—accordingly he sent one of his boats in the next night and took off one of the inhabitants who informed him, that it was known that he was on the coast, and that two expresses had been sent to Kingston in consequence. He therefore determined upon executing the latter part of his instructions, and made his

United States Squadron under Com: Bainbridge returning triumphant from the Mediterranean
in 1815

ENGRAVED FOR THE NAVAL MONUMENT

arrangments accordingly ; landed, place sentinels at the house to prevent alarm, and set fire to the vessel, which was nearly ready to launch ; she was a stout, well built vessel, to mount 14 guns, and would probably have been launched in about ten days. A small store-house, which contained stores for the vessel, was unavoidably burnt, as it was so near the vessel that it took fire from her. The few milita, which had been left to guard the vessel and property, retreated upon the approach of our boats. As soon as the vessel was entirely consumed, Lieut. Gregory re-embarked his men, without having permitted one of them to enter a house. Finding the alarm so general he thought prudent to cross the lake immediately : he stopped one day at Oswego for refreshment, and arrived here last evening, having performed a most difficult service with his usual gallantry and good conduct.

Lieut. Gregory speaks in the highest terms of commendation of Sailing Master Vaughan and Mr. Dixon, as well as the men under his command, for their patient endurance of hunger and fatigue and the zeal with which they perfomed every part of their duty.

I think in justice to these brave men, that they ought to be allowed something for the destruction of this vessel—they have, however, every confidence in the justice and liberality of the government, and submit their case most cheerfully to its decision.

I have the honor to be, &c.

Hon. William Jones.　　ISAAC CHAUNCEY.

———

EXTRACT OF A LETTER FROM COM. CHAUNCEY TO THE SECRETAR'Y OF THE NAVY.

United States Ship Superior off Kingston,
Sir, *August 10, 1814,*

GREAT anxiety of mind and severe bodily exertions have at length broken down the best constitution and subjected me to a violent fever, that confined me for eighteen days. This misfortune was no more to be foreseen than prevented, but was particularly severe at the moment it happened, as it induced a delay of five or six days in the sailing of the fleet.

In the afternoon on the 31st of July, I was taken on board, but it was calm, and I did not sail before the next morning. To satisfy once whatever expectations the public had been led to entertain of the sufficiency of this squadron to take and maintain the ascendency on this lake, and at the same time to expose the futility of promise, the fulfilment of which had been rested on our appearance at the head of the lake, I got under way at 4 o'clock in the morning of the 1st inst. and steered for the mouth of the Niagara. Owing to light winds, I did not arrive off there before the 5th. There we intercepted one of the enemy's brigs running over from York to Niagara with troops, and run her on shore about six miles to the westward of Fort George. I ordered the *Sylph* in, to anchor as near to the enemy as he could with safety, and to destroy her. Capt. Elliott ran in, in a very gallant manner to within from 300 to 500 yards of her, and was about anchoring when the enemy set fire to her and she soon after blew up. This vessel was a schooner the last year, and called the *Beresford*—since they altered her to a brig they changed her name, and I have not been able to ascertain it. She mounted 14 guns, twelve 24lb. carronades and two long 9 pounders.

My anxiety to return to this end of the lake was increased by the knowledge I had of the weakness of Sacket's harbour, and the apprehension that the enemy might receive a large reinforcement at Kingston, and embarking some of the troops on board his fleet, make a dash at the harbour and burn it with all my stores during our absence. When I left the harbour there were but about 700 regular troops fit for duty It is true a few military had been called in, but little could be expected of them, should an attack be made. My apprehension, it seems, was groundless, the enemy having contented himself with annoying in some trifling degree the coasters between Oswego and the harbour in his boats.

I cannot forbear expressing the regret I feel that so much sensation has been excited in the public mind, because this squadron did not sail so soon as the wise heads, that conduct our newspapers, have presumed to think it ought. I need not suggest to one of your experience, that a man-of-war may appear to the eye of a landsman perfectly ready for sea, when she is deficient in many of the most essential points of her armament, nor how unworthy I should have proved myself of the high trust reposed in me, had I ventured to sea in the face of an enemy of equal force, without being ready to meet him in one hour after my anchor was weighed.

It ought in justice to be recollected, that the building and equipment of vessels on the Atlantic are unattended by any of the great difficulties which we have to encounter on this lake—there every department abounds with facilities ; a commander makes a requisition, and articles of every description are furnished in twelve hours; but this fleet has been built and fitted in the wilderness, where there are no agents and chandler's shops and founderies, &c. &c. to supply our wants, but every thing is to be created ; and yet I shall not decline a comparison of what has been done here, with anything done on the Atlantic, in the building or equipment of vessels. The *Guerriere,* for instance, has been building and fitting upwards of twelve months in the city of Philadelphia, and is not now ready. The *President* frigate went into the navy yard at New York for some partial repairs, a few days after the keel of the *Superior* was laid : since then two frigates of a large class, and two sloops of the largest class, have been built and fitted here, and have sailed before the *President* is ready for sea, although every article of their armament and rigging has been transported from New York in despite of obstacles almost insurmountable. I will go farther, sir, for it is due to the unremitted and unsurpassed exertions of those who have served the public under my command, and will challenge the world to produce a parallel instance, in which the same number of vessels of such dimensions have been built and fitted in the same time by the same number of workmen.

I confess that I am mortified in not having succeeded in satisfying the expectations of the public; but it would be infinitely more painful, could I find any want of zeal or exertion in my endeavors to serve them, to which I could in any degree impute their disappointment.

> I have the honor to be, sir, with
> the utmost respect, your most obed't
> and very humble servant,

Hon. WILLIAM JONES,   ISAAC CHAUNCEY.
Secr'y of the navy.

LETTER FROM COM. CHAUNCEY TO SECRETARY OF THE NAVY.

United States Ship Superior off the Ducks,
SIR,   *October 2, 1814.*

HAVING a very commanding breeze yesterday, I sent the *Lady of the Lake* into Kingston to reconnitre. She stood close in with the forts and shipping, keeping just within the range of their shot, and had a fair view. The ships lay in the same position as on the 29th ult. and the large ship still without her sails bent—no visible preparations to embark troops. I shall watch them in this position as long as possible without endangering the fleet.

> I have the honor &c.
> **ISAAC CHAUNCEY.**

TESTIMONIES OF RESPECT.

On Saturday, Sept. 5, 1812, in pursuance to previous arrangements, a public entertainment at Faneuil

Hall was given to Capt. Hull, in celebration of the achievement of the *Constitution* frigate in the destruction of the British frigate *Guerriere*. An unusual assembly of the citizens, amounting to nearly six hundred, without distinction of party, were present on the occasion. Among the distinguished guests, were the officers of Com. Rodger's squadron [the commodore was too much indisposed to attend]. Brig. Gen. Boyd and staff, Judge Benson of New York, and many gentlemen from the southward.

At an early hour in the morning, State-street, and the way in continuation quite down to the end of Long wharf, off which the squadron was lying at anchor, was beautifully decorated by a display of flags, from the tops and windows of the buildings on both sides, and from the masts of vessels.

At 3 o'clock the procession was formed at the Exchange Coffee House, and went from thence, preceded by an excellent band of music, to the hall of entertainment. The Hon. John C. Jones, president of the day, with Capt. Hull on his right and immediately followed by six vice-presidents, formed the head of the procession on its way to the hall. The concourse of citizens in the streets, through which the procession moved, notwithstanding the unpleasant wetness of the day was larger than known on almost any other occasion. These gave three cheers as the procession passed down State Street. The decorations of the hall which were conducted by Col. Henry Sargeant, were in the highest degree brilliant and appropriate. All the arrangements of the day were splendid and elegant, and such as did great credit to the committees by whom they were superintended. So large and respectable a convention of citizens of different political sentiments having mingled together indiscriminately in celebration of an achievement so honourable to their country, was indeed a most interesting spectacle; and in the highest degree honourable to the town of Boston.

The citizens of Philadelphia presented to Capt. Hull a large and elegant piece of plate, on which was

36

the following inscription : *The citizens of Philadel-phia, at a meeting convened on the* v *of Sept.* MDCCCXII, *voted this urn, to be presented in their name to Captain Isaac Hull, commander of the United States frigate Constitution, as a testimony of their sense of his distinguished gallantry and conduct in bringing to action and subduing the British frigate Guerriere, on the* XIX *day of August,* MDCCCXII, *and of the eminent service he has rendered to his country, by achieving, in the first naval conflict of the war, a most signal and decisive victory over a foe, that had, till then, challenged an unrivalled superiority on the ocean, and thus establishing the claim of our navy to the affection and confidence of the nation.*

Engraved by W. Hooker.

They also gave a handsome piece of plate to C. Morris, lieutenant.

The national legislature voted $50,000 and their thanks to Capt. Hull, officers and crew ; also, to Capt. Hull a gold medal, and to each of the officers silver medals, with appropriate devices.

The order of Cincinnati admitted Capt. Hull an honorary member of their society.

The legislatures of New York and Massachusetts voted their thanks to Capt. Hull, officers and crew.

The common council of the city of New-York gave a public dinner, and the freedom of the city, in a gold box, to Capt. Hull ; and their thanks to the officers and crew. The citizens of New York also gave a public dinner to Capt. Hull.

The councils of Albany voted the freedom of the city to Capt. Hull, and thanks to officers and crew.

The councils of Savannah voted their thanks to Capt. Hull, officers and crew.

The citizens of Charleston S. C. presented to Capt. Hull a handsome piece of plate.

The citizens of Portland presented to Lieut. Wadsworth, a native of that place, a handsome sword with suitable devices, in testimony of their high sense of his gallantry in the action with the *Guerriere.*

The legislature of Virginia presented to Lieut. Morgan and Midshipman Tayloe, natives of that state, a valuable sword each, in honor of their valor in the same action.

———

Congress voted $25,000 and their thanks to Capt. Jacob Jones, officers and crew of the *Wasp*, also a gold medal to Capt. Jones, and silver medals to each of the officers, in testimony of their high sense of the gallantry displayed by them in the capture of the British sloop *Frolic*.

The legislature of Deleware presented to Capt. Jones, a native of that state, a rich piece of plate, in testimony of their gratitude for his services in the cause of his country. The plate was designed and executed by Fletcher and Gardiner of Philadelphia, and cost $500.

The citizens of Philadelphia gave a sword, an elegant silver urn, and a public dinner to Capt. Jones, and a sword to each of the lieutenants.

The legislature of Pennsylvania gave a handsome sword to Lieut. Biddle.

The common council of New York gave an elegant sword and the freedom of the city to Capt. Jones, and also a public dinner and thanks to the officers and crew—The citizens of New York also gave a public dinner.

The order of Cincinnati at New York admitted Capt. Jones as a member.

The legislatures of New York and Massachusetts, and the councils of Savannah voted their thanks to Capt. Jones, officers and crew.

———

The national legislature voted their thanks to Com. Decatur, officers and crew of the frigate *United States*, also a gold medal to Com. Decatur, and silver medals to each of the officers, in honor of the brilliant victory gained by the frigate *United States* over the British frigate *Macedonian*.

The legislatures of New York, Pennsylvania, and Massachusetts, and the councils of New London and Savannah voted their thanks to Com. Decatur, officers and crew.

A splendid ball and entertainment were given to Com. Decatur and officers on their arrival at New London.

The common council of New York voted a public dinner and the freedom of the city in a gold box to Com. Decatur, that his portrait be procured and set up in the gallery of portraits belonging to the city, and that thanks be given to the commodore, officers and crew.

A ball was given to Com. Decatur at the city Hotel, New York, on the 2d of January 1813. The decorations of the hall surpassed any thing of the kind ever before witnessed in this country.

On the 7th of January 1813, in pursuance to arrangements made by the corporation of the city of New York, a dinner was given at the city Hotel, to the crew of the frigate *United States*, who had so nobly supported the character of American seamen in the late engagement with the British frigate *Macedonian*. The assembly room was decorated precisely in the same style as at the previous naval entertainment, with this difference, that the reservoir in which floated the miniature frigate, instead of containing water, was filled with grog.

The crew were landed at New Slip precisely at 2 o'clock, and marched in good order to the city Hotel, through Pearl-street, Wall-street, and Broadway, preceded by a band of music, amid the loud and reiterated huzzas of their fellow citizens.

On their arrival at the hotel, they were ushered into the room by the committe of the corporation, and took their seats with perfect regularity at the call of the boatswain's whistle, whilst the band struck up the inspiring tune of Yankee Doodle. After which a handsome address was delivered by Alderman Vanderbilt. To which the boatswain replied nearly in the following words :

"In behalf of my shipmates, I return our sincere thanks to the corporation of the city of New York, for the honor which they have this day done us. Rest assured, that it will be always our wish to deserve the good opinion of our countrymen."

When the boatswain had finished this reply, his shipmates, in token of their approbation, made the room ring with three hearty cheers.

At this moment the transparent paintings, exhibiting our three glorious naval victories, were suddenly displayed by the dropping of the canvas, which before had concealed them. It is impossible for pen to describe the effect which it had upon the minds of the astonished sailors : their admiration was expressed by repeated huzzas, and enthusiastic acclamations. Silence was in a few minutes restored by the boatswain's whistle, when the whole crew, to the number of 400 and upwards, commenced their attack upon an excellent dinner, which was soon demolished, and in such a manner as left no room to doubt, "*that they could have done much more, if more had been required.*"

After dinner the boatswain piped for silence, when the president gave the following toast :

"*American ships all over the ocean.*"

Com. Decatur and his first lieutenant, Mr. Allen, shortly after entered the room, and were received by the seamen in a manner that evinced the affection and delight with which they beheld their brave commander. After remaining a few minutes, the commodore gave as a toast,

"*Free trade and no impressment.*"

After the commodore retired, a variety of volunteer toasts were given by different seamen, in a true nautical style, and at 6 o'clock the company, obedient to the boatswain's call, adjourned to the theatre, without having been guilty of unseamen-like conduct, or a single excess, and perfectly satisfied with the attention that had been shown them.

The jolly tars marched in regular procession to the theatre, in compliance with an invitation from the managers. The front of the theatre was illuminated, and exhibited a transparency of the engagement between the *United States* and *Macedonian.* The house was more crowded than was ever before known. The pit was entirely occupied by the gallant crew of the frigate *United States*, who behaved through the evening with the utmost decorum.

The citizens of New York and Philadelphia gave a public dinner to the commander and officers of the frigate *United States*.

The citizens of Philadelphia presented to Com. Decatur a sword of solid gold, 36 inches in length, and weighing 21 oz. 10 pwts. it cost $700.

The legislature of Virginia presented swords to Com. Decatur, Lieut. W. H. Allen, and Lieut. J. B. Nicholson.

The United States frigate *Constitution*, Com. Bainbridge, after the destruction of the British frigate *Java*, arrived at Boston on the 18th of February 1813. On the following Thursday at 12 o'clock, Com. Bainbridge landed at the long wharf from the frigate *Constitution*, amidst loud acclamations, and roaring of cannon from the shore. All the way from the end of the pier to the Exchange Coffee House was decorated with colors and streamers. In State-street they were strung across from the opposite buildings, while the windows and balconies of the houses were filled with ladies, and the tops of the houses were covered with spectators, and an immense crowd filled the streets, so as to render it difficult for the military escort to march. The commodore was distinguished by his noble figure, and his walking uncovered. On his right hand was the veteran, Com. Rodgers, and on his left, Brig. Gen. Welles; then followed the brave Capt. Hull, Col. Blake, and a number of officers and citizens; but the crowd was so immense that it was difficult to keep the order of procession. The band of music in the balcony of the State Bank, and the music of the New-England Guards had a fine effect.

DINNER IN HONOR OF COM. BAINBRIDGE.

On the 2d of March a splendid public dinner was given in the Exchange Coffee House, Boston, to Com. Bainbridge and the officers of the United States frigate *Constitution* for their gallant achievement in the capture of the British first-rate frigate *Java ;*—to which Com. Rodgers, Capts. Hull and Smith, and the officers of the squadron then in port were invited. The procession was formed in Fanueil Hall, by Maj. Tilden, and was escorted, amidst the applauses of the citizens, to the Coffee House, by a battalion, composed of the Boston Light Infantry and the Winslow Blues, commanded by Col. Sargeant. The hall was completely filled. The Hon. Christopher Gore presided. The Hon. Harrison G. Otis, Hon. Israel Thorndike, Arnold Welles Esq. Thomas L. Winthrop Esq. Hon. Peter C. Brooks, and William Sullivan Esq. assisted as Vice Presidents.

The entertainment was sumptuous, and the style in which it was got up did credit to Mr. Jones, who provided it.

Before sitting down to table the blessing of Almighty God was asked in a most impressive manner by the Rev. M. Holley.

After thanks were returned, the Hon. Mr. Gore addressed the gentleman present on the occasion in a very elegant and impressive manner. *See page* 29.

———

Monday the 8th of March was appointed by the city council of Charleston S. C. as a day of general festival and joy in honor of our splendid naval victories. It was ushered in by the ringing of bells and firing of cannon &c: all business was suspended. At 3 o'clock a grand procession was formed. Banners, exhibiting the names of our most eminent statesmen and naval officers were borne by the most distinguished citizens. About 600 sat down to a splendid entertainment. The room was suitably decorated for the occasion.

Back of the president's chair was a colossal bust of Washington, decorated with flags; and festoons of stars and stripes connected the pillars that support the ceiling. At the bottom of the hall was a transparency, on which was inscribed, " *The defenders of the* CONSTITUTION"—"BAIN." the remainder was supplied by the representation of a BRIDGE, at the end of which was represented the HULL of a ship. Directly under the transparency was an elegant painting, from the pencil of John B. White Esduire.

In the evening the city was illuminated. Many of the houses were adorned with beautiful transparencies.

The congress of the United States voted $50,000 and their thanks to Com. Bainbridge, officers and crew, also a gold medal to Com. Bainbridge, and silver medals to each of the officers of the *Constitution*, with suitable devices.

The corporation of the city of New York bestowed upon Com. Bainbridge the freedom of the city, accompanied with a gold box.

The citizens of Philidelphia subscribed an, elegant piece of plate to Com. Bainbridge.

The legislature of New York and Massachusetts voted their thanks to Com. Bainbridge, officers and crew. The resolve of the legislature of Massachusetts was as follows : " That Commodores Bainbridge and Decatur, Captains Hull and Jones of the U. S. navy, their officers and crews, in the splendid victories by them obtained over the British ships of war, the *Java*, *Macedonian*, *Guerriere*, and *Frolic*, and in their generous conduct to their captured enemies, have acquired for themselves a distinguished title to that consideration and applause of their fellow citizens, which is due to an heroic and able discharge of duty, and which is the legitimate reward of the brave man, who devotes his life to the services of his country."

The crew of the *Constitution* frigate were treated with a theatrical entertainment on the evening of the 9th of April. The brave fellows enjoyed it with great glee. They marched to the theatre in regular order and returned in the same manner to the ship, as their chosen home. They behaved with great decency and decorum. The stage box was filled with the navy officers, *Rodgers, Bainbridge, Smith,* and their lieutenants. Com. Bainbridge addressed the crew, previous to their leaving the ship, in the following terms.

" *Sailors,* in the action with the *Java* you have shown yourselves men. You are this evening invited to partake of the amusements of the theatre ; conduct yourselves well. Suffer me not to experience any mortification from any disorderly conduct on your part. Let the correctness of your conduct equal your bravery, and I shall have additional cause to speak of you in terms of approbation."

The honest tars replied—

"Commodore, we will put out of the pit the first man that misbehaves."

The pit was never more orderly than when it was filled with the sailors and marines of the *Constitution.* The neatness of their dress, (blue jackets, scarlet waistcoats, new-neck-handkerchiefs, and glazed hats) was a pleasing sight. The marines were extremely neat, and conducted themselves with the silence and composure of officers. Our citizens saw with delight, what discipline and self-respect could produce upon the hardy sons of the ocean.

At Portland a public dinner was given to Com. Bainbridge.

The citizens of Georgetown, Col. gave a public entertainment to Com. Bainbridge. Among the guests were Capt. Morris, and Lieutenants M'Call and Forrest.

Com. Bainbridge was received at Philadelphia with a military escort amidst the acclamations of the citizens.

In April our naval victories were splendidly celebrated at the city of Washington. Upwards of 200 gentlemen of the first distinction partook of an ele-

gant entertainment, at which a number of patriotic
toasts were drank, accompanied by music and discharge of artillery.

The congress of the United States passed a resolution, "That the president be requested to present to
the nearest male relative of Capt. James Lawrence a
gold medal, and a silver medal to each of the commissioned officers who served under him in the sloop of
war *Hornet*, in her conflict with the British vessel of
war *Peacock*, in testimony of the high sense entertained by congress, of the gallantry and good conduct
of the officers and crew in the capture of that vessel ;
and that the president be also requested to communicate to the nearest relative of Capt. Lawrence, the
sense which congress entertains of the loss the naval
service of the United States has sustained in the death
of that distinguished officer."

The crew of the *Hornet* were treated with a dinner
and a seat at the theatre by the corporation of New
York, in honor of their good conduct in the battle with
the *Peacock*.

The citizens of Philadelphia subscribed a rich and
beautiful piece of plate for the lamented Capt. Lawrence.   He did not live to receive this token of respect and affection.   It was however finished and presented to Mrs. Lawrence.

The following is the answer of Mrs. Lawrence, to
a respectful note, addressed to her from a committee
of the citizens of Philadelphia.

Gentlemen,   *New York, Jan.* 16, 1816.
Your letter, accompanying "two elegant pieces of
plate, intended to commemorate the capture of the
sloop of war *Peacock* by the American sloop *Hornet*,
under Capt. Lawrence's command," has been received.

From the enlightened citizens of Philadelphia, celebrated for their patriotism, this testimony of respect
for the services of my lamented husband is peculiarly
grateful ; and as the applause of his fellow citizens

was the most acceptable reward he could, while living, receive ; so it is the greatest consolation which my widowed heart is capable of enjoying, that his memory is thought worthy of being cherished with esteem by those for whose rights he offered up his life.

Accept, I pray you, gentlemen for yourselves, and be pleased to communicate to those on whose behalf you act, my sincere thanks and respectful consideration. Your obedient servant,

JULIA LAWRENCE.

GEORGE HARRISON, and
DANIEL WILLIAM COX, Esq'rs.
Committee in behalf of the citizens of Philadelphia.

The congress of the United States presented to the nearest male relative of Lieut. William Burrows and to Lieut. M'Call of the brig *Enterprize*, a gold medal, with suitable emblems and devices, and a silver medal to each of the commissioned officers, in honor of their gallantry and good conduct in the conflict with the *Boxer*.

The citizens of Portland gave a dinner to the crew of the *Enterprize* in honor of their bravery in capturing the *Boxer*.

An entertainment was given at Baltimore to Lieut. M'Call on whom the command of the *Enterprize* devolved, after the death of Lieut. Burrows. Among the guests invited, were Capts. Ridgley and Spence, of the United States sloops *Erie* and *Ontario*.

The legislature of South Carolina presented a sword to Lieut. M'Call, as a mark of respect entertained by his native state for his distinguished gallantry and good conduct in the battle with the *Boxer*. They also voted a sword to Lieut. Tillinghast, a native of that state, in honor of the good conduct he exhibited in the same engagement. Also the citizens of Columbia, S. C. the native place of Lieut. Tillinghast, presented to him an elegant sword.

Matthew L. Davis Esq. of New York, passing through Portland on a tour to the eastward, acciden .

tally took a walk into the burying ground. His attention was attracted to the neglected grave of the late Lieut. Burrows. The only guide to the spot, where are deposited the remains of one who deserved so much of his country, was the tomb stone of his deceased competitor, Capt. Blythe. This was erected two years since by the surviving officers of the *Boxer*. Mr. Davis immediately gave orders for an elegant marble monument to be erected over the grave of Burrows, to be finished by his return, and without sparing labour or expense. It was soon completed and put up. Its style of execution does much credit to the ingenious artist, Mr. Bartlett Adams of Portland. The inscription is highly creditable to the taste, judgment and modesty of the generous donor, and worthy the hero, whom it is designed to commemorate.

The congress of the United States voted their thanks to Com. Perry, and through him to the officers, petty officers, seamen, marines, and infantry, serving as such, attached to the squadron under his command, for the decisive and glorious victory of Lake Erie, also gold medals to Com. Perry and Lieut. J. D. Elliott, and silver medals with suitable devices, to each of the commissioned officers, either of the navy or army, serving on board, and a sword to each of the midshipmen and sailing masters, who so nobly distinguished themselves on that memorable day; also, a silver medal to the nearest male relative of Lieut. John Brooks, of the marines, a sword to the nearest male relative of Midshipmen Henry Laub, Thomas Claxton, jr. and John Clark, and three month's extra pay to all the petty officers, seamen marines, and infantry, who were in the engagement.

A splendid public dinner was given by the citizens of Boston to Com. Perry. The company assembled in the Senate Chamber of the State house, from whence the whole proceeded to the Exchange Coffee House.

The dinner was served up in Mr. Jones' best style, and the hall was very elegantly and appropriately de-

corated.   After dinner appropriate toasts, occasionally relieved by songs sung by Messrs. Stebbins and
Messinger, were drank amidst cheers of applause, and
followed by airs from a full band of musick.

Com. Perry was received with the greatest respect
by the citizens of Albany.   The common council voted
him the freedom of the city in a gold case, with an elegant sword.

The legislature of Pennsylvania voted their thanks
to Com. Perry with a gold medal ; to Lieut. Elliott
their thanks, with a like medal ; and to those citizens
of Pennsylvania, who volunteered their services, a silver medal of the weight of two dollars, with each person's name subscribed thereon.

A splendid entertainment was given to Com. Perry
at Tammany Hall, New York.

An entertainment was given to Com. Perry at Barney's "Fountain Inn," Baltimore.   The room was
decorated with elegant transparent paintings, representing the battle of Lake Erie, and exhibiting the
names of our naval heroes, &c.

The cities of Hudson, N. Y. Philadelphia, Rich-
mond and Charleston, S. C. were splendidly illuminated in honor of Perry's victory.

The citizens of Newport R. I. presented to Com.
Perry, a native of that place, a rich piece of plate of
the value of $700.

The legislature of South Carolina gave an elegant
sword to Lieut. Thomas Holdup, for his gallantry in
the battle of Lake Erie.

The citizens of Boston presented to Com. Perry a
service of plate, consisting of nearly forty pieces, which
cost $1600.

A piece of plate of the value of $300 was subscrib-
ed for Com. Perry by the citizens of Fredicksburgh, Va.

The citizens of Philadelphia and Savannah presented to Com. Perry a handsome sword, with appropriate engravings.

The Congress of the United States resolved, that
their thanks be presented to Com. Macdonough, and

through him to the officers, petty officers, seamen, marines, and infantry serving as marines, attached to the squadron under his command, for the decisive and splendid victory gained on Lake Champlain ; that gold medals be struck, emblematical of the actions between the two squadrons, and presented to Com. Macdonough, Capt. Robert Henley, and Lieut. Stephen Cassin ; that silver medals, with appropriate devices be bestowed on each of the commissioned officers of the navy and army, who were in the engagement, and a sword on each midshipman and sailing master. A silver medal was also voted to the nearest male relative of Lieut. Peter Gamble and Lieut. John Stansbury, who fell in the action.

The legislature of New York gave to Com. Macdonough a thousand acres of land.

The legislature of Vermont gave to Com. Macdonough a tract of land adjoining Lake Champlain, from which may be seen that part of the lake where the battle was fought.

The common council of New York presented to Com. Macdonough the freedom of the city in a gold box, and their thanks to his officers and crew. They also requested of the commodore his portrait to be placed in the gallery of paintings.

The citizens of Plattsburg gave a public dinner to Com. Macdonough.

The citizens of Salem gave a public entertainment to Capt. Charles Stewart, of the frigate *Constitution*. The officers of the frigate were among the guests. Every thing was conducted in an elegant style. Com. Rodgers and our naval victors were honorably complimented, and the lamented dead, Lawrence, Burrows, Alwyn, and Budd were not forgotten.

Capt. Porter, on his return from the Western ocean, landed at New York, where he was received with enthusiasm. The people took the horses from his carriage, and, amidst the shouts of thousands, hauled him to his lodgings.

A part of the crew, late of the *Essex*, received a

public entertainment at Tammany Hall, New York. Some of the wounded attended the procession in carriages. Their whole number was 184. The toasts of these men show their love to their country and to their commander.

Capt. Porter was received at Philadelphia by tens of thousands. He entered the city in a carriage with the mayor, preceded and followed by an immense cavalcade of officers, civil and military, and citizens of all ranks. The streets were hung with stripes and stars. When the crowd arrived opposite Christ's Church in Second-street, it was met by a large body of respectable seamen, who fastened another rope to the carriage in which the people were hauling the gallant captain; (for long before they had unharnessed the horses) and the whole moved through the city with continual shouts. When they arrived at the mansion house hotel, the sailors took him on their shoulders and carried him in with huzzas.

Congress voted their thanks to Capt. Lewis Warrington, officers and crew of the *Peacock*, for the skill and bravery displayed in the capture of the *Epervier*. They also gave to Capt. Warrington a gold medal with emblematic devices : to each of the commissioned officers, a silver medal, with like devices, and to each of the midshipmen and sailing masters a sword.

The president of the United States, at the request of congress presented to Capt. Johnston Blakeley of the sloop-of-war *Wasp*, a gold medal with suitable devices, and a silver medal, with like devices, to each of the commissioned officers ; and also a sword to each of the midshipmen and sailing masters of that vessel, in testimony of the high sense entertained by the legislature of the nation, of their gallantry and good conduct in the action with the British sloop of war *Reindeer*.

A public dinner was given to Capt. Biddle of the sloop-of-war *Hornet*, at Tammany Hall, New York. The company was numerous, the guests distinguished, and the toasts American.

The congress of the United States passed a resolution expressive of the high sense entertained by that body of the gallantry and good conduct of Com. Daniel T. Patterson and Maj. D. Carmick, and of the officers, seamen, and marines under their command, in the defence of New Orleans.

The corporation of New York voted the freedom of that city in a golden box, to Capt. Charles Stewart, of the frigate *Constitution*, for his gallantry and nautical skill displayed in the capture of the British ships *Cyane* and *Levant ;* and also the thanks of the corporation to the officers and crew of the frigate for the brave manner in which they engaged, fought and conquered on that occasion.

The *Constitution*, when entering Boston harbour, fired a salute, which was immediately returned from Fort Independence. On anchoring, this glorious vessel was welcomed to her native place by federal salutes from the Washington Artillery, and a company of citizens. Capt. Stewart then left the ship in his barge, accompanied by several officers belonging to the squadron under a salute ; and was received at Long Wharf, by his assembled fellow citizens, with repeated huzzas, and other hearty demonstrations of gratitude and respect. The officers of the Boston brigade, being that day on duty, proceeded in a body to the place of landing, and through their commander, Gen. Welles, paid their respects and congratulations to their gallant and meritorious fellow countrymen. An escort, composed of the Boston Fusiliers and Winslow Blues, under Capt. Fairbanks, conducted Capt. Stewart, and the other officers of the ship, to the Exchange Coffee House, amidst the repeated cheers of the citizens of both sexes, who filled the streets, wharves and vessels, and occupied the houses. The procession was closed by a large number of citizens. A repast was provided at the Coffee House, (where Capt. Stewart received the congratulations of a great number of citizens and strangers) during which a full band of music played national airs and marches ; and the ships, wharves, and State-street were beautifully decorated with the colors of all nations.

WAR WITH ALGIERS.

THIS WAR was declared on the 2d of March, 1815, and was brought to an honorable termination in the short space of four months. We have room to insert only the following documents relative to it.

COPY OF A LETTER FROM COM. DECATUR TO THE SECRETARY OF THE NAVY.

U. S. Ship Guerriere, Bay of Tunis,
SIR,   *July* 31, 1815.

I HAVE the honor to inform you, that upon my arrival at this anchorage, I was made acquainted with the following transactions, which had taken place here during our late war with Great Britain.

Two prizes, which had been taken by the *Abœllino* privateer, and sent into this port, were taken posession of by a British vessel of war while lying within the protection of the Bey of Tunis. The consul having communicated to me information of this violation of our treaty with Tunis, I demanded satisfaction of the Bey. After some hesitation, and proposing a delay of payment for one year, my demand was acceded to, and the money amounting to $46,000, was paid into the hands of the consul, Mr. Noah, agent for the privateer.

I shall proceed immediately for Tripoli, and will give you early information of the further proceedings of this squadron. The Bey of Tunis has now lying in this harbour, nearly ready for sea, three frigates and several small vessels of war.

I have the honor to be,
with great respect, sir, your obe't serv't,
STEPHEN DECATUR.

Hon. B. W. CROWNINSHIELD.
Secretary of the navy.

38

U. S. Ship Guerriere, Messina, Aug. 13, 1815

I HAVE the honor to inform you, that immediately after the date of my last communication I proceeded to Tripoli. Upon my arrival off that place, I received from our consul a letter; in consequence of the information contained in this letter, I deemed it necessary to demand justice from the Bashaw. On the next day the governor of the city of Tripoli came on board the *Guerriere*, to treat in behalf of the Bashaw. He objected to the amount claimed by us, but finally agreed to our demands. The money, amounting to the sum of $25,000, has been paid into the hands of the consul, who is agent for the privateer.

The Bashaw also delivered up to me ten captives, two of them Danes, and the others Neapolitans.

During the progress of our negotiations with the states of Barbary, now brought to a conclusion, there has appeared a disposition on the part of each of them, to grant as far as we were disposed to demand.

I trust that the succesful result of our small expedition, so honorable to our country, will induce other nations to follow the example; in which case the Barbary states will be compelled to abandon their piratical system.

I shall now proceed with the squadron to Carthagena, at which place I hope to find the relief squadron from America.

COPY OF A LETTER FROM COM. BAINBRIDGE TO THE SECRETARY OF THE NAVY.

U. S. Ship Independence, off the Bay of Tunis,
September 6, 1815.

I HAD the honor of making communications to you from Carthagena on the 10th ultimo, from which place I sailed with the *Independance, Congress, Erie, Chippewa,* and *Spark,* destined for Tripoli, having learned that a misunderstanding existed between the Bashaw of that place, and our consul residing there.   On my way I called at Algiers to exhibit this additional force off there, presuming it would have some weight in pre-serving the peace which had just been made; for the only mode of convincing these people is by occular demonstration.

On my arrival off Tripoli, I learned that Com. De-cature had been there with the first squadron, and had adjusted our differences, which existed at that place. Our consul at Tripoli informed me, that the exhibiting of our naval force before Trpoli had produced a most favorable change in the disposition of the Bashaw for preserving the peace with us.

At Tripoli, learning that the Bey of Tunis was rest-less towards the United States, I immediately pro-ceeded with the vessels with me for that place.

On my arrival at Tunis, I learned by a letter from our consul there, that the Bey and his officers were friendly disposed towards us.

Having agreeably to your instructions, exhibited the force under my command to all the Barbary powers, (and which I believe, will have a tendency to prolong our treaties with them,) I have only now, in further obedience to those instructions, to return with the squadron to the United States.

EXTRACT OF A LETTER FROM THE SAME TO THE SAME.

U. S. Ship Independance, Malaga,
September 14, 1815.

I arrived here yesterday, under the expectation of meeting here the first squadron; but to my regret, Com. Decatur has not yet come down the Mediterranean, and where the squadron with him is I know not; for the last I learned of them was off Tripoli, which place they left on the 9th ultimo.

As the squadron has to return this autumn, in pursu-ance of your orders, it is very desirable that it should leave this sea as soon as possible, to avoid the inclem-ency of the winter on our coast, particularly on ac-count of the smaller vessels.   The *Independence,*

Congress Boxer, Saranac, Chippewa, and *Spark* are here; the *Erie* I expect every hour from Malta, where, I had sent her; the *Torch* and *Lynx* are at Carthagena. All these vessels will be prepared immediately to return; but they cannot sail till the other squadron has joined us.

Copy of a letter from Com. Decatur to his excellency the Marquis Cercello, Secretary of State and Minister of Foreign affairs to his Majesty the King of Naples.

SIR, *U. S. Ship Guerriere, Naples, Sept. 8, 1815.*

I HAVE the honor to inform your excellency, that in my late negociation with the Bashaw of Tripoli, I demanded and obtained the release of eight Neapolitan captives, subjects of his majesty the king of the two Sicilies. These I have landed at Mesina. It affords me great pleasure to have had it in my power, by this small service, to evince to his majesty the grateful sense entertained by our government of the aid formerly rendered to us by his majesty, during our war with Tripoli.

With great respect and consideration, I have the honor to be your excellency's most obedient servant,
STEPHEN DECATUR.

His Excellency the Marquis Cercello,
Secretary of State, &c. &c.

SIR, *Naples, Sept. 12, 1815.*

Having laid before the king my master, the paper which you have directed me, dated the 8th inst. in which you were pleased to acquaint me, that in your last negociation with the Bey of Tripoli, you had freed from the slavery of that Regency eight subjects of his majesty, whom you had also set on shore at Mesina; his majesty has ordered me to acknowledge this peculiar favor, as the act of your generosity, which you have been pleased to call a return for the trifling assistance which the squadron of your nation formerly received from his royal government during the war with Tripoli.

In doing myself the pleasure of manifesting this sentiment of my king, and of assuring you in his name, that the brave American nation will always find in his majesty's ports the best reception—I beg you will receive the assurances of my most distinguished consideration.

Marquis CERCELLO,
Secretary of State and Minister of Foreign Affairs.

Com. DECATUR, *Commander of the Squadron of U. S. of America.*

EXTRACT OF A LETTER FROM AN OFFICER OF THE U. S. NAVY.

Bay of Naples, Sept. 10, 1815.

THIS being the first opportunity since we left Algiers, I use it. We left Algiers the 8th July, and on the 15th arrived at Cagliari, for water and refreshments ; on the 25th sailed for Tunis, and on the following day anchored in the bay, in a fine position. The commodore immediately made his compliments to the Bey, signifying to him that, as he had permitted two brigs, prizes to the United States flag, to be taken from under his batteries by an English ship of war, contrary to the usages of war and civilized nations, he having power to resist this violation of this port; the purpose of his visit was to demand indemnity for this breach of good faith, and he would expect it to be sent on board by a given hour on the day named : the commodore sent an estimate of the value of the prizes, and although there appears to have been great consternation, the demand was promptly complied with, and the indemnity sent on board ; having accomplished this service by the 2d of August, we sailed for, and on the 5th anchored before Tripoli, where we had a similar ceremony to perform, and which was conducted in the same smooth, cool, decided way without any palaver, which would leave room to doubt that we should do as we said. The Bey of Tripoli appears not to have had so much of the ready at command, but showed equal readiness with his neighbour to comply with the demand : falling short of the indemnity required, he signified that there was a Danish family in his posession, consisting of nine persons, and two other Europeans, whom he was willing to deliver up to make good the indemnity demanded ; the commodore did not hesitate a moment, and we had the satisfaction to see them soon after arrive on board our squadron. I need not say how gratifying this cruise must be to every American soul : how delightful it was to see the stars and stripes holding forth the hands of retributive justice to the barbarians, and rescuing the unfortunate, even of distant but friendly European nations, from slavery.

On the 10th, we arrived at Syracuse, and on the 20th at Messina, where we underwent some repairs, and on the 2d September arrived at this place.

EXTRACT OF A LETTER FROM AN OFFICER ON BOARD THE UNITED STATES BRIG ENTERPRIZE.

"We remained at Malaga about two days, and then returned to Gibralter—here we were joined by all Com. Decatur's squadron, excepting his own ship. Our fleet now consisted of the *Independence, Macedonian, United States, Constellation, Congress, Ontario, Erie, Enterprize, Chippewa, Saranac, Boxer, Firefly, Flambeau, Torch, Spitfire, Spark,* and *Lynx.* It was a proud sight for an American to see in a British port just at the close of a war with her, which the English thought would have been the destruction of our navy, a squadron of seventeen sail, larger perhaps than our whole navy at the commencement of that war. At Malaga the governor waited on Com. Bainbridge on board his ship an honor which he had never deigned to pay to any admiral before. On our arrival at Gibralter the commodore fired a salute of seventeen guns, which was returned.

" You have no idea of the respect which the American character has gained by our late wars. The Spaniards especially, think we are devils incarnate :

as we beat the English, who beat the French, who beat them, whom nobody ever beat before—and the Algerines whom the devil himself could not beat.

ANECDOTES.

At the time Decatur arrived in sight of Gibralter, a great number of British officers and citizens, and among them an American gentleman, were assembled on an eminence to view the American fleet. Decatur entered the harbour with his squadron in a very hand-some style; sailed round, and went out again, with-out coming to anchor—his object being merely to make signals to the sloop of war *Ontario*. The Brit-ish officers were very desirous of knowing the different names of the vessels of the squadron as they approach-ed. The shrewd American pretended to know every vessel the moment he saw her broadside, and they crowded around him for information. The first frig-ate, he said, was the *Guerriere* ; the second, the *Mace-donian* ; the third, the *Java* ; the next was the *Eper-vier* ; the next the *Peacock* ; and the next—" oh, damn the next," they exclaimed, and immediately moved off, highly disgusted with the names of the vessels of the Yankee squadron.

It is said the Dey of Algiers very reluctantly gave up all idea of receiving tribute from the Americans, and alleged among other things, that other nations, if he consented, might take advantage of it, and perhaps unite and occasion his destruction. It was not the amount or value of the sum he was particular about, but the receiving something annually of the Ameri-cans would add to his security, if it were only a little powder. Com. Decatur observed, that he thought it very probable, if he insisted upon receiving powder of the Americans as tribute, his wishes would be grati-fied, but he must certainly expect to receive balls with it. His Deyship very wisely gave up the point.

When Com. Decatur's squadron was before Tunis, exacting payment from the Bey, for the restored prizes, there were in the harbour 6 Tunisian frigates, 6 corvetts and brigs, and 50 gun-boats. Capt. Gordon was employed to receive the money of the Bey.

The American Commissioners to the Dey of Algiers.

THE undersigned have the honor to inform his highness, the Dey of Algiers, that they have been appointed, by the president of the United States of America, commissioners plenipotentiary to treat of peace with his highness, and that pursuant to their instruction, they are ready to open a negotiation for the restoration of peace and harmony between the two countries, on terms just and honorable to both parties; and they feel it incumbant on them to state explicitly to his highness, that they are instructed to treat upon no other principle than that of perfect equality, and on the terms of the most favored nations; no stipulation for paying any tribute to Algiers, under any form whatever will be agreed to.

The undersigned have the honor to transmit herewith a letter from the President of the United States, and avail themselves of this occasion to assure his highness of their high consideration and profound respect.

Documents accompaning the message of the President transmitting to the senate the treaty of peace with Algiers.

U. S. Ship Guerriere, Bay of Algiers,
SIR, *July 4, 1815.*

WE have the honor to refer you to the official reports of Com. Decatur to the navy department, for an account of the operations of this squadron previous to our arrival off Algiers on the 28th ultimo.

Having received information, that the Algerine squadron had been at sea for a considerable time longer than that to which their cruises usually extended, and that a dispatch boat had been sent from Gibraltar to Algiers to inform them of our arrival in the Mediterranean, we thought that they might have made a harbour where they would be in safety. We therefore, whilst they were in this state of uncertainty, believe it a proper moment to deliver the President's letter, agreeably to our instruction. Accordingly, on the 20th ult. a flag of truce was hoisted on board the *Guerriere* with the Swedish flag at the main. A boat came off about noon with Mr. Norderling, consul of Sweden, and the captain of the port who confirmed the intelligence we had before received, and to whom we communicated information of the capture of their frigate and brig. The impression made by these events was visible and deep. We were requested by the captain of the port (Mr. Norderling declaring he was not authorized to act,) to state the conditions on which we would make peace, to which we replied, by giving the letter of the President to the Dey, and by a note from us to him, a copy of which (No. 1) we have the honor to transmit herewith. The captain of the port then requested that hostilities should cease, pending the negotiation, and that persons authorized to treat should go on shore, he and Mr. Norderling both affirming that the minister of marine had pledged himself for our security and return to our ships when we pleased. Both these propositions were rejected, and they were explicity informed that the negotiation must be carried on board the fleet, and that hostilities, as far as they respected vessels, could not cease— They returned on shore. On the following day the same persons returned and informed us, that they were commissioned by the Dey to treat with us on the proposed basis, and their anxiety appeared extreme to conclude the peace immediately. We then brought forward the model of a treaty, which we declared would not be departed from in substance, at the same time declaring, that although the United States would never stipulate for paying tribute under any form whatever, yet that they were a magnanimous and generous nation, who would upon the presentation of consuls do what was customary with other great nations, in their friendly intercourse with Algiers. The treaty was then examined and they were of opinion, that it

39

would not be agreed to in its present form, and particularly requested that the article, requiring the restitution of the property they had captured, and which had been distributed, might be expunged, alleging that such a demand had never before been made upon Algiers. To this it was answered, that the claim was just, and would be adhered to. They then asked whether, if the treaty should be signed by the Dey, we would engage to restore the captured vessels, which we refused. They then represented that it was not the present Dey who had declared the war, which they acknowledged to be unjust, conceding that they were wholly in the wrong, and had no excuse, and requested we would take the case of the Dey into consideration, and upon his agreeing to terms with us more favorable than had ever before been made with any other nation, to restore the ships, which they stated would be of little or no value to us, but would be of great importance to him, as they would satisfy the people with the conditions of the peace we were going to conclude with him.

We consulted upon this question, and determined that, considering the state of those vessels, the sums that would be required to fit them for a passage to the United States, and the little probability of selling them in this part of the world, we would make a compliment of them to his highness in the state they then were, the commodore engaging to furnish them with an escort to this port. This however, would depend upon their signing the treaty as presented to them, and could not appear as an article of it, but must be considered as a favor conferred on the Dey by the United States.

They then requested a truce, to deliberate upon the terms of the proposed treaty, which was refused; they then pleaded for three hours. The reply was, "not a minute; if your squadron appears in sight before the treaty is actually signed by the Dey, and the prisoners sent off, ours would capture them." It was finally agreed that hostilities should cease, when we perceived their boat coming off with a white flag hoisted ; Swedish consul pledging his word of honor not to hoist it unless the treaty was signed and the prisoners in the boat. They returned on shore, and although the distance was full five miles, they came back within three hours, with the treaty signed, as we had concluded it, and the prisoners.

During the interval of the absence, a corvette appeared in sight, which would have been captured if they had been detained one hour longer. The treaty has since been drawn out anew, translated by them, and duly executed by the Dey, which we have the honor to transmit herewith.

Mr. Shaler has since been on shore, and the cotton and money mentioned in the fourth article, have been given up to him. They now show every disposition to maintain a sincere peace with us, which is doubtless owing to the dread of our arms ; and we take this occasion to remark, that, in our opinion, the only secure guarantee we can have for the maintenance of the peace just concluded with those people, is the presence, in the Mediterranean, of a respectable naval force.

As this treaty appears to us to secure every interest within the contemplation of the government, and as it really places the United States on higher ground than any other nation, we have no hesitation on our part, in fulfiling such of its provisions as are within our power, in the firm belief that it will receive the ratification of the President and Senate.

We have the honor to be, with respect,

Sir, your obedient servants.

STEPHEN DECATUR.

Hon. James Monroe,   WILLIAM SHALER.

JAMES MADISON.

PRESIDENT OF THE UNITED STATES OF AMERICA.

To all and singular to whom these Presents shall come.... Greeting:

WHEREAS a Treaty of Peace and Amity, between the United States of America and his Highness Omar Bashaw, Dey of Algiers, was concluded at Algiers on the thirtieth day of June last, by Stephen Decatur and William Shaler, citizens of the United States, on the part of the United States and the said Omar Bashaw, Dey of Algiers, and was duly signed and sealed by the said parties, which Treaty is in the words following, to wit:

TREATY of Peace and Amity, concluded between the United States of America and His Highness Omar Bashaw, Dey of Algiers.

Art. 1. There shall be, from the conclusion of this treaty, a firm, inviolable and universal peace and friendship between the President and the citizens of the United States of America, on the one part, and the Dey and Subjects of the Regency of Algiers in Barbary on the other, made by the free consent of both parties, on the terms of the most favorable nations: and if either party shall hereafter grant to any other nation any particular favor or privilege in navigation or commerce, it shall immediately become common to the other party, freely when it is freely granted to such other nations; but when the grant is conditional, it shall be at the option of the contracting parties to accept, alter, or reject such conditions, in such manner as shall be most conducive to their respective interests.

Art. 2. It is distinctly understood between the contracting parties, that no tribute, either as biennial presents, or under any other form or name whatever, shall ever be required by the Dey and Regency of Algiers from the United States of America, on any pretext whatever.

Art. 3. The Dey of Algiers shall cause to be immediately delivered up to the American squadron, now off Algiers, all the American citizens, now in his possession, amounting to ten, more or less ; and all the subjects of the Dey of Algiers, now in possesion of the United States, amounting to five hundred, more or less, shall be delivered up to him, the United States, according to usages of civilized nations, requiring no ransom for the excess of prisoners in their favors.

Art. 4. A just and full compensation shall be made by the Dey of Algiers, to such citizens of the United States, as have been captured and detained by Algerine cruisers, or who have been forced to abandon their property in Algiers in violation of the twenty-second article of the treaty of peace and amity concluded between the United States and the Dey of Algiers, on the 5th of September, 1795.

And it is agreed between the contracting parties, that in lieu of the above, the Dey of Algiers shall cause to be delivered forthwith into the hands of the American consul, residing at Algiers, the whole of a quantity of bales of cotton left by the late consul general of the United States in the public magazines in Algiers, and that he shall pay into the hands of the said consul the sum of ten thousand Spanish dollars.

Art. 5. If any goods, belonging to any nation with which either of the parties is at war, should be loaded on board vessels belonging to the other party, they shall pass free and unmolested, and no attempts shall be made to take or detain them.

Art. 6. If any citizens or subjects with their effects, belonging to either party, shall be found on board a prize vessel taken from an enemy by the other party, such citizens or subjects shall be liberated immediately, and in no case, on any other pretence whatever, shall any American citizen be kept in captivity or confinement, or the property of any American citizen, found on board of any vessel belonging to any other nation, with which Algiers may be at war, be detained from its lawful owners after the exhibition of sufficient proofs of American citizenship and of American property by the consul of the United States, residing at Algiers.

Art. 7.   Proper passports shall immediately be given to the vessels of both the contracting parties, on condition that the vessels of war belonging to the Regency of Algiers, on meeting with merchant vessels belonging to the citizens of the United States of America, shall not be permitted to visit them with more than two persons besides the rowers ; these only shall be permitted to go on board, without first obtaining leave from the commander of said vessel, who shall compare the passport, and immediately permit said vessel to proceed on her voyage ; and should any of the subjects of Algiers insult or molest the commander or any other person on board a vessel so visited, or plunder any of the property contained in her, on complaint being made by the consul of the United States residing in Algiers, and on his producing sufficient proof to substantiate the fact, the commander of Rais of said Algerine ship or vessel of war, as well as the offenders, shall be punished in the most exemplary manner.

All vessels of war belonging to the United States of America, on meeting a cruiser belonging to the Regency of Algiers on having seen her passports and certificates from the consul of the United States, residing in Algiers, shall permit her to proceed on her cruise unmolested, and without detention.   No passport shall be granted by either party to any vessel, but such as are absolutely the property of citizens or subjects of the said contracting parties, on any pretence whatever,

Art. 8.   A citizen or subject of either of the contracting parties having bought a prize vessel condemned by the other party, or by any other nation, the certificates of condemnation and bill of sale shall be a sufficient passport for such vessel for six months, which considering the distance between the two countries, is no more than a reasonable time for her to procure proper passports.

Art. 9.   Vessels of either of the contracting parties, putting into the ports of the other, and having need of provisions or other supplies, shall be furnished at the market price ; and if any such vessel should so put in from a distance at sea, and have occasion to repair, she shall be at liberty to land and re-embark her cargo without paying any customs or duties whatever ; but in no case shall she be compelled to land her cargo.

Art. 10.   Should a vessel of either of the contracting parties be cast on shore within the territories of the other, all proper assistance shall be given to her crew : no pillage shall be allowed.   The property shall remain at the disposal of the owners, and if reshipped on board of any vessel for exportation, no customs or duties whatever shall be required to be paid thereon, and the crew shall be protected and secured, until they can be sent to their own country.

Art. 11.   If a vessel of either of the contracting parties shall be attacked by an enemy within cannon shot of the forts of the other, she shall be protected as much as possible.   If she be in port she shall not be seized or attacked, when it is in the power of the other party to protect her ; and when she proceeds to sea, no enemy shall be permitted to pursue her from the same port, within twenty-four hours after her departure.

Art. 12.   The commerce between the United States of America and the Regency of Algiers, the protections to be given to merchants, masters of vessels, and seamen, the reciprocal rights of establishing consuls in each country, and the privileges, immunities and jurisdiction to be enjoyed by such consuls, are declared to be on the same footing in every respect with the most favored nations respectively.

Art. 13.   The consul of the United States of America shall not be responsible for the debts contracted by citizens of his own nation, unless he previously gives written obligations so to do.

Art. 14.   On a vessel or vessels of war, belonging

to the United States, anchoring before the city of Algiers, the consul is to inform the Dey of her arrival, when she shall receive the salutes which are by treaty or custom given to the ships of war of favored nations, on similar occasions and which shall be returned gun for gun ; and if after such arrival, so announced, any Christians whatsoever, in Algiers make their escape and take refuge on board any of the ships of war, they shall not be required back again, nor shall the consul of the United States, or commander of said ships, be required to pay any thing for the said Christians.

Art. 15. As the government of the United States of America has in itself no character of enmity against the laws, religion or tranquility of any nation, and as the said States have never entered into any voluntary war or act of hostility, except in defence of their just rights on the high seas, it is declared by the contracting parties, that no pretext arising from religious opinions shall ever produce an interruption of the harmony existing between the two nations ; and the consuls and agents of both nations shall have liberty to celebrate the rites of their respective religions in their own houses.

The consuls respectively shall have liberty and personal security given them to travel within the territories of each other both by land and sea, and shall not be prevented from going on board any vessels they may think proper to visit ; they shall likewise have the liberty to appoint their own drogoman and broker.

Art. 16. In case of any dispute arising from the violation of any of the articles of this treaty, no appeal shall be made to arms, nor shall war be declared on any pretext whatever ; but if the consul, residing at the place where the dispute shall happen, shall not be able to settle the same, the government of that country shall state their grievance in writing, and transmit the same to the government of the other, and the period of three months shall be allowed for answers to be returned, during which time no act of hostility shall be permitted by either party; and in case the grievances are not redressed, and a war should be the event, the consul and citizens, and subjects of both parties respectively, shall be permitted to embark with their effects unmolested, on board of what vessel or vessels they shall think proper, reasonable time being allowed for that purpose.

Art. 17. If in the course of events, a war should break out between the two nations, the prisoners captured by either party shall not be made slaves; they shall not be forced to hard labor, or other confinement than such as may be necessary to secure their safe keeping, and shall be exchanged rank for rank ; and it is agreed that prisoners shall be exchanged in twelve months after their capture, and the exchange may be effected by any private individual legally authorized by either of the parties.

Art. 18. If any of the Barbary states or other powers at war with the United States, shall capture any American vessel and send it into any port of the Regency of Algiers, they shall not be permitted to sell her, but shall be forced to depart the port, on procuring the requisite supplies of provision: But the vessels of war of the United States, with any prizes they may capture from their enemies shall have liberty to frequent the port of Algiers, for refreshment of any kind and to sell such prizes, in the said ports, without any other customs or duties, than such as are customary on ordinary commercial importation.

Art. 19. If any of the citizens of the United States, or any persons under their protection, shall have any disputes with each other, the consul shall decide between the parties, and whenever the consul shall require any aid or assistance from the government of Algiers to inforce his decisions, it shall be immediately granted to him ; and if any disputes shall arise between any citizens of the United States and the citizens or subjects of any other nation having consul or agent in Algiers, such disputes shall be settled by the consuls or agents of the respective nations; and any

40

disputes or suits at law that may take place between any citizens of the United States and the subjects of the Regency of Algiers, shall be decided by the Dey in person and no other.

Art. 20. If a citizen of the United States should kill, wound, or strike a subject of Algiers, or, on the contrary a subject of Algiers should kill, wound, or strike a citizen of the United States, the law of the country shall take place, and equal justice shall be rendered, the consul assisting at the trial ; but the sentence of punishment against an Amerinan citizen shall not be greater, or more severe, than it would be against a Turk in the same predicament, and if any delinquent should make his escape, the consul shall not be responsible for him in any manner whatever.

Art. 21. The consul of the United States of America shall not be required to pay any custom or duties whatever on any thing he imports for a foreign country for the use of his house and family.

Art. 22. Should any of the citizens of the United States of America die within the limits of the Regency of Algiers, the Dey and his subjects shall not interfere with the property of the deceased, but it shall be under the immediate direction of the consul, unless otherwise disposed of by will. Should there be no consul, the effect shall be deposited in the hands of some person worthy of trust, until the party shall appear who has a right to demand them, when they shall render an account of the property ; neither shall the Dey or his subjects give hindrance in the execution of any will that may appear.

Now therefore be it known, that I James Madison, President of the United States of America, having seen and considered the said Treaty, have by and with the advice and consent of the Senate, accepted, ratified and confirmed the same, and every clause and article thereof.

In testimony wherefore I have caused the seal of the United States to be hereunto affixed, and (L. S.) have signed the same with my hand. Done at the City of Washington this twenty-sixth day of December, A. D. one thousand eight hundred and fifteen, and of the Independence of the United States the fortieth.

JAMES MADISON.

By the President, JAMES MONROE, Secretary of State.

The following list comprises the names of all the vessels belonging to the United States navy in 1812, before the late war with Great Britian. Those marked in italics were lost during the war. The *Boston*, burnt at Washington, was a mere hulk, not worth repair as was also the *New York*, which escaped the flames.

Ship	Rate.		Rate.
Ship United States	44	Hornet	18
President	44	*Wasp*	18
Constitution	44	Brig Adams	18
Chesapeake	36	Onedia	16
Constellation	36	*Syren*	16
Congress	36	*Argus*	16
New York	32	Enterprize	14
Adams	42	*Rattlesnake*	14
Boston	32	*Nautilus*	14
Essex	32	*Vixen*	14
John Adams	24	*Viper*	12
Louisiana	18	Sch'r *Vixen*	8

Besides gun-boats, bombs, &c.

NAVAL REGISTER FOR 1815.

Names and Rank.		Dates of Commissions.		
CAPTAINS.				
Alexander Murray		1	July	1798
John Rodgers		5	March	1799
James Barron		22	May	"
William Bainbridge		20	do	1800
Hugh G. Campbell		16	Oct.	"
Stephen Decatur		16	Feb.	1804
Thomas Tingey		23	Nov.	"
Charles Stewart		22	April	1806
Isaac Hull		23	do	"
Isaac Chauncey		24	do	"
John Shaw		27	Aug.	1807
John H. Dent		29	Dec.	1811
David Porter		2	July	1812
John Cassin		3	do	"
Samuel Evans		4	do	"
Charles Gordon		2	March	1813
Jacob Jones		3	do	"
Charles Morris		5	do	"
Joseph Tarbell	No. 1	24	July	"
Arthur Sinclair	No. 2	24	o	"
Oliver Hazard Perry		10	Sept.	"
Thomas Macdonough		11	do	1814
Lewis Warrington		22	Nov.	"
Joseph Bainbridge		23	do	"
William Crane		24	do	"
Johnston Blakeley		25	do	"
James T. Leonard		4	Feb.	1815
James Biddle	No. 1	28	do	"
Chs. G. Ridgley	No. 2	28	do	"
R. T. Spence	No. 3	28	do	"
Dan. T. Patterson		28	do	"
MASTERS COMMANDANT.				
Samuel Anges	No. 4	24	July	1813
M. T. Woolsey	No. 7	24	do	"
J. O. Creighton	No. 9	24	do	"
Ed. Treachard	No. 10	24	do	"
John Downes	No. 11	24	do	"
J. D. Henley	No. 14	24	do	"
Jesse D. Elliott	No. 15	24	do	"
Robert Henley		12	Aug.	1814
Stephen Cassin		11	Sept.	"
Dan'l S. Dexter	No. 1	10	Dec.	1814
James Renshaw	No. 2	10	do	"
David Deacon	No. 8	10	do	"
Lewis Alexis	No. 4	10	do	"
M. B. Carroll	No. 1	4	Feb.	1815
Sidney Smith		28	do	"

Names and Rank.		Dates of Commissions.		
Thomas Brown		1	March	"
William Lewis		3	do	"
LIEUTENANTS.				
Nathaniel Haraden		31	March	1807
Francis I. Mitchell		18	Feb.	1809
George Merrill		30	April	"
Samuel Woodhouse		4	May	"
Chs. C. B. Thompson		15	do	"
Joseph Nicholson		15	June	"
Alex. S. Wadsworth		21	April	"
John Pettigrew		22	do	"
George W. Rodgers		24	do	"
George C. Read		25	do	"
Henry E. Ballard		26	do	"
Thomas Gamble		27	do	"
William Carter, Jr.		28	do	"
B. I. Neale	No. 2	4	June	"
J. I. Nicholson	No. 3	4	do	"
Walter Stewart	No. 4	4	do	"
Wolcott Chauncey		7	do	"
John H. Elton		8	do	"
Edmund P. Kennedy		9	do	"
Jesse Wilkinson		10	do	"
Alexander J. Dallas		13	do	"
John B. Nicholson		20	May	1812
Bekman V. Hoffman		21	do	"
George Budd		23	do	"
Thomas A. C. Jones		24	do	"
Joseph S. Macpherson		26	do	"
John Porter		27	do	"
John T. Shubrick		28	do	"
William Finch		4	Jan.	1813
William B. Soubrick		5	do	"
Henry Wells		6	do	"
Benjamin W. Booth		7	do	"
Alexander Claxton		8	do	"
Enos R. Davis		10	May	1813
Charles W. Morgan		3	March	"
Samuel P. Macomber		4	do	"
Raymond H. J. Perry		5	do	"
Lawrence Kearney		6	do	"
William H. Watson		7	do	"
Thomas Hendry, Jr.		8	do	"
Foxall A. Parker		9	do	"
Edward R. M'Call		11	do	"
Daniel Turner		12	do	"
Wm. H. Allen	No. 1	24	July	"
S. D. M'Knight	No. 2	24	do	"

Names and Rank.		Dates of Commissions.		
David Conner	No. 3	24	July	1813
John Gallagher	No. 4	24	do	'
Thomas Holdup	No. 5	24	do	'
Jas. A. Dudley	No. 7	24	do	'
Jas. T. Creeders	No. 8	24	do	'
Wm. M. Hunter	No. 9	24	do	'
John D. Sloat	No. 10	24	do	'
John Duckett	No. 11	24	do	'
W. H. Cocke	No. 12	24	do	'
J. J. Yarnall	No. 13	24	do	'
Mat. C. Perry	No. 14	24	do	'
C. W. Skinner	No. 15	24	do	'
Jasper Wragg	No. 16	24	do	'
James Sanders	No. 17	24	do	'
James Renty	No. 18	24	do	'
S. W. Adams	No. 19	24	do	'
J. R. Madison	No. 21	24	do	'
D. Taylor	No. 22	24	do	'
George Pearce	No. 23	24	do	'
Fred W. Smith	No. 24	24	do	'
H. S. Newcomb	No. 25	24	do	'
N. D. Nicholson	No. 26	24	do	'
T. Conaghnot	No. 27	24	do	'
Otho Norris	No. 29	24	do	'
J. T. Newton	No. 30	24	do	'
P. A. J. P. Jones	No. 31	24	do	'
Samuel Henley	No. 32	24	do	'
A. Crackling	No. 33	24	do	'
Joseph South	No. 34	24	do	'
L. Rousseau	No. 36	24	do	'
G. W. Storer	No. 37	24	do	'
Henry B. Rapp	No. 40	24	do	'
Lewis German	No. 41	24	do	'
Joseph Cassin	No. 42	24	do	'
Rob. M. Rose	No. 43	24	do	'
R. Kennon	No. 44	24	do	'
Edward Shubrick		9	Oct.	'
Charles A. Budd		18	June	1814
Francis H. Gregory		28	do	'
Wm. H. Ovenheimer		16	July	1814
Edward Barewell		22	do	'
John M. Maury *		9	Dec.	'
Frederick Baury		9	do	'
Benjamin Cooper		9	do	'
Philip F. Voorhees		9	do	'
Henry Gilliam		9	do	'
John H. Clark *		9	do	'
William D. Salter		9	do	'
William A. Spencer		9	do	'
William L. Gordon		9	do	'
David Geisinger		9	do	'
Richard Winter		9	do	'
John T. Wade		9	do	'
John Percival		9	do	'
James Ramage		9	do	'
William V. Taylor		9	do	'
Maxime Mix		9	do	'
Thomas N. Newell		9	do	'
Edward Haddaway		9	do	'
Charles F. M'Cawley		9	do	'
John H. Bell		9	do	'
Dulany Forrest		9	do	'
Bladen Dulany		9	do	'
Tho. W. Magruder		9	do	'

Names and Rank.		Dates of Commissions.		
Francis B. Gamble		9	July	1814
Richard Dashiel		9	do	'
John Taylor		9	do	'
George B. M'Culloch		9	do	'
Robert Spedder		9	do	'
Thomas T. Webb		9	do	'
Walter G. Anderson		9	do	'
Stephen Champlin		9	do	'
Charles T. Stallings		9	do	'
James M'Gowan		9	do	'
William Lowe		9	do	'
E. A. F. Vallette		9	do	'
John H. Aulick		9	do	'
Charles T. Clarke		9	do	'
Silas Duncan		9	do	-
Thomas Cunningham		9	do	'
Isaac M'Keever		9	do	'
Robert F. Stockton		9	do	'
Nat L. Montgomery		9	do	'
Walter N. Monteath		9	do	'
A. C. Stout		9	do	'
Silas H. Stringham		9	do	-
George Vancleave		9	do	'
Paul Zantzinger		9	do	'
John W. Gibbs		9	do	'
John T. Drury		9	do	'
Charles E. Cowley		9	Dec.	1814
William Laughton		9	do	'
Nelson Webster		9	do	'
Wm. A. C. Farragut		9	do	'
Richard G. Edwards		9	do	'
William Merwin		4	Feb.	1815
William K. Latimer		4	do	'
Gustavus W. Spooner		4	do	'
Isaac Mayo		4	do	'
William H. Prailsford		4	do	'
William Eliott		4	do	'
Thomas Crabb		4	do	'
Edward B. Babbit		1	May	'
George Hamersley		5	do	'

SURGEONS.

Names and Rank.		Dates of Commissions.		
Edward Cutbush		24	June,	1799
Peter St. Medard		14	July,	'
Samuel R. Marshall		16	Jan.	1800
Lewis Heerman		27	Nov.	1804
Joseph G. P. Hunt		27	do	'
Jonathan Cowdery		27	do	'
Samuel D. Heap		27	do	'
Robert L. Thorn		3	March,	1809
Samuel R. Trevett. Jr.		3	do	'
Wm. P. C. Barton		28	April,	'
Joseph W. New		18	June,	'
Joseph S. Schoolfield		18	do	'
George Logan		14	April,	1810
Amos A. Evans		20	do	'
Robert Morrell		31	May,	'
Robert S. Kearney		28	July,	'
James Page		5	March,	1811
John D. M'Reynolds		2	Oct.	'
Thomas Harris		6	July,	1812
William Turk	No. 1	24	July,	1813
Hyde Ray	No. 2	24	do	'
William Baldwin	No. 3	24	do	'

* The relative rank of those officers whose commissions are dated the 9th of December, 1814, has not been established.

Names and Rank.		Dates of Commissions.		
Wm. W. Buchanan	No. 4	24	July	1813
Samuel Ayer	No. 5	24	do	"
E. L. Lawton	No. 6	24	do	"
Charles Cotton	No. 7	24	do	"
Gerard Dayers	No. 8	24	do	"
William Caton	No. 9	24	do	"
Robert A. Barton	No. 10	24	do	"
Benj. P. Kissam	No. 11	24	do	"
John A. Kearney	No. 13	24	do	"
Richard C. Edgar	No. 14	24	do	"
B. Washington	No. 15	24	do	"
Wm. M. Clarks	No. 16	24	do	"
Tho's Chidester	No. 17	24	do	"
Jas Inderwicke	No. 18	24	do	"
Geo. T. Kennon	No. 19	24	do	"
Walter W. New		6	Oct.	"
Samuel Horsley		15	April	1814
Robert C. Randolph		15	do	"
Charles B. Hamilton		15	do	"
Usher Parsons		15	do	"
William Swift		15	do	"
J. M. S. Conway		27	June,	"
Richard K. Hoffman		16	July,	"
Richmond Johnson		1	March	1815
Thomas B. Salter		22	May	"

SURGEONS' MATES.

Names and Rank.		Dates of Commissions.		
John Harrison		16	Jan.	1805
Stith Lewis		23	do	1809
Gustavus R. Brown		1	March	"
Manuel Philips		18	July	"
William Barnwell		28	do	1810
William Belt		23	Sept.	1811
Donaldson Yeates		14	May	1812
John D. Armstrong		27	do	"
William C. Whittlesey		7	July	"
Peter Christie		8	do	"
John Young, Jr.		9	do	"
Samuel Jackson		10	do	"
Andrew B Cook		21	Dec.	"
James C. Garrison		22	do	"
E. D. Morrison	No. 2	24	July	1813
Horatio S. Warring	No. 3	24	do	"
John H. Gordod, Acting Surgeon	No. 5	24	do	"
Samuel M. Kissam	No. 6	24	do	"
Leonard Osborne	No. 9	24	do	"
Tho's Williamson	No. 7	24	do	"
John Dix	No. 10	24	do	"
Benj. Austin, Jr.	No. 15	24	do	"
Thomas Cadle	No. 16	24	do	"
Leuco Mitchell	No. 17	24	do	"
Silas D. Wickes	No. 18	24	do	"
Isaac Balwin. Jr.	No. 19	24	do	"
Wilmot F. Rodgers	No. 20	24	do	"
Thomas Rogerson		25	Oct.	"
George S. Sproston		8	Nov.	"
John C. Richardson		17	May	1814
John W. Peaco		28	June	"
Archimedes Smith		5	July	"
Ale'r M. Montgomery		16	do	"
Oliver LeChevalier		10	Dec.	"
William Butler		10	do	"
Thomas M'Kissoch		10	do	"

Names and Rank.		Dates of Commissions.		
John Wise		10	Dec,	1814
Thomas I. H. Cushing		10	do	"
John H. Steel		10	do	"
S. B. Whittington		10	do	"
Francis Gerrish		10	do	"
Edward Woodward		10	do	"
Benjamin A. Welles		10	do	"
Frederick P. Markham		10	do	"
William D. Conway		10	do	"
James N. Turnstale		10	do	"
Davis G. Tuck		10	do	"
Robert C. Wardle		10	do	"
James Norris		10	do	"
Thomas C. Gardner		10	do	"
William F. Bradbury		10	do	"
Benajah Tickner		10	do	"
William P. Jones		10	do	"
Thomas G. Peachy		10	do	"
John Mairs		10	do	"
John M'Adam		10	do	"
John S. Merseon		10	do	"
Charles Chase		10	do	"
Thomas V. Wiesenthal		10	do	"
George B. Doane		10		"
Amos King		10		"
Pliny Morton		10		"
Benjamin S. Tyler		10		"
Nathaniel Miller		6	Jan.	1815
William Burchmore		10	do	"
Solomon D. Townsend		3	May.	"
Richard Derby, Jr.		8	do	"
John R. Martin, acting Surgeon		9	May	"
James R. Royce, acting Surgeon's Mate		10	Jan.	"
David H. Fraser, acting Surgeon's Mate,		22	Feb.	"

PURSERS.

Names and Rank.		Dates of Commissions.		
Isaac Garreston		25	April	1812
Clement S. Hunt		25	do	"
Gwinn Harris		25	do	"
John H. Carr		25	do	"
Nathaniel Lyde		25	do	"
James R. Wilson		25	do	"
Samuel Robertson		25	do	"
Samuel Hambleton		25	do	"
Robert C. Ludlow		25	do	"
Robert Pottinger		25	do	"
John B. Timberlake		25	do	"
Thomas I. Chew		25	do	"
Thomas Shields		25	2o	"
Richard C. Archer		25	de	"
Lewis Deblois		25	do	"
George S. Wise		25	do	"
Francis A. Thornton		25	do	"
Edwin T. Satterwhite		25	do	"
James M. Halsey		25	do	"
Edward Pitzgerald		25	do	"
Alexander P. Darragh		25	do	"
Edward W. Turner		25	do	"
Robert Ormsby		25	do	"
Henry Dennison		25	do	"
Ludlow Dashwood		52	do	"

Names and Rank.	Dates of Commissions.			Names and Rank.	Dates of Commissions.		
William S. Rogers	26	Feb.	1813	Belt, William I.	1	Sept.	"
Henry Fry	27	do	"	Belches, John A. A. L.	1	do	"
John R Shaw	27	do	"	Berry, Charles	1	do	"
Samuel P. Todd	1	March	"	Boerum, William	1	do	"
Nathaniel W. Rothwell	2	do	"	Barron, Samuel	1	Jan.	1812
George Beall	24	July	"	Bryden, John	1	do	"
James H. Clark	24	do	"	Bowyer, Thomas H.	1	do	"
William P. Zantzinger	24	do	"	Bryan, Benjamin	1	do	"
Joseph North	24	do	"	Beatty, Horatio	1	do	"
Joseph Wilson, Jr.	24	do	"	Brashears, Richard	1	do	"
Herman Thorn	24	do	"	Ballinger, Franklin	1	do	"
Thomas Waine	24	do	"	Baldwin, William	1	do	"
Lewis Fairchild	24	do	"	Bonneville, Thomas N.	1	do	"
John S. Skinner	26	March	1814	Baker, Yorrick	18	July	"
Joseph B. Wilkinson	26	do	"	Bell, William H.	18	do	"
Ezekiel Solomon	26	do	"	Ball, Eliphalet	18	do	"
Benjamin F. Bourne	26	do	"	Biglow, Abraham	18	do	"
William Sinclair	26	do	"	Boden, William	18	do	"
Richard T. Timberlake	26	do	"	Benson, John C.	22	Aug.	"
Samuel Livermore	26	do	"	Beck, Samuel	12	April	1813
Matthew C. Atwood	26	do	"	Baldwin, Russell	17	May	"
Gerome K. Spence	8	April	"	Brown, Thomas H.	9	Nov.	"
Melancton W. Bostwick	16	July	"	Bruce, Henry	9	do	"
John N. Todd	1	March	1815	Bubier, John	9	do	"
Timothy Winn	17	May	"	Byrne, Edmund	1	Feb.	1814
William M. Sands	20	do	"	Bird, John D.	16	April	"
Thomas Breese	8	July	"	Benham, Timothy G.	30	Nov.	"
Joseph H. Terry, acting Purser				Brewster, Benjamin	30	do	"
				Branch, Cyrus A.	30	do	"
CHAPLAINS.				Bartholomew, Benjamin	30	do	"
				Barr, James	30	do	"
Andrew Hunter	5	March	1811	Bubbidge, John P.	30	do	"
David P. Adams	10	May	"	Boughan, James	11	Jan.	1815
John Cook	19	do	1812	Buchanan, Franklin	28	do	"
William H. Briscoe	11	July	"	Bainbridge, Arthur	23	Feb.	"
Colden Cooper	24	April	1815	Boardley, John M.	7	March	"
Cheever Felch	12	May	"	Bowman, Joseph	8	July	"
A. Y. Humphreys, acting Chaplain				Cutler, William	15	Nov.	1809
				Chaille, William H.	17	Dec.	1810
MIDSHIPMEN.				Caton, Richard, Jr.	9	June	1811
				Cross, Joseph	9	do	"
Adams, James	16	Jan.	1809	Caldwell, Charles H.	1	Sept.	"
Adam, Robert	18	May	"	Cook, John A.	1	Jan.	1812
Armstrong, James A. L.	15	Nov.	"	Chauncey, John S.	1	do	"
Alexander, Albert A.	1	Sept.	1811	Conover, Thomas A.	1	do	"
Abbot, Walter	1	Jan.	1812	Campbell, Archibald	1	do	"
Allison, William R.	1	do	"	Cranston, Robert	1	do	"
Abbot, Joel	1	do	"	Crary, Lodowick	1	do	"
Avery, George	28	do	"	Cornwall, Joseph S.	1	do	"
Ashbridge, Joseph H.	14	Aug.	1813	Cuthbert, Lachlan	1	do	"
Adams, Henry A.	14	March	1814	Cocke, Harrison	18	June	"
Andrews, Alex'r. M'Kim	13	April	"	Childs, Enos	18	do	"
Armistead, Robert	30	July	"	Curtis, James F.	18	do	"
Allen, William H.	30	Nov.	"	Cambreling, John P.	18	do	"
Alexander, Nathaniel	30	do	"	Carter, Nathaniel, Jr.	18	do	"
Armstrong, William H.	30	do	"	Cooke, John, Jr.	18	do	"
Abbot, Thomas C.	6	Dec.	"	Connor, James	18	do	"
Adams, Roderick R.	2	March	1815	Cutts, James M.	18	do	"
Bond, Samuel	20	Jan.	1806	Curtis, Thomas B.	28	Sept.	"
Brown, Thomas S.	17	Dec.	1810	Cummings, John L.	8	Oct.	"
Brown, I. A. D.	17	do	"	Carpenter, Edward	10	July	1813
Berry, William	17	do	"	Carpenter, Benjamin	10	do	"
Breese, Samuel L. A. L.	17	do	"	Channings, John M.	9	Nov.	"
Boarman, Charles	9	June	1811	Carter, Hill	9	do	"

Names and Rank.	Dates of Commissions.			Names and Rank.	Dates of Commissions.		
Cotts, Augustus	9	Nov.	1818	Freeman, Edgar	9	June	1811
Cottineau, Hercules	9	do	"	Field, Robert	1	Sept.	"
Chew, John (or Benj.)	1	Feb.	1814	Fischer, John D.	18	June	1812
Carson, Robert	1	do	"	Freelon, T. W.	18	do	"
Conyngham, David	1	do	"	Fenimore, Thomas E.	20	Feb.	1818
Cochran, Joshua W.	1	do	"	Freeman, James M.	24	May	1814
Cannon, Joseph S.	26	do	"	Follet, Benjamin	6	Dec.	"
Campbell, James	30	Nov.	"	Goodwin, John D.	16	Jan.	1809
Colter, James	30	do	"	Gwinn, John A. L.	18	May	"
Cunningham, Robert B.	30	do	"	Greenwell, Edward	9	June	1811
Corlis, Charles	30	do	"	Gibbon, Frederick S.	9	do	"
Collier, John	30	do	"	Gaunt, Charles	1	Sept.	"
Cutts, Joseph	6	Dec.	"	Goodwyn, Peterson	1	Jan.	1812
Coxe, James S.	10	Jan.	1815	Griffin, Allen	1	do	"
Childs, Charles B.	28	do	"	Gray, Henry	1	do	"
Cochran, Richard	7	Feb.	"	Greenlaw, James	18	June	"
Cambridge, William E.	6	March	"	Goodrum James	18	do	"
Crowninshield, Jacob	11	do	"	Graham, John H.	18	de	"
Clinton, James H.	24	April	"	Goldsborough, Lewis M.	18	do	"
Doyle, Thomas	4	July	1805	Gilmeyer, Jacob	1	Jan.	1818
De Hart, Gosen	15	Nov.	1809	Greeves, Thomas	9	Nov.	"
De Lion, Abraham	17	Dec.	1810	Goodwin, Daniel	30	do	1814
Dowse, Edward	17	do	"	Grimke, Benj. Secundus	30	do	"
Dayton, T. W. H.	1	Sept.	1811	Green, Willis M.	30	do	"
Downing, Samuel W.	1	do	"	Gerry, Thomas R.	6	Dec.	"
Dulany, James W.	1	do	"	Gardner, Walter	6	do	"
De Vaux, Maximilian	1	do	"	Gardner, William H.	6	do	"
Dunham, Peleg K.	1	Jan.	1812	Gaillard, Daniel S.	4	Feb.	1815
Davis, Oscar	1	Feb.	,	Gedney, Thomas R.	4	March	"
Dale, John Montgomery	18	June	,	Humphreys, Julius	16	Jan.	1809
Dobbin, James H.	18	do	"	Hill, John, Jr. A. L.	6	Feb.	"
Dennis, John, Jr.	18	do	"	Hall Warren	17	Dec.	1810
Daily, Thomas W.	9	Nov.	1813	Heath, Richard	17	do	"
Derby, Charles P.	9	do	,	Haslett, Andrew	17	do	"
De Saussure, Daniel S.	9	do	"	Harrison, Thomas P.	9	June	1811
Davis, Owen	1	Feb.	1814	Hedges, F. E.	9	do	"
Downing, Mahlon M.	8	March	"	Hunter, Richard	1	Sept.	"
Dominick, Richard	30	April	"	Harper, William J.	1	do	1812
Duzenberry, Samuel	16	July	"	Higgins, Jesse	1	Jan.	"
Dangerfield, William	30	Nov.	"	Harrison, Benjamin	1	do	"
Dana, Charles	30	do	"	Hall, William	1	do	"
De Wolf, Francis L.	30	do	"	Harper, Joseph L.	4	June	"
Dodd, George D.	30	do	"	Hunter, Moses	18	do	"
Davezac, de Castera G.	30	do	"	Hunter, David	18	do	"
Delany, Hugh	30	do	"	House, William	18	de	"
Dyson, Henry	1	Jan.	1815	Higinbothom, Delozier	18	do	"
Dodge, Edwin I.	18	do	"	Harby, Levi	18	do	"
Dornin, Thomas	2	May	"	Hardy, I. C.	18	do	"
Eli, Guy	16	Jan.	1809	Hamilton, Edward W.	18	do	"
Egerton, Richard	15	Nov.	"	Hodges, James	9	Nov.	1818
Essex, Edwin	15	do	"	Hall, A. S.	9	do	"
Evans, John	17	Dec.	1810	Hull, Joseph	9	do	"
Eastburn, Joseph	9	June	1811	Handy, Thomas B.	28	Jan.	1814
Elzy, James	1	Sep.	"	Howell, John F.	1	Feb.	"
Eskridge, Alexander	1	Jan.	1812	Hunter, George W.	1	do	"
Ellery, Frank	1	do	"	Hollins, George N.	1	do	"
Eakin, Samuel A.	18	June	"	Hopkins, John L.	26	do	"
Ellery, Charles	18	March	1814	Hart, Ezekiel B.	30	April	"
Emmet, Christopher T.	1	Oct.	"	Hayes Thomas	16	June	"
Engle, Frederick	6	Dec.	"	Heth, John.	25	do	"
Field, Ambrose	1	Dec.	1809	Homer, William H.	30	Nov.	"
Farragut, David G.	7	do	1810	Horton, Samuel	30	do	"
Forrest, French	9	June	1811	Hunter, Harry D.	30	do	"
Fitzhugh, Andrew	9	do	"	Harvey, William	30	do	"

41

Names and Rank.	Dates of Commissions.			Names and Rank.	Dates of Commissions.		
Hunt, John	30	Nov.	1814	M'Caw, John	1	Sept.	1811
Harris, John L.	30	do	"	M'Cawley, George	1	do	"
Harris, William S.	30	do	"	Mitchell, Robert	1	do	"
Hobart, George	6	Dec.	"	M'Intosh, James M'K.	1	do	"
Hoffman, Ogden	31	do	"	Minchin, Charles W.	1	Jan.	1812
Howard, William L.	10	Jan.	1815	M'Cluney, William	1	do	"
Holts, Hubbard H.	4	March	"	M'Clean, William	1	do	"
Jones, Charles	6	July	1803	Mackall, Richard	1	do	"
Jasper, William	1	Jan.	1808	Mott, William H.	1	do	"
Johns, Enoch H.	16	do	1809	M'Neil, Archibald	1	do	"
Jamesson, William	1	Sept.	1811	Morales, Joseph	1	do	"
Innian, William	1	Jan.	1812	Montgomery, John B.	4	June	"
Jackson, James T.	1	do	"	Mitchell, David	18	do	"
Isaacs, G. W.	1	do	"	Mason, James	18	do	"
Jarvis, Joseph R.	18	June	"	M'Clintock, Henry	18	do	"
Jamesson, Skeffington	18	do	"	Macley Daniel H.	16	April	1813
Jones, Richard A.	18	do	"	Mourehead, Joseph	9	do	"
Ingraham, Duncan N.	18	do	"	M'Rorie, D. W.	1	Feb.	1814
Israel, Israel	9	Nov.	1813	M'Cauley, Daniel S.	1	do	"
Jarrett, Frederick	8	March	1814	Moore Sharp D.	18	July	"
Jones, Walter F.	11	June	"	Mahoney, Michael	30	Nov.	"
Justin, Joshua H.	30	Nov.	"	Matterson, Joseph	30	do	"
Johnson, Edward S.	30	do	"	M'Kean, Wm. W	30	do	"
Jacobs, Edward	30	do	"	M'Kenzie, William	30	do	"
Keene, Lewis	1	Jan.	1812	M'Intosh, William A.	30	do	"
Kuhn, Adam S.	1	Feb.	1814	Merchand, Nicholas	30	do	"
Kelle, John	1	do	"	Myers, Joseph	6	Dec.	"
Keasbey, John R.	4	Nov.	"	Mercer, Samuel	4	March	1815
Knight, James D.	30	do	"	Martin, Robert F.	2	May	"
Keogh, Matthew	6	Dec.	"	Nicholson, James	1	Dec.	1809
Lacy, Charles	16	Jan.	1809	Nichols Robert,	1	Sept.	1811
Linch, Greene	16	do	"	Nicholson, James	1	Jan.	1812
Lewis, John I. H.	15	May	"	Newcomb, Walter	1	do	"
Lecompte Charles	18	do	"	Nixen, Z. W.	18	June	"
Ludlow, James H.	15	Nov.	"	Newton, Henry C.	18	do	"
Luckett, John M.	17	Dec.	1810	Nicholson, Wm. C.	18	do	"
Lee, William A.	9	June	1811	Newman, Wm. D.	1	Feb	1814
Lowe, Enoch	1	Sept.	"	Nones, J. B.	1	do	"
Leib, Thomas I.	1	do	"	Nicholson, Wm. B.	17	March	"
Latimer, Arthur	1	Jan.	1812	Nelson, Armtstead	10	Nov.	"
Loveday, John	1	do	"	Nicholas John S.	6	June,	1815
Lecompte, Samuel	4	June	"	Olmstead, Edward	17	Dec.	1810
Lufborough, Alex. W.	18	do	"	Ogden, Henry	1	Sept.	1811
Lewis, William G.	18	do	"	Oneale, Richard	1	Jan.	1812
Leverett, George H.	18	do	"	Overton, Patrick H.	30	Nov.	1814
Long, John C.	18	do	"	Patton, George	15	Nov.	1809
Langdon, Henry S. Jr.	18	do	"	Page Banjamin	17	Dec.	1810
Lee, John H.	18	do	"	Perry, James Alex.	9	June	1811
Lansing, Edward A.	18	do	"	Paulding, Hiram	1	Sept.	"
Legare, James F.	18	do	"	Pottenger, William	1	do	"
Lovell, H. S.	9	Nov.	1813	Page, Hugh N.	1	do	"
Lord, William R.	1	Feb	1814	Patter Richard M.	1	Jan.	1812
Lyman, James R.	16	July,	"	Pendergrast, Garret	1	do	"
Lassalle, Stephen B.	4	Nov.	"	Pettigrew, Thomas	1	do	"
Lowndes, Charles	18	March	1815	Prentiss, Nathaniel A.	18	June	"
Livingston, Richard P.	29	do	"	Pratt Shubal	18	do	"
Myers, William	16	Jan.	1809	Platt, Charles T.	18	do	"
Motley, A.	16	do	"	Price, Edward	5	April	1813
M'Kinney, Wm. E.	9	June	1811	Phelps Samuel B.	20	May	"
M'Neir, Thomas	9	do	"	Prentiss, John E.	9	Nov.	"
Morris, James L.	9	do	"	Paine, John H. S.	9	do	"
Mazyck, P. R.	9	do	"	Pattern, Thomas	9	do	"
M'Alister, John	1	Sept.	1811	Patterson, William	1	Feb.	1814
M'Chesney, William	1	do	"	Pollard, William	8	March	"

Names and Rank.	Dates of Commissions.			Names and Rank.	Dates of Commissions.		
Pelot, John F.	10	June,	1814	Sweeney, Hugh S.	18	June	1812
Pinkham, Alex. B.	17	do	"	Sullivan, John M	1	March	1813
Pinckney, Richard S.	3	Aug	"	Shute John B.	16	April	"
Porter, David H.	4	do	"	Skiddy, William	9	May	"
Pickte, Richard	30	Nov.	"	Spaulding, James	9	Nov.	"
Postell, Edward	30	do	"	Swartwout, John	9	do	"
Palmer, John W.	30	do	"	Stewart. Archibald M.	9	do	"
Potter, William H.	6	Dec.	"	Stout, Matthew W.	12	do	"
Potter, Robert	2	March	1815	Stevenson, John	1	Feb.	1814
Pearson, Frederick	11	March		Stewart, David R.	1	do	"
Pennock, William H.	20	April	"	Summers, R. M.	1	do	"
Parker, George	6	June	"	Shields, William	2	do	"
Renshaw, Samuel	4	July	1805	Smith, William P.	17	March	"
Roney, James	4	July	1807	Shubrick, Irvine	12	May	"
Roberts, L. Q. C.	16	Jan.	1809	Stearns, Joshua B.	28	Sept.	"
Rogers, James	15	Nov.	"	Storer, Frederick	30	Nov.	"
Randolph, R. B.	15	Aug.	1810	Strong, Peter Y.	30	do	"
Ritchie, John T.	17	Dec.	"	Shaler, Egbert	30	do	"
Ramsay, William W.	1	Sept.	"	Sherburne, Jona. W.	30	do	"
Ray, James W. H.	1	do	"	Street, Miles	30	do	"
Roberts, James	1	do	"	Shaw, Roger C.	30	do	"
Randolph, William B.	1	Jan.	1812	Scott, Merit	30	do	"
Ridgeway, Ebenezer	1	do	"	Somerville, G. W.	30	do	"
Russel, Edmund M.	18	June	"	Stockton, Horatio	24	Jan.	1815
Russel, Charles C.	18	do	"	Sanderson, Francis	3	Feb.	"
Randall, Henry	18	do	"	Smith, Jesse	11	March	"
Rogers, Samuel	9	Nov.	1813	Story, Frederick W. C.	11	do	"
Rodgers William T.	9	do	"	Tippet, Thomas A.	9	June	1811
Rice, William	9	do	"	Ten Eick, Abraham	1	Sept	"
Ritchie, Robert	1	Feb.	1814	Temple, William	1	do	"
Rutter, Solomon	26	do	"	Titus, Ira	1	do	"
Ross, Thomas	17	March	"	Taylor, James B.	1	Jan.	1812
Rogers, Clement	16	April	"	Tyler, Tobias	1	do	"
Randolph, Victor M.	11	June	"	Thompson, Joseph	1	do	"
Rudd, John	30	Nov.	"	Taylor, William	1	do	1812
Roane, William	30	do	"	Tatnall, Josiah	1	do	"
Rutgers, Herman	30	do	"	Toscan, Frank	18	June	"
Rittenhouse. W. W.	30	do	"	Tilton, Nehemiah	9	Nov.	1813
Rutledge, Edward	30	do	"	Tardy, Henry	9	do	"
Reed, John	30	do	"	Thwing, Samuel	14	May	1814
Rousseau, John B.	30	do	"	Toscan, Messidor	1	Sept	"
Rand, Isaac H.	25	Jan.	1815	Townsend, John S.	18	Nov.	"
Randolph, Burwell S	2	Feb.	"	Tuttle, John P.	30	do	"
Smith, Edward	16	Jan.	1809	Turner, Henry E.	30	do	"
Stewart, James	15	Nov.	1810	Toole, John	30	do	"
Saunders, John	15	do	"	Tompkins, John	30	do	"
Stewart, Richard	15	do	"	Thorniley, Wm. F.	30	do	"
Smoot, Joseph	1	Dec.	"	Tilden, Thomas B.	1	Jan	1815
Suggette, Thomas	1	do	"	Tallmage, Benj. Jr.	4	do	"
Smith, Charles	17	do	1810	Taylor, Wm. G. B.	13	Feb.	"
Stevens, Clement	9	June	1811	Vanzandt, Ira	16	Jan.	1809
Springer, Charles L.	1	Sept.	"	Voorhees, Ralph	11	Sept.	1811
Spiknall, Joseph	1	Jan.	1812	Voshell, James	1	Jan.	1812
Swartwout, Augustus	1	do	"	Varnum, Frederick	18	June	"
Searcy, Robert	1	do	"	Vallette, James Kirk	1	do	1815
Snelson, Robert L.	1	do	"	Washington, Sam'l W.	15	Nov.	1809
Steele, William	1	do	"	Wayne, William C.	17	Dec.	1810
Simonds, L. E.	1	do	"	Wish, John	17	do	"
Sawyer, Horace B.	1	do	"	Wyman, Thomas W.	17	do	"
Street, Miles	1	do	"	Weaver, Wm. A.	14	Feb.	1811
Stribbling, Cornelius	18	June	"	Walker, Daniel R.	9	June	"
Sands, Joshua R.	18	do	"	Williams, James	1	Sept.	"
Stallings, Otho	18	do	"	Williamson, J. D.	1	do	"
Scott, Beverly R.	18	do	"	Williamson, Chas. L.	1	do	"

Names and Rank.	Dates of Commissions.		Names and Rank.	Dates of Commissions.	
Wall, Albert G	1	Jan. 1812	Dunston, William	3	April 1815
Winlock, Ephraim	1	do	Ellison, Francis H.	3	July 1813
Wilson, Stephen B.	1	do	Ferris, Jonathan D	28	Feb. 1809
Washington, W. S. L.	5	Feb.	Ford, Augustus	28	March 1810
Whetmore, Wm. C.	18	June	Fisk, Spence	7	May 1812
Whittington, Clement	18	do	Fleetwood, William	7	do
Wolbert, Frederick	18	do	Ferguson, James	27	do 1814
Watts, Edward	18	do	Gerry, Samuel R.	17	Jan. 1809
Whipple, Pardon M	18	do	Green, William	26	June 1812
White, Joshua	18	do	Godfrey, Thomas	18	April 1815
Warner, Henry R.	28	do	Herbert, Joshua	4	Aug. 1807
Ward, Henry	1	Oct.	Halburd, John	11	Feb. 1809
Wheaton, Seth	4	March 1814	Hutton, John S.	24	do
White, James	29	Aug.	Hammersley, Thomas	14	Jan. 1812
Weiser, William	30	Nov.	Henry, Henry A. L.	1	July
Wood, Oliver W.	30	do	Hallowell, George	5	Dec. 1812
Wilson, Cesar R.	30	do	Hixon, Samuel C.	30	April 1814
Wright, Edward	30	do	Hill, Henry D.	16	June
Watkins, Erasmus	6	June 1815	Haller, Isaac	7	July
Yates, Charles	1	Jan. 1812	Hawksworth, G. T.	Act'g. S. master.	
Young, John	1	do	Heartie, Isaac T.	do	do
			Jones, Edward	26	Jan. 1809
SAILING MASTERS.			Jennings, Nathaniel	30	March 1812
			Jones, Daniel	8	May
Arundell, Robert	20	May 1812	Jenkins, John D.	26	do
Akin, Thomas C.	26	June	Johnston, Robert	10	do 1813
Adams, James H.	10	July	Johnson, William	6	June 1815
Adams, Samuel W.	3	do 1813	Kingston, Simon	29	June 1812
Arnold, John	3	do	Knox, Robert	20	July
Brooks, Samuel	17	Oct. 1803	Kemper, Sylvester	30	Oct.
Barry, Edward	28	Feb.	Kitts, John	15	May 1813
Brown, Eli	25	April 1812	Levy, Uriah	21	Oct. 1812
Bloodgood, Abraham	35	June	Looming, Janus	11	Nov.
Bennet, Cornelius	9	Dec.	Luckett, Alexander	15	Dec.
Briggs, Samuel R.	3	July 1813	Lowe, Vincent	20	March 1813
Baker, Nicholas	3	do	Lindsey, Joseph	17	do 1814
Brun, Philip	13	Feb. 1813	Lee, William	30	April 1815
Basset, James	18	April 1814	Mooney, John	23	Jan. 1809
Bowie, Henry	Act'g. S. master		Mull, Jacob	13	Feb.
Carr, James E.	4	Aug. 1807	Mork, James A. L.	14	July 1812
Catalano, Salvadore	9	do 1809	M'Carty, William D.	18	do
Chambers, Thomas	24	Feb. 1812	Moliere, Henry	1	Aug.
Carter, John K.	9	May	Moliere, Lucas	1	do
Coit, William	26	do	M'Connell, William	2	Nov.
Cox, Richard J.	23	June	Mix, Elijah	12	June 1813
Cooper, Jas. B. A. L.	9	July	Mullaby, Francis	3	July
Caldwell, W. M. A. L.	27	March 1813	Mulford, Richard	3	do
Clough, John	3	July	Mallone, William F.	4	April 1814
Chamberlain, S. P.	8	Jan. 1814	M'Lachlin, Philip	28	July
Collins, William	3	Feb.	Meyers, Stuben	18	Nov.
Cansler, William	29	March	Miller, William	28	Jan. 1815
Croft, George	17	Aug.	M'Night, William	Act'g. S. master.	
Dudley, Linton	25	Jan. 1809	Maynadier, Daniel	do	do
Dealy, Richard	14	Feb. 1811	Nantz, John	7	July 1812
Doxey, Biscoe	24	June 1812	Nicholson, William	14	Aug. 1813
Davis, George	20	July	Northrop, Job	22	Jan. 1815
Dove, Marmaduke	29	Aug.	Nichols, Thomas	Act'g. S. master.	
Dobbins, Daniel	16	Sept.	Owings, John C.	15	Sept. 1806
Dill, J. H.	10	April 1813	Osgood, Joseph	3	July 1813
Dodge, Billy	3	July	Phillips, David	1	Jan. 1801
De la Roche, Geo. F.	3	Aug.	Prentiss, Jabez	4	Feb. 1809
Dorgan, Andrew	11	Sept.	Page, Lewis B.	9	March
Downes, Shubal	12	do	Potts, James B.	24	July 1812
Drew, John	6	Dec. 1814	Payne, Thomas	10	Oct.

Names and Rank.	Dates of Commissions.			Names and Rank.	Dates of Commissons.		
Polk, William W.	18	July	1814	Tew, Henry	28	March	1814
Rogers, James	6	April	1810	Tatem, Robert S.	21	July	"
Robins, William M.			1812	Terry, James	20	April	1815
Romey, Edward	18	Nov.	"	Ulrich, George	4	Dec.	1809
Rinker, Samuel	3	Sept.	1813	Van Voorhis, Rob't B.	28	Feb.	"
Sountag, George S.	4	Aug.	1807	Vaughan, William	22	Aug.	1812
Stevens, Joseph	8	May	1812	Verney, Henry	5	Dec.	"
Smith, Horace	17	July	"	Williamson, James L.	4	Aug.	1807
Smith, William P.	26	Dec.	"	Watts, Thomas	9	Feb.	1809
Story, Thomas W.	27	April	1813	Wilkinson, Henry	1	Jan.	1812
Sheed, William W.	5	May	"	Wilson, George M.	24	July	"
Stoodley Nathaniel	14	Aug.	"	Waldo, Charles F.	10	March	1813
Stellwagen, D. S.	14	May	1814	Warner, John	15	Sept.	"
Shoemaker, David, Jr.	19	Oct.	"	Wright, James B.	19	Nov.	"
Spilman, James	3	Feb	1815	White, John	2	Dec.	"
Trant, James	10	Apr	1799	Williston, Joseph	26	Nov.	1814
Taylor, James	16	May	1812	Warren, Nahum	6	Feb.	1815
Taylor, Joseph	14	July	"	Worthington, Henry	2	May	"
Topham, Philip M.	27	do	1813	Young, Edward L.	9	May	1812

MARINE CORPS.

Names and Rank.	Dates of Commissions.			Names and Rank.	Dates of Commissions.		
LT. COL. COMMANDANT.				P. B. D. Grandpre No 8	18	June	1815
Franklin Wharton	7	March	1804	Lyman Kellogg No 5	18	do	"
				Sam'l E. Watson No 6	18	do	"
MAJORS.				W. L. Brownlow No 7	18	do	"
Daniel Carmich	7	March	1809	Leon'd J. Boone No 8	18	do	"
John Hall	8	June	1814	Tho's W. Legge No 9	18	do	"
				W. H. Freeman No 10	18	do	"
CAPTAINS.				Jos. L. Kuhne No 11	18	do	"
Anthony Gale	{ 24	April	1804	Henry Olcott No 12	13	do	"
	} Brev. Major			C. M. Broome No 13	18	do	"
Robert Greenleaf	19	Jan	1811	B. Richardson No 15	18	do	"
Archibald Henderson	1	April	"	F. B. White No 16	18	do	"
Richard Smith	{ 13	Mar.	1812	William Nicoll No 17	18	do	"
	} Brev Major			Wm. L. Boyd No 18	18	do	"
Robert Wainwright	29	Sept	"	Charles Lord No 19	18	do	"
Wm. Anderson No 1	18	June	1814	Levi Twiggs No 20	18	do	"
Tho's R. Swift No 2	18	do	"	Edmund Brooke No 21	18	do	"
Samuel Miller No 3	{ 18	do	"	John Harris No 22	18	do	"
	} Brev. Major			Samuel B. Johnson	16	July	"
John Crabb No 4	{ 18	do	"				
	} and Paym'r			**2ND LIEUTENANTS.**			
Henry H. Ford No 5	18	do	"	Penry Stephens No 1	28	Feb.	1815
John M. Gamble No 6	18	do	"	Thos. A. Linton No 2	28	do	"
Charles S. Hanna No 7	18	do	"	Richd Auchmuty No 3	28	do	"
Alexander Sevier No 8	{ 18	do	"	Joseph Busque No 4	28	do	"
	} Brev. Major			James Edelen No 5	1	March	"
Alfred Grayson No 9	{ 18	do	"	Christopher Ford No 6	18	do	"
	} & Qr. Master			James J. Mills No 7		do	"
Wiliam Strong No 10	18	do	"	Francis A. Bond No 8		do	"
James Heath No 11	18	do	"	Park. G. Howle No 9		do	"
Samuel Bacon No 12	18	do	"	Geo. B English No 10		do	"
H. B. Breckenridge No 1	10	Dec.	"	H. W. Kennedy No 11		do	"
William Hall No 2	10	do	"	R. D. Green No 12		do	"
F. W. Sterne No 3	10	do	"	S. Duvall No 13		do	"
				Chas Snowden No 14		do	"
1ST. LIEUTENANTS.				I. G. Singeltary No 15		do	"
F. B. D Bellevite No 1	18	June	1815	Wm. F. Swift No 16		do	"
J. R. Montegul No 2	18	do	"	Gillies Thompson	12	April	"
				Edward S. Nowell	9	May	"

LIST OF THE AMERICAN NAVY.

Guns	Names of Vessels.	Commanders.	Guns	Names of Vessels.	Commanders.
		Com. Bam-	12	Spark	F. Gamble
74	Independence	bridge, Capt.	11	Spitfire	A. J. Dallas
		Crane	10	Torch	W. Chauncey
74	Washington	Cap. I Chauncey	14	Nonsuch	Trant
74	Franklin	Lieu. Morgan	17	Ticonderoga	
		first officer since	10	Lady Prevost, l. B.	
		the death of	9	Prometheus	A. S. Wadsworth
		Capt. Smith	9	Tom Bowline	Hoffman
74	New-Orleans		9	Alligator	
74	Chippewa		7	Roanoke	
44	Guerriere, flagship	Com.S. Decature	19	Hunter, late British	
		Capt. Lewis	7	Firebrand	
44	United States	J. Shaw	7	Surprise	
44	Constitution		5	Hornet	
44	Java	O. H. Perry	5	Ghent	
44	Pittsburgh		3	Caledonia, late B.	
44	Superior		5	Lynx	
36	Constellation	C. Gordon	3	Despatch	
36	Congress	C. Morris	3	Asp	
36	Macedonian, late B.	J. Jones	3	Porcupine	
32	Mohawk		2	Gov. Tompkins	
32	Confiance, late B.		8	Conquest	
24	Cyane	do	4	Ranger	
24	Saratoga		3	Lady of the Lake	
24	John Adams	E. Trenchard	1	Ontario	
24	General Pike		—	Raven	
20	Madison		—	Asp,	
20	Alert, late British	W. Stewart	3	Pert	
18	Hornet*	J. Riddle	4	Fair America	
18	Wasp*	J. Blakeley	1	Amelia	
18	Peacock	L. Warrenton	11	Finch, late British	
18	Ontario	J. D. Elliott	11	Chubb, do	
18	Erie	C. Ridgeley	7	Preble	
18	Louisiana		6	Montgomery	
18	Niagara		5	Camel	
18	Detroit, late British		5	Buffalo	
18	Lawrence		—	Tickler	
18	Eagle		12	President	
18	Jefferson		2	Galley Centipede	
18	Jones		2	Nettle	
18	Epervier,* late B.	J. T. Shubrick	2	Viper	
16	Chippewa	G. C. Read	2	Borer	
16	Saranac	J. Elton	2	Allen	
16	Boxer	J. Porter	2	Burrows	
16	Lennet, late British		1	Alwyn	
16	Troup		1	Ballard	
16	Sylph		1	Ludlow	
16	Qu. Charlotte, l. B.		1	Wilmer	
14	Enterprize	L. Kearney		Ketch Spitfire	
14	Oneida			Vesuvius	
12	Fleambeau	J. B. Nicholson		Vengeance	
12	Firefly	G. W. Rogers			

INDEX.

Im The Story
personalised classic books

"Beautiful gift.. lovely finish. My Niece loves it, so precious!"

Helen R Brumfieldon

★★★★★

UNIQUE GIFT

FOR KIDS, PARTNERS AND FRIENDS

Timeless books such as:

Kids

Alice in Wonderland · The Jungle Book · The Wonderful Wizard of Oz
Peter and Wendy · Robin Hood · The Prince and The Pauper
The Railway Children · Treasure Island · A Christmas Carol

Adults

Romeo and Juliet · Dracula

Highly Customizable · **Change** Books Title · **Replace** Characters Names with yours · **Upload** Photo for inside page · **Add** Inscriptions

Visit
Im The Story .com
and order yours today!